Sanity Plea
Schizophrenia in the
Novels of Kurt Vonnegut

Sanity Plea

Schizophrenia in the
Novels of Kurt Vonnegut

Revised Edition

Lawrence R. Broer

The University of Alabama Press

Tuscaloosa and London

Copyright © 1989
The University of Alabama Press
Revised Edition Copyright © 1994
The University of Alabama Press
All rights reserved
Manufactured in the United States of America

Cover art ©1994 by Lucy Karl

∞

The paper on which this book is printed meets the minimum requirements of
American National Standard for Information Science-Permanence of Paper for
Printed Library Materials, ANSI Z39.48-1984.

Library of Congress Cataloging-in-Publication Data

Broer, Lawrence R.
    Sanity plea : schizophrenia in the novels of Kurt Vonnegut /
  Lawrence R. Broer. — Rev. ed.
        p.   cm.
    Includes bibliographical references and index.
    ISBN 0-8173-0752-4
        1. Vonnegut. Kurt Knowledge Psychology. 2. Mental illness in
literature. 3. Schizophrenia in literature.   I. Title.
PS3572.05Z55   1994
813'.54—dc20   94-1075

        British Library Cataloguing-in-Publication Data available

for
Joshua and Wesley McKean

"This is a very bad book you're writing," I said to myself behind my leaks.

"I know," I said.

"You're afraid you'll kill yourself the way your mother did," I said.

There in the cocktail lounge, peering out through my leaks at a world of my own invention, I mouthed this word: schizo-phrenia.

I did not and do not know for certain that I have that disease . . . I was sick for a while, though.

I am better now.
Word of honor: I am better now.

Breakfast of Champions

Contents

x   Contents

Preface

"I would not be surprised—if it turned out that gifted people culled for mental illness have given the world more works of art worth saving than those culled for other reasons."

Fates Worse Than Death

In the two books Kurt Vonnegut has published since *Sanity Plea* appeared in 1989, *Hocus Pocus* (1990) and *Fates Worse Than Death* (1991), the author affirms what I describe in *Sanity Plea* as his dominant literary impulse from *Player Piano* to *Hocus Pocus:* to hold a sanity hearing for himself, his characters, and his readers—but mainly for his protagonists who represent himself. "My goodness!" he exclaims. "What a lot of heavy psychological stevedoring I have done so early on!" *(Fates* 54).

Telling the American Psychiatric Association of the psychoanalytical novel he planned to write, Vonnegut refers, in essence, to the story he tells all along—the spiritual evolution of one man, Kurt Vonnegut, battling his despair over a world that seems unyielding in its suffering and destructiveness. That novel would be called, he says, *SS Psychiatrist,* about a worker in the field of mental health, asked to cure people in cultures and societies that have gone insane *(Fates* 32). Vonnegut, I have tried to show, *is* that "worker," the "eclectic" psychoanalyst, "a little Jungian, a bit Freudian, a little Rankian" *(Palm Sunday* 243), probing his own subconscious, as well as the sociopathic madness of "this corrupt and bloody century" *(Fates* 200). But he is also the shaman, treating society's ills not, as he says, with "lithium, Thorazine, Prozac, or Tofranil" *(Fates* 31), but with that basic prescription for sanity he promulgates from *Player Piano* to *Hocus Pocus:* kindness, respect, humor, intelligence, and communal caring.

Though at the end of *Hocus Pocus,* the author calls "dumb" and "humorless" those who believe that Tralfamadorian fatalism reflects his own sense of the human condition, readers continue to see him as a pessimist or defeatist. Salman Rushdie, who should know better, feels that the Tralfamadorian presence in *Hocus Pocus* proves that Vonnegut's attitude to *Homo sapiens* is bleaker than ever, summed up in three words: "So it goes" (358). Civilization for Vonnegut no longer smolders, says John Skow, it "has burned itself out" (8). Certainly in the trenchant social criticism and intensely personal revelations of *Fates* (which might be subtitled "Family Secrets") and in *Hocus Pocus* (whose biggest character is "myself, of course" [130]), Vonnegut tests his sanity and that of his readers more directly than ever before. Though Vonnegut remains ambivalent about the causes of mental illness (all is "muddled," many things are plausible, he says *[Fates* 206]), it is once again the specter of "a terrible childhood" *(Fates* 33) that dominates the author's most recent family portraits— described in *Hocus Pocus* as "the family image problem" (7). Though both Eugene Debs Hartke and Vonnegut appear more forgiving than condemning of the father Vonnegut says was turned from "sleeping beauty" to "Rip Van Winkle" *(Fates* 241), the author numbers both deeply unhappy parents among the "living dead": the mother who goes insane, whose hatred is like "hydrofluroic acid" *(Fates* 28), and the artistically failed father, so desperate for love, so disappointed by life, he loses his will to live. We learn in *Fates* that it is not only the father, the "unfulfilled Prince," the suicidal mother, and Mark, the briefly schizophrenic son, who suffer the pathological retreat from life that typically affects Vonnegut's protagonists, but his first wife, her mother, and finally the author himself, who, in an effort to "get out of life entirely," wound up in a locked ward at St. Vincent's hospital *(Fates* 93). Vonnegut offers as a moral, "whatever you do, don't marry anybody named Vonnegut" *(Fates 34).*

Ironically, Vonnegut's willingness to deal openly and compassionately with painful family experience suggests, as do the autobiographical prefaces and texts of his later novels, that his own mental health was well on the mend. In a letter responding to *Sanity Plea,* Vonnegut remarks,

> In my line of work it is no help to understand what one *is really* doing. Au contraire. It seems to me that you have solved what had long been to me a mystery: why my work is so offensive to some readers. I have said that getting mad at a work of art is like getting mad at a banana split. I thought maybe the issue was my quite conventional religious skepticism or my undying love for the National Recovery act. But . . . I now understand that it's my violation of the commandment that we honor our fathers and mothers. (February 12, 1990)

As to the madness of that larger society Vonnegut calls diseased and disgraced *(Fates 44),* his verdict is less forgiving but still hopeful. Vonnegut indicts the Reagan-Bush years for the mean-spirited and "batty fantasies," the "crazy quilt of ideas" *(Fates* 77, 78), that emanate from politicians who conduct racist political campaigns and "show business" wars to divert the public from crimes at home. To wit, it was good for civilians to buy assault rifles; the Contras in Nicaragua were a lot like Thomas Jefferson and James Madison; Palestinians were to be called "terrorists" at every opportunity; the contents of wombs were government property; the American Civil Liberties Union was a subversive organization; people with AIDS asked for it; and anything like the Sermon on the Mount was socialist or communist—insanity on a par with the reign of Caligula, Vonnegut concludes, or the Council of Trent *(Fates* 77, 78). But even nuttier than the "technological nincompoopery" *(Fates* 116) that boasts of knocking down missiles from the Evil Empire with laser beams or satellites or "flypaper," or legislating the love of a piece of cloth, Vonnegut warns of the idiocy of religious leaders, including the president, whose ethical pronouncements distill to two commandments: "Stop thinking!" and "Obey!" *(Fates* 158). Only a person, Vonnegut says, who has given up the power of reason to improve life here on earth could accept such commandments.

Do expressions of contempt for such inhuman or insane ideas make Vonnegut a pessimist, or rather the canary bird in the coal mine whose "bleak impoliteness," John Irving says, provokes us to be more thoughtful, creative, and kind *(Kurt Vonnegut and His Crimes* 41)? Vonnegut sees the world of the 1980s as increasingly unhappy, destructive, and ailing, led by those "sickies," the "war preparers," and their state-of-the art wounding and killing machines, and by the "Neo-Cons" (Neo-Conservatives) who cleaned out the savings banks. He worries that mankind's epitaph may yet be: "We probably could have saved ourselves, but were too damn lazy to try very hard" *(Fates* 116). But, he declares, "That doesn't mean the Sermon on the Mount must now be considered balderdash" (132). In that hopeful spirit, Vonnegut cheers to the fact that America's experiment with freedom and justice is just beginning, that people can learn to be kind as well as mean (46), and that rather than surrender their will and their common sense to quacks and racketeers and charismatic lunatics they might cure their loneliness through membership in those big, warm, life-support systems Vonnegut calls artificial extended families, the author's "Holy Grail," as essential to health as vitamin C, in whose communal values he continues to believe.

Let the closing argument be made by the brilliant defense attorney, Vonnegut's close friend and famous war buddy, Bernard V. O'Hare. They (Vonnegut's critics) "don't know that what they read is only his reactions to the sight of the world gone mad and rushing headlong toward Dresden to the hundredth power. And they miss his message in which he pleads that the world governments found their rule on something more akin to the Sermon on the Mount than the preachings of those who lead the world to Armageddon" *(Fates* 206). If such warnings constitute pessimism, O'Hare says, it is too bad there is not an "epidemic" of it.

In *Hocus Pocus* Eugene Debs Hartke contemplates a sanity hearing in which his lawyer expects the damaged war veteran to cop an "insanity plea." Instead, Hartke and Vonnegut plead their case for psychic wholeness, their hope that they have been more compassionate than cynical or uncaring, and ask to be fairly judged. It is a humanistic appeal Vonnegut makes directly in *Fates,* in which he promises to bring forth a book in which "everything is contained" and through which the *"hocus pocus* laundromat" (72) of creative imagination will transform cruel vengeance to kindness and forgiveness. It is the shaman's, the artist-priest's, career-long plea—one we ought finally to heed.

LAWRENCE BROER

Acknowledgments

Thanks first to my colleagues Herb Karl and Irving and Harriet Deer for their early encouragement and always dependable insight. I am grateful to Kathryn Hume, Robert Merrill, Richard Erlich, Thomas Dunn, and Robert Scholes for their editorial assistance, to my editors at UMI, and to the author himself for his praise and support. To Pat Schuster and Barbara Lamphere, special thanks for preparing this manuscript. Chapters 7 and 10 have appeared in slightly altered form in *Clockwork Worlds: Mechanized Environments in Science Fiction,* edited by Richard D. Erlich and Thomas P. Dunn (Westport, Conn.: Greenwood Press, 1988). I wish to thank these editors and the publishers of Greenwood Press for permission to reprint. I am indebted to the University of South Florida for providing the research time to write this book. And finally I am grateful for the enthusiasm and research assistance of those students whose help I could not have done without: Mark Lamb, Ernest Suarez, Faye McBurney, Terry Tomalin, Sharon Arnstein, Robin Rawlings, and Betty Alvarez.

Introduction:
Madness in a Modern Mode

The young writer is faced, from the moment he begins his first novel, with the unavoidable fact that the only hope for a successful dramatic effect lies today in the depiction of the grotesque and abnormal; for it is there and there only that the tragic situation of modern life exists.

John Aldridge, *After the Lost Generation*

She said to him that the whole world suddenly seemed to be going crazy.

He commented that there was nothing sudden about it, that it had belonged in a prison or a lunatic asylum for quite some time.

Bluebeard

George Bernard Shaw accounted for the savage unreasonableness of mankind by suggesting that some alien world was using the earth as its insane asylum, dropping lunatics off at regular intervals. For such writers as John Barth, Joseph Heller, Thomas Pynchon, and Kurt Vonnegut, Shaw's observation of madness at the center of human affairs becomes a disturbingly literal estimate of the human situation in the latter half of the twentieth century. The times are no longer out of joint; they are unimaginable—an ongoing nightmare of violence and unpredictability in which the writer's conception of his world changes from that of Matthew Arnold's "battle-ground" in "Dover Beach" to the lunatic asylum of Ken Kesey's *One Flew over the Cuckoo's Nest*, Beckett's *Watt*, or Vonnegut's *God Bless You, Mr. Rosewater*.

Joseph Wood Krutch characterized the pre–Second World War hero as "enfeebled,"[1] but Ihab Hassan dubs the character to emerge from the pathological present as "a grotesque effigy to the rule of chaos,"[2] someone isolated, violent, defeated, tortured, and warped. Even the extreme and dreadful titles of studies of contemporary fiction, such as *Landscape of Nightmare, Lunatic in the Drawing Room, Desperate Faith,* and *Radical Innocence,* suggest that a significantly new element of warpedness has come to dominate the writer's depiction of character, that the most revealing image of our times is that of overwhelming madness. In *The Holocaust and the Literary Imagination,* Lawrence L. Langer argues that the present age, characterized by sudden gratuitous violence, terrorism, and anarchy, is indeed worse—more distorted and disillusioning—than its predecessors. Death and dying, atrocity and warpedness, are viewed as routine, not as exceptional. Name any value, Langer says, including the prohibition against the violation of children, and the age has exhibited that, far from being inviolate, it was violated as a matter of course. Langer concludes that the atrocities of the death camps and those that have succeeded Auschwitz represent a continuity of terror that may almost be called a new tradition, one in which the phantasmagoric and horrific is real and the gentle and generous a prodigy to be remarked with amazement.[3] The phantasmagoric and horrific realities of recent times—tragic political assassinations, racial violence, the political madness of Watergate, the foul brutalities of Viet Nam, political fanaticism, mad religions, a monolithic, frequently irresponsible technology, the absence of moral absolutes, dehumanizing theories of human behavior—explain why Alfred Kazin describes contemporary fiction as a series of "apologies for abnormality, designed to make us sympathize with the twig as it is bent the wrong way." The novel becomes "not a series of actions which the protagonist initiates because of who he is, but a series of disclosures, as at a psychoanalyst's."[4] The paranoiac antics of the Portnoys, Yossarians, Slothrops, McMurphys, Molloys, and Pilgrims support the grim view of Bellow's Mr. Sammler that the world has become a "merry-go-round cemetery," a prison of ungovernable lunatics in states of "mad perdition," "agitated spirits" casting themselves into chaos.[5] Responding to the recent writer's obsession with warpedness in what he calls "the literature of 'Extremis,' " Kurt Vonnegut explains, "We all respond with a sort of shriek to the ghastliness of news today.... It is typical of people who have a gruesome history, who have seen many invasions, a large number of dead people, and many executions."[6]

While these "shrieks" of madness in contemporary fiction occur with important variations, two extremes persist: that which in his essay "The White Negro" Norman Mailer terms "The Psychic Outlaw" or "Sexual Adventurer"—the rebel-victim con-men of J. P. Donleavy and Joseph Heller, and the walking dead of Samuel Beckett and Kurt Vonnegut, dangerously withdrawn if not catatonic characters who lapse into complete helplessness and paralysis. In Mailer's view, the continuing violence and irrationality following the nightmare of Hiroshima and the concentration camps has bred a new, psychopathic hero given to extremes of violence and self-centeredness, reverting even to savagery at times to combat the sterilizing effects of technology, the corporation, and the machine. Referring to a clinical text on criminal psychopathy, Mailer describes this manifestation of the lunatic hero as a man who denies complex social realities in favor of the radical, hedonistic realities of self. Nihilism, frenzied self-affirmation, or martyrdom—some perverted or pathological state of mind—are the norms toward which he tends.[7]

While such egomaniacs seek emotional abandonment and exotic extremism to save themselves, the emotionally depleted heroes of Beckett and Vonnegut are so profoundly alienated from society and self, so utterly overwhelmed by feelings of futility and shame, they lapse into complete helplessness. The spiritual and physical indignities of a pointless and inhumane world render Beckett's "gallery of moribunds" literally prostrate, victims of a tortuous introspection that leads nowhere except to immobility and spiritual or emotional paralysis. In his book *Samuel Beckett,* G. C. Barnard shows that Beckett's characters suffer from all the standard clinical symptoms and phases of schizophrenia—disorder of thought, incongruous or blunted emotional reactions, bizarre delusions, deep depression and withdrawal, and hallucinations with a persecutory, nihilistic, or grandiose content.[8] Similarly, the war-scarred, death-haunted heroes of Vonnegut are so dehumanized by anonymous bureaucracies, computers, and authoritarian institutions, and so immobilized by guilt and fear, they too turn into disembodied creatures with disintegrating minds—as if to confirm John Aldridge's declaration that the typical narrative today sets the scene for suicide and nervous collapse.[9]

Probably no characters in contemporary fiction are more traumatized and emotionally damaged than those of Kurt Vonnegut. There are dozens of suicides; psychopathic violence is commonplace; all major protagonists suffer periods of deep depression—some existing nebulously on the edge of sanity, with periodic breakdowns, others losing touch with reality entirely and requiring psychiatric care and hospitalization. Vonnegut gives specific names to the numerous forms of mental collapse that overtake his characters—"combat fatigue," "demonic depression," "echolalia," "sexual mania," "masochism," "catalepsis," "samaritrophia," "dementia praecox," "paranoia," "catatonia," and "Hunter Thompson Disease."

Vonnegut's prototypal fragmented hero, Eliot Rosewater or Billy Pilgrim (they share more than a room in a mental hospital),[10] is ominously familiar with psychiatrists and mental wards. He is a man with a tortured conscience, deeply repressed hostilities toward his mother and father, feelings of insignificance, and a feeble will to live. The shock of war, coupled with tragically disillusioning childhood experiences, cripple his ability to lead any kind of normal life—to love or be loved, to believe in people, work, society, or God.[11] Life's "shitstorms" have driven him so deeply within himself that those moments of intense sexual experience which come to rescue Sebastian Dangerfield, Yossarian, or Mailer's Rojack, are unknown or purely perfunctory. Vonnegut's people become automated shadows, responding only mechanically to offers of love or affection. The only womb that interests them is that which offers some cozy hiding place—a state of blankness or indifference to anything and everything. As Paul Proteus suggests in *Player Piano* (1952), one without responsibilities would do nicely.[12]

The words of Howard Campbell in *Mother Night* (1962) describe the dominant impulse of all Vonnegut's art: to show us "what makes people go crazy" and "the different ways they go crazy."[13] On the one hand, Vonnegut's interest in craziness appears primarily social and figurative in character. Insanity becomes the most graphic and compelling metaphor for a society hell-bent upon self-destruction, whose cruelty and aggression threaten to take us the way of the mastodon and the megatherium.[14] This is the demonic world of free enterprise and the vicious class system it creates; the cold and ruthless efficiency of big business conglomerates indifferent to human suffering or the destruction of natural resources; attendant corporate legal viciousness; the lunacy of irresponsible mechanization; the amassing of nuclear weapons in the pursuit of peace; the bizarre quest for God and spiritual salvation through material acquisitions and technological advance; the patriotic madness that makes war gladly; self-serving religions that believe in pure good or evil; the incompetence of nearly all political leadership; and finally, as Vonnegut says, the horror of "plain old death."[15]

Part of Vonnegut's artistic purpose has been to serve his society as a "Shaman," a kind of spiritual medicine man whose function is to expose these various forms of societal madness—dispelling the evil spirits of irresponsible mechanization and aggression while encouraging reflectiveness and the will to positive social change. It is this almost mystical vision of himself as spiritual medium and healer that Vonnegut intends by calling himself a "canary bird in the coal mine"—one who provides spiritual illumination, offering us warnings about the dehumanized future not as it must necessarily be, but as it surely would become if based on the runaway technology of the present.[16]

Both roles—Shaman and canary bird—meet Vonnegut's major criterion for himself as artist—that writers are and biologically have to be agents of change, specialized cells in the social organism.[17] Functioning as the projective imagination of the Life Force, Vonnegut shapes us a more benign and creative future—one in which human beings feel their common humanity at a deep and emotional level of being. Such a future community would have kindness, awareness, mercy, fairness, charity, and mutual respect at its core, symbolized by gentle people sharing a common bowl.[18] It is on behalf of this saner world that Vonnegut directs his satirical missiles, warning us with visions of apocalyptic fury that we are a doomed species unless we learn to replace lunatic aggression and cruelty with gentleness and restraint.

While Vonnegut's role as social critic is not to be denied, his reputation as America's most popular prose satirist has obscured the more personal and intensely psychological nature of his art. It is this psychic dimension—what Kathryn Hume calls "the infernal subdepths" of Vonnegut's fiction[19]—where Vonnegut's art functions most ingeniously and where he achieves his most compelling emotional effects. Only when we plumb the buried tensions of this more chilling Kafkaesque underworld—the purpose of this study—can we understand the bizarre phobias, paranoid delusions, masked aggression, and desperate escapist compulsions of Vonnegut's psychically maimed heroes.

Part of Vonnegut's critical success is in fact the achievement of a story whose message of psychic and social trauma is perfectly fused. It is the bedlam of violence and social chaos that induces the personal dissolution and incipient madness of Vonnegut's dazed and pliant heroes. A legacy of endless destruction—brutality, injustice, lovelessness, indifference to suffering—leaves them feeling will-less and morbidly withdrawn, often with a desire to die. All arrive at that state of emotional desolation described by Howard Cambell in *Mother Night* as "Nobody and nothing inside," a state of "catalepsis" likened to that of a "friendly robot" who must be told where and when to move next (185).[20] In *God Bless You, Mr. Rosewater* (1965), Vonnegut describes the lobotomized condition of his prototypal war-damaged hero Eliot Rosewater as a state of indifference to anything and everything, signaled by the "big click" and a period of total blankness that lands him in an asylum.[21]

Eventually the question the reader-turned-psychoanalyst must ask about Eliot Rosewater is one that must be asked about each Vonnegut protagonist in turn: is he "a flamboyantly sick man" who needs to be institutionalized, or is he one of the sanest characters in Vonnegut's fiction (23)? At a sanity hearing at the close of *God Bless You, Mr. Rosewater,* the testimony is ambiguous—divided between those who see Eliot as "irrevocably bananas," (33) and those who see him as "the sanest man in America" (64). Some evidence—Eliot's physical deterioration,[22] his alcoholism, his hallucinations—suggests that Eliot is indeed ready for an asylum, "crazy as a loon," according to the family lawyer, Norman Mushari (10). Yet what Mushari sees as a clear indication of Eliot's insanity, the reader may see as an exposé of the utter moral ruthlessness and criminal exploitation underlying the Rosewater family fortune.

If this novel were merely about the obvious sanity of Eliot's humanity versus the obvious insanity of greed and cruelty of his tormentors, its hold on us—which comes from the complexity of Eliot's psychological condition—would be far less compelling. Vonnegut discourages easy categorizations because he knows that in the context of the present pervasive madness that we call normality, sanity, freedom, love, *all* our frames of reference are ambiguous and equivocal. Distinctions between sanity and insanity, between the schizoid individual and the psychotic, are problematical. It is difficult to say, for instance, when the schizoid manifestations of characters like Paul Proteus, Eliot Rosewater, Billy Pilgrim, or Malachi Constant cross the borderline into psychosis—that is, when they can no longer control their split with reality and thus become a danger to themselves and others and require care and attention in a mental hospital.[23] As a character says in a recent novel by John Del Vecchio, "he could be both sane and crazy. In these days nobody can tell which is which."[24]

Vonnegut's problematizing, then, stimulates a more intimate and creative relationship between reader and text. Skilled at what Robert Scholes and Patricia Waugh call "defamiliarization," Vonnegut, says Scholes, "pounces on a tired platitude or cliché like a benevolent mongoose and shakes new life into it."[25] The resulting instability, openness, and flexibility require the reader not only to rethink routine assumptions about and definitions of reality, often exploitative and dehumanizing, but to grow aware of the way meaning and value are constructed and therefore challenged or changed. Waugh observes that Vonnegut's novels are fictional *Mythologies,* which like Roland Barthes's work aim to unsettle our convictions about the relative status of truth and fiction. Involving us in a matrix of contradictions, ambiguities, and inconsistencies, Vonnegut forces us into an active dialogue with the characters themselves—challenging us to finish the text by providing new definitions of what is sane or not sane.[26]

Yet there actually comes a moment in every Vonnegut novel when the hero is driven to or over the edge of insanity—when contrasts between the world as orderly, rational, and humane and the world as a slaughterhouse of ongoing violence and cruelty become too unbalancing to endure.[27] Such a symbolic moment occurs in *Slaughterhouse-Five* (1969) at Billy Pilgrim and Valencia's anniversary party. Billy listens to a barbershop quartet of optometrists singing first about "sweethearts and pals," which mocks Billy's own lonely, loveless life, and then a bitter song of social injustice, with the words, "Things gettin' worse, driving all insane" (172). Billy experiences tortured "psychosomatic responses to the changing chords." The world's insane refusal to make sense makes life finally so unendurable for Billy that he retreats "upstairs in his nice white house" (176), which gives every appearance of being an asylum. It is now that he calls upon the consolations and the alleged wisdom of the Tralfamadorians.

In exactly this manner, usually at the promptings of an alien, dangerously fatalistic inner voice, each of Vonnegut's heroes crawls into a kind of schizophrenic shell, a deliberate cultivation of a state of death-in-life existence that isolates and divides him against himself.[28] It is in this sense that the protagonist comes by the psychic malaise described in *Mother Night* as that "wider separation of my several selves than even I can bear to think about" (136). Elsewhere, after numerous hints of such a condition have accumulated, Howard Campbell, contemplating suicide, tells us how he has been able to cope with the world's horrors only "through that simple and widespread boon to modern mankind— schizophrenia" (133).

In *Slaughterhouse-Five,* Vonnegut tells us that the protagonists's withdrawal from the real world is "a screen," or what in psychiatry is called a "mask," a deliberately cultivated strategy of maintaining personal freedom by withdrawing behind some sort of protective shield, and putting another, false self forward.[29] The danger of such an inner, defensive maneuver is that the mask may become compulsive, and hence more a threat than a safeguard to the sanity it is meant to preserve. Withdrawal from an outer world of people and things into one of phantom fulfillment may lead to a total inability to act and finally to a state of nonbeing and a desire for death. R. D. Laing likens such a fate to living in "a concentration camp," in which the imagined advantages of safety and freedom from the control of others is tragically illusory. By putting a "psychic tourniquet" on his ailing soul, Laing says, the individual's detached self develops a form of "existential gangrene."[30] In this light, it is no small coincidence that Billy Pilgrim should confuse a building on the grounds of his Dresden prison camp with a building on Tralfamadore, that both environments should be filled with poison gas, that the prison should have sliding glass doors just as Billy's living space on Tralfamadore is surrounded by glass, that one prison guard at both places should converse with Billy in English, that Billy should serve as an object of ridicule and entertainment for Dresdeners and Tralfamadorians alike, that similar objects should show up in both places—e.g., horseshoes, dentures—and finally that both places should come to an end by fire as a result of apocalyptic explosions. Vonnegut's point is that one hell holds Billy prisoner as surely as the other, but in the case of his Tralfamadorian fantasy, Billy himself holds the key to the locked doors of bedlam inside his own mind.

Amazingly, particularly in light of the popular notion that Vonnegut is so simple, his philosophy so accessible, the standard reading of this book represents a major misunderstanding of Vonnegut's work—the view that Vonnegut is a writer of "pessimistic" or "defeatist" novels. Critics from David Goldsmith to Josephine Hendin have argued that the philosophic determinism of Tralfamadore represents Vonnegut's own sense of the futility of the human condition. It is the wisdom of Tralfamadore, they say, based upon the belief that human events are inevitably structured to be the way they are and hence do not lend themselves to warnings or explanations, that allows both Billy and the author to adjust to their traumatic memories of Dresden.[31]

In the recent comprehensive study of contemporary literature, *The Harvard Guide to Contemporary American Writing,* Josephine Hendin contends that

Vonnegut "celebrates" the themes of detachment and meaninglessness as devices for diminishing the emotional charge of painful experience.[32] Vonnegut's pessimism, she says, adds up to a vision of people doomed by a mechanical programming they cannot resist or change. Hence Vonnegut offers only "passivity, acceptance, resignation, and denial" as solutions to the sense of helplessness life engenders.[33] Like so many critics before her, Hendin fails to see that Vonnegut writes precisely to show men and women the dangers of "burying themselves at the bottom of the pool, bottom of the earth, bottom of the universe" as a defensive system against pain.[34] The Tralfamadorian view of reality is the very antithesis of Vonnegut's position that artists should be treasured as alarm systems—specialized cells for giving warning to the body politic—and as biological agents of change. The Tralfamadorians eventually blow up the universe while experimenting with new fuels for their flying saucers. They do not improve Billy's vision but rather ensure his schizophrenic descent into madness. Caged in a zoo, turned into a puppet for the entertainment of mechanical creatures whose own world is both physically and morally sterile, seduced into renouncing whatever vestige of free will he has left, Billy Pilgrim becomes the very embodiment of what Vonnegut has warned against for years. Insulated from pain, Billy has simply abdicated his humanity, trading his dignity and integrity for an illusion of comfort and security, and becoming himself a machine.

The tendency to see Vonnegut's work as pseudo–science fiction has diverted attention from the deeper sources of Vonnegut's art while fostering a view of him as artistically simple and philosophically glib, lacking the imaginative reach and technical sophistication of his more praised contemporaries, Beckett, Barth, Pynchon, and Heller.[35] It has been almost axiomatic that the more central the novel's psychological plot, the more uncomprehending and hostile the critical response. In a *New York Times* review of Vonnegut's novel *Deadeye Dick* (1982), Christopher Lehmann-Haupt projects the typically negative criticism Vonnegut's recent novels have received by saying that there is "something ill-defined or unspoken . . . lying just beneath the surface of events" in *Deadeye Dick,* which he suspects "accounts for why all of Mr. Vonnegut's novels since *Slaughterhouse Five* seem to have grown increasingly facile and mannered."[36] He concludes, *"Deadeye Dick* is better than *Jailbird* (1979), which was in turn an improvement on *Slapstick* (1976). But that's not really saying much." About the "something ill-defined or unspoken," he adds sarcastically, "I honestly don't know what this something is."

It is usually these same patronizing critics who, failing to understand the psychological function of Vonnegut's exotic settings and imaginary worlds, see Vonnegut as a "facile fatalist" and associate such fantasy creations as Titan, Tralfamadore, Mars, San Lorenzo, or Shangri-La with frivolity and superficiality. Hendin, for example, can believe that Vonnegut uses the "immense canvas of intergalactic space to magnify the pointlessness of human effort in any direction"[37] because she fails to see that, in a novel like *Sirens of Titan* (1959) or *Slaughterhouse-Five,* what is seemingly outer space is actually the tortuous, subterranean passages of the protagonist's own mind. Such fantasies are invariably the product of paranoid delusions in which the protagonist believes himself to be guided or ruled over by voices from above—voices of hallucinated father figures, agents of doom like Bokonon, Winston Niles Rumfoord, and Frank Wirtanen, who weave seductive fatalist sophistries. John Weir Perry calls such schizophrenic episodes experiences of "apotheosis," delusions of grandeur in the form of messianic callings, sacred marriages, or other illusions of special destiny. The individual sees himself as royalty, or divinity, as King or Queen, deity or saint, hero or heroine, messiah.[38]

Failing to see that these devious prophets and mad escapist visions warn against fatalism rather than affirm such a philosophy Hendin subsequently ignores the complexly interwoven systems of metaphor by which these warnings are conveyed. She fails to notice that in *Sirens of Titan,* for instance, numerous allusions to glass—portholes, windows, mirrors, crystals, and transparency—and to doors, caves, and tunnels show objective reality to be a mirror reflection of the nightmarish experiences occurring within the tormented mind of Malachi Constant. Such mirror reflections reinforce Vonnegut's position that the insane world of soulless materialistic lusts for fame and money, of suicidal wars and self-serving religions that we presently inhabit, is a world of our own lunatic invention. We become our own victims by becoming entrapped and enslaved by dehumanized, mechanistic systems of control which we ourselves largely create.[39]

It is doubtful too that Hendin notices Vonnegut's ingenious use of spiral images to represent these hellish mechanisms—militaristic, philosophic, religious, socioeconomic, genetic—to which Vonnegut's characters are dangerously lured. On the one hand, these cones, fountains, caves, whirlpools, staircases, rollercoasters, clocks, and cocoons appear too pervasive and powerful to escape; on the other, they seem superficially benign and alluring. The latter Vonnegut calls in *Sirens of Titan* "a dynamite bouquet" (290), defined in *Cat's Cradle* (1963) as "what looked like a wonderful idea then—what looks like a hideous idea in retrospect" (55). These so-called bargains come in a variety of packages: the desirability of a utopia of perfect peace, beauty, and understanding; the quest for God and spiritual salvation through material acquisitions and technological advance; the quest for brotherhood through bloodshed (stockpiling doomsday weapons to keep the world safe); uncritical patriotism as a test of love of country. To Vonnegut's traumatized, susceptible narrators, these seductive escapist illusions promise relief from the painful complexity of human identity and the anguish of choice, but as with Billy Pilgrim, entrapment in self-imprisoning spirals puts the protagonist into a dizzying spin downward toward moral oblivion, engendering a robotlike identity and endangering the very sanity he tries to preserve.

Vonnegut warns of such a fate—the final loss of self, of human identity and personal freedom—through still another set of ominous psychic references: vivid images of petrification, destruction by fire, and death by drowning. The schizophrenic's dread of dissolution often manifests itself in terms of human nullification, e.g., being disembodied, emptied out of an inner self, made vacuumlike, being turned into someone else's thing. Vonnegut's characters experience precisely this feeling of depersonalization, believing themselves "petrified" or "frozen" by dehumanizing social, militaristic, or religious machinery or by the deadliest spiral of all—their own pessimism. At various times the protagonist experiences the loss of moral identity, represented in drowning imagery, being engulfed, or swallowed up.[40] Hence characters see themselves "deluged," overwhelmed by "tidal waves," sucked into whirlpools or sewers. That Vonnegut should use the exact imagery and phraseology of schizophrenia to portray the suffering of his characters suggests a more than casual insight into this condition.[41]

In fairness, those writers who see Vonnegut as a fatalist are partially right. The author's fictional voice is dualistic—"split . . . right up the middle," as is said of Paul Proteus in *Play Piano* (226)—into a self that affirms and a self that denies. It is the fierce combat of these warring identities—referred to by Freud in *Beyond the Pleasure Principle* as a battle between the forces of Eros, the life instinct, and Thanatos, the death instinct, that the tormented Howard Campbell calls "schizophrenic." Attempts at resolving this conflict constitute the psychoanalytic plot central to each of Vonnegut's novels and to his work as a whole.[42] Significantly, a major disorder trait present in schizophrenic patients is the compulsion to negate immediately any positive statement the patient makes; as soon as one portion of the split psyche affirms, the other portion must contradict.[43] This dichotomous struggle of simultaneous assertion and denial of the value of existence, in which the individual is torn between the yes of the will to live and the no of the will to cease, has baffled critics, leading them to allege self-contradictions and philosophical inconsistencies in Vonnegut's work, but accounts for the self-induced neutralization of ego and purposeful absence of resolution at the end of Vonnegut's early novels.

This failure to discern the nature of Vonnegut's divided fictive selves has led to the critical myopia that sees Vonnegut as a cosmic pessimist. While a majority of critics heed the more audible and visible nihilistic voice in Vonnegut's protagonists—the self filled with "lie down and die"—they miss or ignore altogether its spiritual twin—the efforts of a healthier, yearning, creative self to brave the life struggle, to develop the awareness and courage to act against self-imprisoning cat's cradles and to determine its own identity in a world of mechanistic conformity and anonymity.[44] Thus it is that the dynamic psychic drama of Vonnegut's fiction takes form—the struggle for possession of the protagonist's agonizingly divided soul by the opposing forces of optimism and pessimism. In one novel after another, we witness the sometimes despairing, sometimes hopeful efforts of Vonnegut's fragmented protagonists to put their disintegrated selves together again—to resist the various forms of moral escapism that paralyze their creative will and to achieve a wholeness of spirit.

On the one hand, the protagonist's idealistic voice encourages him to maintain youthful idealisms: to nurture a drive or awareness, self-possession, and moral responsibility, and to pursue dreams of a more just and harmonious social order. On the other hand, the protagonist's lunatic experience breeds a potentially incapacitating despair which undermines his drive for autonomy and social reform. A paralyzing fatalism prompts him to forsake all hope of improvement in the human condition. Hence arises that compulsive search for refuge from life's storms which causes the protagonist to drug himself to reality—to dream dangerous fantasies of perfect peace and harmony, which may relieve him from dealing with painful experience but which threaten to condemn him to the "existential gangrene" spoken of by R. D. Laing. As long as he muffles the cry of conscience and relinquishes his will to others, the protagonist can experience only a self-induced hatred and a kind of moral petrification of spirit. Whether he will manage to find a bridge between his several selves— what psychologists call "homeostasis"[45]—and develop the awareness and courage to follow his conscience and act against the deforming mechanisms that threaten to engulf him is the fundamental concern of every Vonnegut novel.

Vonnegut's first schizoid hero, Paul Proteus, appears partially successful at best in resisting the system of machines that threatens his sanity. The problem is that despite his inherent resistance to, as he puts it, "carrying out directions from above," Paul ultimately lacks the strength of will and the courage to follow a partially awakened conscience and to act against the totalitarian machinery that he himself helps to administer. As soon as his positive voice asserts itself, the pessimistic voice nullifies it, creating a kind of spiritual stalemate. This self-neutralization of ego leaves him feeling like what he eventually becomes, "an unclassified human being" (239). Yet if Paul is unable to resolve his personal crisis, he is sufficiently aware at the close of *Player Piano* to deliver Vonnegut's affirmative message: that "the main business of humanity is to do a good job of being human beings; not to serve as appendages to machines, institutions, and systems" (297). That Paul's struggle for autonomy is itself life-affirming is confirmed by Lasher in his closing comment to Paul, "It doesn't matter if we win or lose, Doctor. The important thing is that we tried" (315).

While we leave Paul Proteus in limbo, the element of hope in his last name signals a potential for growth realized by future heroes, each of whom becomes increasingly successful in combating defeatism, in struggling against tyrannical systems of control, and in putting his disintegrated self and world together again. The denouement to Paul's psychodrama is still to come—not in *Player Piano* and not until the dialectical struggle between hope and despair that begins with Paul is worked out in a process of exorcism and renewal through such extensions of the Vonnegut hero as Malachi Constant, Howard Campbell, Eliot Rosewater, Billy Pilgrim, and Kilgore Trout. The sense of this crystallizes when we recognize that, as Vonnegut himself explains, the struggle of these later heroes should be perceived in light of the spiritual evolution of one man—a single, fragmented psyche—seeking to overcome defeatism and to discover a faith, a course of action, that will result in a more positive, creative identity. That man, a traumatized survivor of Dresden, trying to adjust to an absurd world after the war, battling his despair over a world that seems unyielding in its suffering and destructiveness, is Kurt Vonnegut. No wonder that Vonnegut should say to us, "I find myself turning all my books into one book";[46] "The big show is inside my own head";[47] "I myself am a work of fiction."[48]

This "magical lunatic" has been telling us for years that his "career has been about craziness," and that the basic plot of his fiction is the "losing and regaining" of his own equilibrium.[49] "I have always thought of myself as an over-reactor," Vonnegut says, "a person who makes a questionable living with his mental diseases." When asked about his work as personal therapy, he replied, "That's well known. Writers get a nice break in one way, at least: they can treat their mental illnesses every day." In *Breakfast of Champions* (1973) Vonnegut decided to address his "creative craziness" directly—putting a name to it—thus illuminating the profound suffering of all his major characters and explaining the crucial stimulus to his own creative drive. Telling us in a dialogue with himself that he is afraid he will kill himself the way his mother did, he writes, "Here in the cocktail lounge, peering out through my leaks at a world of my own invention, I mouthed the word: schizophrenia. The sound and appearance of the word had fascinated me for many years—I did not and do not know for certain that I have that disease—I was sick for awhile, though. I am better now. Word of honor: I am better now" (210).

As we shall see, it is very likely that the therapeutic purging of the Billy Pilgrim within himself—his fatalistic voice—is the process by which the author has become "better." Just as Ernest Hemingway and Joseph Heller acknowledged using their typewriters as psychoanalysts to work out the psychologically damaging effects of war, so Vonnegut, a traumatized survivor of the allied bombing of Dresden, has used his writing as a way of purging himself of the terrors of war and adjusting to a postwar world just as absurd in its suffering and destruction as the war itself.

Addressing the subject of this book in a personal letter to me, Kurt Vonnegut said he hoped I didn't think he was crazy. He had not, he said, had any genuinely schizophrenic episodes in his life.

I haven't ever hallucinated, or been hospitalized or incapacitated for mental illness of any sort. I have been profoundly depressed, but have always been able to keep working somehow. The medical school at the University of Iowa did a study of established writers at the Writer's Workshop, myself included, and learned that we were all depressives—from families of depressives. There was scarcely an hallucinator in the lot.[50]

In fact, Vonnegut's recent work testifies that he has more than survived what in *Breakfast of Champions* he called the "spiritual crossroads of his career"—a battle with personal despair. With the help of his work as therapy, he has learned to create for himself and for us that "humane harmony" whose absence may nearly have driven him crazy. Vonnegut's "creative craziness" has done more than serve him as personal therapy, more even than to make for "beautiful accidents in art."[51] Vonnegut's creative life adjustments in a mad and aggressive world are those by which we may learn to regain our own equilibrium. Artur Sammler in *Mr. Sammler's Planet* asks, "Is the world crazy, so crazy that lunar voyages will be easier than to straighten out the chaos man has made on earth?"[52] Vonnegut opts for voyages of a different kind—descents into self for the knowledge and wisdom to combat the chaos within and the chaos without.

According to the testimony of Leon Trout at the end of *Galápagos* (1985), there is still hope for mankind, even in the darkest of times. For the characters of *Galápagos,* says Leon, it is too late to "crawl from the ruins of *their* creation."[53] But for us, by learning "to give a damn" (80), there is time to steer the floundering *Bahía de Darwin* (the ship of human destiny) in a more humane and intelligent direction—to eschew the dynamite bouquet of mindlessness, to change our minds about experiments with destruction, and to experiment instead with kindness, intelligence, and restraint. Mechanistic structures—ticks of the clock, lovelessness and apathy, the stockpiling of weapons of destruction, the pessimism of Kilgore Trout—all are open to revision. Noting that the "Galápagos Islands could be hell in one moment and heaven in the next," Leon Trout asserts that it is we who are responsible for our creations, that it is we, as a character first says in *God Bless You, Mr. Rosewater,* who "are right now determining whether the space voyage for the next billion years or so is going to be a Heaven or Hell" (18).

Part I

The Struggle

The big show is inside my head.

Breakfast of Champions

We may well heave a sigh of relief that it is . . . vouchsafed to a few to salvage . . . from the whirlpool of their own feelings the deepest truth, toward which the rest of us have to find our way through tormenting uncertainty and with restless groping.

Civilization and Its Discontents

1

Player Piano:
A Looney Tune for the Masses

Some of the greatest prophets were crazy as bedbugs.
                                                    The Shah of Bratpuhr

*Those who know how close the connection is between . . . courage
and hope, or lack of them—will understand that the sudden loss
of hope and courage can have a deadly effect . . . that a person
doesn't continue to live very long physically after hope is lost.*
                                    Viktor Frankl, *Man's Search for Meaning*

In his essay "The Theme of Mechanization in *Player Piano*," Thomas Hoffman
shows us that much of the success of Vonnegut's first negative utopia comes
from the pervasiveness with which the machine is shown to have infiltrated
society and robbed people of their sense of usefulness, meaning, and dignity.[1]
In the post-EPICAC era people have come to feel useless, their very souls
having been hollowed of substance.[2] Spiritual and libidinal energies have been
so totally regimented and perverted in mechanical activities that a manager,
Garth, is described as standing in relation to the corporate image as a lover;
Anita, wife of hero Paul Proteus, is shown lying back in "a rainbow colored
nest of control wires" (270) satisfied not so much by her husband's sexual
attention as by the "social orgasm of, after . . . the system's love play, being
offered Pittsburgh" (13). Such examples of libidinal displacement occur repeatedly throughout Vonnegut's work as the central expression of emotional inca-
pacitation.[3]

   Professor Hoffman suggests that in offering us warnings about the dehumanized future, not as it must necessarily be but as it surely would become if
based on the runaway technology of the present, Vonnegut writes "more like a
social scientist than a novelist," presenting us with "sociology expressed in

fictional form."[4] We are shown that while the book's main theme is "machine-made loneliness" resulting from the protagonist's struggle for awareness and independence from machinelike controls, Paul's story is used more to highlight the problems and actions of an entire society than of one man.[5] To illustrate the predominantly sociological character of the novel, Professor Hoffman reminds us of the tripartite division of Vonnegut's microcosmic American society that has been fragmented into hopelessly alienated parts in the name of simplified planning and production—the managers and engineers on one side of the river, the workers on the other; near the managers, the machines.[6]

> In the northwest are the managers and engineers and civil servants and a few professional people; in the northeast are the machines; and in the south across the Iroquois River, is the area known locally as Homestead, where almost all of the people live. (9)

Certainly Paul's particular plight—his isolation from all that had once given his life meaning: his job, his father, his wife, and his best friend—represents the plight of his society as a whole. Paul is intensely guilt-ridden, in fact, over being part creator of the sterile, unproductive lives of those little people for whom he professes a generalized love and whose certain hatred troubles him deeply. Just after we meet him, he is looking on unhappily at the mechanical hands, electric eyes, and punch press jaws of the machinery of the Ilium works—machines that are no longer controlled by men but by other machines. The human loss most ominous to Paul because it mirrors his own condition is that, like the piano keys, like puppets, the citizenry has become so regulated and standardized by the ruling technocracy that they themselves have become mindless pieces of machinery, unable to believe in anything better and hence no longer capable of human change or growth.

This is particularly the plight of the workers—of the Reconstruction and Reclamation Corps, or Reeks and Wrecks, and those relegated to mindless enslavement in the army—who have been mechanically determined to be un-blessed with sufficiently high IQ and thus spat out by the great computer-God EPICAC XIC to the far side of the river, the area known as Homestead. Since the machines do all the hiring and firing and positions are irrevocable, these people either exist in self-hatred and contempt for their enslavers (reconciling themselves to their lot as if cast by an act of God), or they commit suicide or anesthetize themselves to the pain of uselessness and alienation with clichés of well-being provided by governmental propagandists. Kroner, the High Priest of Industrial Efficiency, may extol the wonders of the Second Industrial Revolution with its increase of production, but Ed Finnerty observes that drug abuse, alcoholism, and suicide are all up in direct proportion to the increase in automation (58). Dr. Halyard may explain the splendors of American mechanization to the Shah of Bratpuhr, but the reader sees that the supposed beneficiaries of such mechanization have been swallowed up and regurgitated like Paul's cat early in the novel.

These contrary perceptions of reality—mechanization as splendorous to Halyard but as enslavement to the Shah—function as what Patricia Waugh calls a process of "defamiliarization."[7] Vonnegut inverts the science-fiction convention whereby humans are depicted attempting to comprehend the values of an alien world. Ilium is the "alien" world to the Shah. Oblivious to its established value systems or moral codes, the Shah defamiliarizes the machine-ridden society that the inhabitants of Ilium take for granted, exposing amoral assumptions and consequences of a governmental propaganda machine that calls people without jobs or dignity, people "liberated" (28) from production.

Halyard complains that "this guy thinks of everything he sees in terms of his own country" (7). But the reader sees that Halyard exploits the Homesteaders' inability to decode governmental language to keep them docile and fatalistic—enforcing the view that "nothing of value changed, that what was true was always true" (122).[8] What the Shah exposes as arbitrary and manipulative systems of language and belief, Halyard portrays as absolute and irresistible. The isolation and paralysis of the Homesteaders is determined as much by the subtle machinations of language as by more obvious social constrictions. An understanding of the arbitrary, pluralistic, and symbiotic nature of reality and language, signs and signifiers, becomes a central expression of the moral and mental development of Vonnegut's hero—the ability to analyze mechanistic structures, psychical, social, and linguistic, and to construct realities of his own. The hero becomes increasingly adept at what Jacques Lacan cites as basic to dynamic psychic life, the playful use of language as puns, jokes, metaphors, irony, paradox, and dream vision.[9]

Vonnegut himself has said that his guiding purpose as an artist has been to serve as "the canary bird in the coal mine"—as an alarm system to warn society of its technological dangers—so his role as social critic or as a writer of "sociological" novels is not to be denied. But there is another dimension in this novel—one personal and intensely psychological in nature—that explains more precisely the profound "loneliness" experienced by its protagonist Paul Proteus and that may come closer than Hoffman's explanation to helping us understand the author's long uphill struggle against the dehumanizing power of machines. For once, the blurb on a Vonnegut book cover has it right: "Paul Proteus had it made. Why did he feel as if he were going insane. . . . What kind of nut was he, anyway?" Before he can solve the larger social conflicts of the novel represented by the split between the managers and engineers and those who live across the river, Paul must first heal his own agonizingly divided soul. To Ed Harrison, a potential managerial defector like himself, Paul offers a warning: if Ed tries the stratagem of living partly on the job and partly in dreams, he will be split "right up the middle" before he can decide which way to go. When Ed asks if something like this happened to him, Paul answers in the affirmative (9). There is hence a psychological as well as a political and sociological meaning to Paul's cry, "we must meet in the middle of the bridge" (114). Whether Paul will manage to find a bridge between *his* several selves—to develop the awareness and courage to follow his conscience and to act against the machinery that threatens to engulf him—is the main issue to be decided by the end of this novel. In fact, it is the most fundamental concern of every Vonnegut novel.

If, as I suggest, *Galápagos* (1985) was the last of Vonnegut's purely therapeutic books, the last schizophrenic invention as well as the last session on the couch for the author, then *Player Piano* is surely the first—the first in which Vonnegut holds a sanity hearing for himself, for his characters, and for the bizarre world in which he tries to maintain a precarious "equilibrium." Early in *Player Piano,* Ed Finnerty feels something snap inside him and sits for hours with Paul's cocked gun in his mouth. "You think I'm insane?" he asks Paul. "You're still in touch." "I guess that's the test," Paul replies (85–86). Ironically, Finnerty, who has begun to rebel openly against the system of machines that threatens his sanity, worries that Paul is not more shaken by the unholy mechanistic society he helps administer. Actually Paul is less in touch with his surroundings and with himself than he or Finnerty suspects. Longing for a time when things were less impersonal and more human, he suffers frequently from depression, swigs regularly from a bottle of whiskey in his bottom desk drawer for solace, and speaks of being in need of a psychiatrist and of committing suicide. As he contemplates the emotional void in his marriage, he comes to suspect that his wife's feelings are shallow but considers that his suspicions are part of his sickness (25).[10] As he contemplates his sickness, Paul lives through one of the most revealing symbolic episodes in all Vonnegut's work. On the very first page of the book we read of Paul's befriending of a small black cat. Wandering in the Ilium Works, the cat is caught and eaten by an automated sweeper. The machine spits the cat down a chute and into a freight car outside the factory. Momentarily it seems the cat will survive, but as Paul races desperately to help, the cat scrambles up the side of an electrically charged fence and, with a pop and a green flash, is sent sailing high into the air, "dead and smoking, but outside" (20–21).

The moral is obvious, but nonetheless ominous. The omnipresent machinery of Paul's society is deadly to living things, and the possibility of escaping its influence is slight. But what Vonnegut shows us through the symbolic death of the cat is that Paul's sickness, his immense depression, is the result of fearing that his *own* fate is to be as terrible and inevitable as that of the cat with which he identifies, that is, that he will be gobbled up by the omnipresent emotional vacuum cleaner, the corporate personality. At one point, for instance, Paul sees himself as if overwhelmed by a tidal wave, deluged, like the toy boat he watches moving toward its doom in the "dark, gurgling unknown" of the sewer (253).

The image is particularly foreboding in light of R. D. Laing's description of the schizophrenic as one who typically experiences a loss of self—of identity or freedom—in the form of drowning, of being engulfed or swallowed up.[11] Paul at various times sees himself "deluged," overwhelmed by a "tidal wave," and sucked into the devouring storm sewer (253). However vaguely sensed by Paul at first, his fear of being absorbed forever into the dehumanizing machinery of the corporation has been contingent in his mind upon accepting the Pittsburgh job, the most important position in his field and the sole maniacal obsession of his wife, Anita. As Anita is badgering him once again about showing more enthusiasm for the Pittsburgh promotion, he begins to reflect upon her shallowness and his own loss of interest in everything around him. Hanging up the telephone, he puts his head down and closes his eyes. When he opens them again, they are fixed directly on the dead cat in the basket (25).

Ironically Paul's instinctive aversion to the pervasive mechanization of life around him—the replacement of people with machines and the mechanical behavior of people who have been turned into machines—has driven him into an emotional vacuum that is just as defeating as the misery he seeks to escape. He recognizes that any attempt at achieving an emotional life for himself is pure pretense, that shows of affection are just shows, mechanical and insincere. He knows, for instance, that his reactions to his wife are mere reflex. Anita, too, has reduced marriage to a set of mechanical conventions, as when she manipulates expressions of warmth from Paul whenever she feels him pulling free from her influence. And when Paul is with Finnerty, he only pretends to share the man's emotional enthusiasms, while observing that Finnerty uses words such as *love* and *affection* to describe his feelings, words Paul can never bring himself to use (87). Even when Finnerty makes his commitment to helping the people on the opposite side of the river, Paul finds himself without any sort of appropriate feeling for Finnerty's important announcement (139). When Finnerty accuses him of being afraid to live, Paul acknowledges that he is indeed without belief of any kind (140).[12]

From within his self-spun cocoon, Paul lacks sufficient awareness, conviction, and moral strength either to continue playing convincingly the role of loyal and happy plant manager, fellow high-priest with Kroner and Baer to the Great God EPICAC, or to repudiate this higher calling passed on to him by his father and openly resist the system that threatens to destroy his will to live. Either prospect leaves him feeling like "an unclassified human being" (239), lonely and dispossessed. It is partly in this sense that Paul comes by that agonizingly divided soul, that separation of his several selves that eventually causes Howard Campbell of *Mother Night* to commit suicide. The problem is that despite his inherent resistance to, as he puts it, "carrying out directions from above" (128), Paul's drive toward selfhood is always counterbalanced by a moral paralysis brought on by institutional conditioning and a fatalistic philosophy. We find him continuously relinquishing his will to others, reacting like the keys on the player piano (38), or else allowing a partially awakened conscience to be lulled easily to sleep.

As the son of Ilium's most famous industrial leader, the virtual founder of modern mechanization, Paul has been so long programmed to accept and perpetuate the divine right of machinery that he wonders at his own unnaturalness at being disgruntled with the system. He even longs for an overwhelming fervor like that of his dead father and Kroner in the unquestioning faith that his is indeed a golden age. Occasionally Paul finds himself mindlessly assimilating the clichés of progress and *esprit de corps* mouthed so easily by Kroner, Baer, and Shepherd, and by Mom and Anita. He tries hard to believe in the sanctity of machines and industrial organization, and even begs to be refuted as he pours out his misgivings to his surrogate father, Kroner. The point is, though, that no refutations are needed. The corporate will, however detestable to Paul, is stronger than his own; when Paul stands before Kroner, he senses that he is actually in the presence of his father and powerless to resist the old man (48). Even Anita, for whom things are relevant or irrelevant, moral or immoral, only as they secure or hinder social advancement, is capable of controlling Paul's behavior. To insure that Paul gives the proper, corporate responses during a social outing with his boss, Anita prepares him an outline. Paul does not read it, but when Kroner mentions the Pittsburgh job to him, Paul responds as he thinks Anita wants him to (127).

Paul's potentially fatal mistake is deciding to play dead, to muffle the cry of conscience through a variety of anesthetizing devices. If the conflict of divided loyalties and the inability to commit himself is simply too overwhelming, he will withdraw from it in the fashion described by Edmond L. Harrison. That is, he will crawl into the nearest suitable womb (266). And so it is no surprise that when Anita presses him about the Pittsburgh job, Paul curls up tighter and tighter in "the dark, muffled womb" of his bed (134).[13]

Ironically, it is Anita, whose love he finds so detestably mechanical, who provides the major opiate for Paul's uneasy conscience. Her sexuality becomes his only enthusiasm in life; he feels the "drugging warmth" of her bosom and feels himself to be merging his "consciousness" with that of his wife (177, 178). Once, having made a decision to quit, he asks Anita whether she is ever bothered by conscience. She chides him playfully and pulls him down to kiss her, but then play turns into something very much like hypnotism: "I don't want my little boy to worry. You're not going to quit, sweetheart. You're just awfully tired" (178). Paul feels as if he is drugged, surrenders to fatigue and thinks of Edgar Allan Poe's "Descent into the Maelstrom," as "he [gives] himself over" to the unfailing rhythm of sex (270).

Paul finds another comforter or blinder of sorts in the fantasy world portrayed in the adventure books he reads, and into which he literally tries to withdraw. Described as retreating into "phantasmagoria within the privacy of his closed eyelids" (143), he identifies with romantic pioneer heroes who depend not upon machines but upon basic cunning and physical strength for survival (114). Paul tries to make his fantasy real by purchasing an isolated, backwater farmhouse, "a patch of the past" he thinks Anita will love. But when she finds it hideous and thinks of appropriating its quaint contents to her own home, Paul's dream is quickly aborted. Drowning imagery provides Paul with an unconscious forewarning of spiritual stagnation and the dissolution of ego such isolation may produce. Contemplating his backwater paradise, Paul notices that the word "deluge" sticks in his mind (148). Jacques Lacan would refer to this as an instance in which the subject is "spoken" rather than speaking.[14]

But Paul's moral paralysis, his will-lessness, is reinforced by something even more threatening to his sanity than his flight from technology. On trial as leader of the Ghost Shirt Society, Paul confesses that his rebellion against organizational machinery is partly Oedipal in origin—the unconscious repression of erotic love for his mother, and fear and anger toward the censoring, primal father.[15] The prosecutor asks if Paul's hatred of machinery and "injustice to humanity" isn't motivated by something less abstract. "I'm talking about your hate for *someone*," he says, "one of the greatest true patriots in American history, your father." The prosecutor submits that Paul is still a spiteful boy to whom the American economy, "this civilization of ours," has become a symbol of the father Paul subconsciously would like to destroy (298). When the prosecutor asks Paul to deny this, Paul admits that he can't (299). The voice of the prosecutor (or persecuting authority) is only a "whisper," a signal, perhaps, sent up from Paul's own unconscious mind, the onset of cathartic unburdening of buried fear and guilt. The exposure, however, leaves Paul feeling defenseless and alone, believing that the problem is "singularly" his own (299).

Paul's compassion for the Reeks and Wrecks is real, but he also projects his own desperate hunger for love when he observes that the strongest need of the little, common people of Ilium was for understanding, beauty, and simple, earthy love. When he claims that this had been hidden to him all his life "by the walls of his ivory tower" (102), we see that his own deepest yearnings have been equally enigmatic. During these musings, Paul is confronted by two young women from the Ilium underworld, and he loves them "instantly" (103). Paul's vague surmise is right: he *is* "voracious for love—Anita's love, vividly imagined love, vicarious love—any love, whatever was immediately available" (236). The latter thought occurs as Paul watches Anita primping before a "booby trap" mirror whose lights suddenly flash on. Fascinated by her breasts "ingeniously hidden," Paul watches her image a long time, changing forms, "turning this way and that" (236). When she catches Paul looking, she jumps and folds her arms "across her bosom in a protective gesture."

The unconscious sexual implications of the scene are profoundly Oedipal—

for Paul and for all Vonnegut's protagonists to follow.[16] Just as the prosecutor at Paul's trial discloses Paul's obsession with social injustice as something less abstract, so Paul's yearnings for "any love" disguise a compulsion far more personal: it is not even the warmth and fragrance of Anita's bosom he seeks, but his mother's. Both literally and figuratively, the mirror is "booby" trapped. It literally highlights breasts Paul associates with maternal safety, contentment, and ideal beauty, and it adumbrates the futility of his quest to recapture such contentment through illusory mothers and substitute wombs—fantasies of mindless Edenic happiness.[17]

Paul's impulse to throw off the trappings of civilization and retreat to a golden age of the past correlates with his Oedipal breast and womb fixations, a time and space of perfect contentment. The location of Paul's farmhouse is "a completely isolated backwater, cut off from the boiling rapids of history, society, and the economy. Timeless" (147). The emotional release Paul seeks in this womblike, precivilized, or subconscious world is conspicuously sexual: "Here was a place where he could work with his hands, getting life from nature without being disturbed by any human beings other than his wife" (149). Other than his *mother,* he should have said. For a long time Anita accepts her status as Paul's substitute mother. She frequently speaks "baby talk" to Paul "as though he were a lazy little boy coaxed into doing a small favor for his mother" (42). At the start of their marriage, she merges her identity with Paul's mother by hanging his father's picture in the bedroom (66). She worships the image with idolatrous if not erotic fervor. She later turns her affection to Lawson Shepherd, whom she claims is the exact image of Paul's father (67). Finally, she withdraws from Paul's mother-fantasy by accusing him of not desiring her at all but "something . . . shaped like a woman" (237). Her warmth, then, is doubly "counterfeit" (25). But Paul's love is equally dishonest, and she rightly rebels against being treated like a "machine." Aware that it is her "counterfeit" image in the mirror that attracts Paul, Anita asserts her own selfhood by covering her bosom, denying him his most passionate need: the maternal, erotic breasts. Paul also pays for these forbidden longings with nightmarish visions of an angry, punishing father. Awakening in the middle of the night alongside his mother-wife, he thinks he sees the father he seeks to replace glowering at him from the foot of the bed (246).

Anita is right to accuse Paul of taking pleasure from making things up to feel guilty about (43). However unconscious, Paul's sense of wrongdoing is so strong he grows masochistic—condemning not only himself but all humanity.[18] "I'm no good," he announces; mankind is motivated by something "sordid." "That's what it is to be human" (299). Paul is more right than he knows. His anger toward his father is as natural as the anxiety resulting from the loss of his mother's love. Freud says about the son's inevitable ambivalence and guilt toward the primal authority,

His sons hated him, but they loved him, too. After their hatred had been satisfied by their act of aggression, their love came to the fore in their remorse for the deed. It set up the super-ego by identification with the father; it gave that agency the father's power, as though as punishment for the deed.[19]

Paul's struggle for autonomy is complicated by a nonnurturing mother and a father with whom it is impossible to identify. The absence or coldness of both parents is typical of the case history of schizophrenics.[20] Such parents deny the child a secure and reliable model of behavior and growth, frustrate his or her feeling of internal and external harmony, and create an inability to differentiate illusion from reality. Lacan explains that to escape the Oedipal relationship with the mother and constitute his own identity, the subject must acquire the name ("the paternal metaphor") of the father. But how does Paul achieve this through a father coldly aloof, mechanical, and unloving, whose values Paul rightly defies? According to Lacan's mirror theory of ego-formation,[21] Paul's image of himself through the eyes of his parents is fragmented, disembodied, or invisible. When Paul should be assimilating his parents' constraints and ideals, his mother withholds affection, and his father literally isn't there. Niles Finnerty wonders what a psychiatrist would say about Paul's unconscious swipes at his father, and asks, "Was your father a bastard?" "How do I know who my father was?" Paul says. "The editor of *Who's Who* knows about as much as I do. The guy was hardly ever home." (85).

If Paul is to achieve the love and self-possession he seeks, he must resist simplistic readings of and escapist solutions to the painful demands of being human. He must resolve "the unpleasant business between me and the memory of my father" by bringing Oedipal tensions to consciousness and recognizing neither that these forbidden wishes make him "bad" nor that such a condition is "singularly" his own.[22] Rather, as Paul acknowledges when Lasher says, "Some sons do hang themselves" (97), "This is as old as life itself." Not only have sons always rebelled against the authority of the father, but a certain amount of the guilt and repression Paul suffers serves the course of civilization itself—allowing the individual to mediate primal aggression, warring urges between Eros and Thanatos.[23] Paul's understanding of his own declaration that "what distinguishes man from the rest of the animals is his ability to do artificial things" (295) is critical to his personal evolution and to the struggle of all civilized life. He must take the authority and conscience of a father onto himself, controlling his instincts and repudiating "the lawlessness of machines" (299) for which his father stands.[24] He must use the power to create, the path of the artist, the power of Eros, to preserve and extend life rather than to sustain the unfeeling, mechanical world of his father and such surrogate fathers as Kroner and Baer.

Paul will continue, however, to be fearful of reality, neurotically guilty, disillusioned, and emotionally withdrawn as long as he believes that the soulless mechanization of his life is a matter of historic or biological inevitability and infant sexual love remains his "one unqualified enthusiasm in life," his proto-type for happiness. Shepherd is not far wrong when he tells Anita that instead of being filled with get up and go, Paul is dangerously filled with "lie down and die" (166). Even as Paul wonders if he has the capital to stop being a pawn of history, he cannot imagine that same history having "led anywhere else" (41). He views himself as so inescapably a part of the machinery of society and history that he can move in one direction only to determine his own identity (41). In this very way he rationalizes his joyless life with Anita, deciding that, whatever her failings, she is his inevitable fate, to love as well as he can (133). Even at the end of the book, we find Paul not very different from Ewing I. Halyard, wondering about the mechanics of being human, "mechanics far beyond the poor leverage of free will" (300–301).

Given Paul's record of moral evasion, it is not surprising that he should so easily fall prey to such paralyzing fatalism. The philosophic consolations of fatalism can be devilishly alluring since one need not struggle to be aware of or to change that which is believed unchangeable. It is a particularly deadly form of self-loss because by such paralysis the individual may well perpetuate his own doom at the hands of whatever totalitarian entity attempts to consume him. This, in fact, is precisely Paul's fate at the conclusion of *Player Piano*—at the Meadows, two weeks of superficial comaraderie and brotherhood for "the not yet complete"(44), and as titular head of the Ghost Shirt Society. Both mini psychodramas test Paul's courage and will to combat machinery within and without, which he fails. The lack of higher imaginings than fantasized boobies and substitute wombs leads Paul further into narcissistic isolation and away from that "fresh, strong identity" he feels stirring within (102).

While the "Meadows" conveys womblike associations of softness, natural-ness, and contentment, the life it engenders is grotesquely mechanical. Manu-factured opportunities for friendship produce only further alienation and loneli-ness. Members are given ten minutes to get to know one another, and expres-sions of intimacy and individuality of feelings are as counterfeit as the love of Anita and Paul's father. The machinelike designs of the corporation are met by mass producing conformist robotic personalities whose values and conscience belong to the organization. As for Paul's struggle for selfhood, "It was impos-sible to tell where one ego left off and the next began" (191).

Paul's secret "detachment," his "variously amused or cynical outlook" (134) seems momentarily to save him from assimilation into the group, but assumption of an alien identity, what Laing, Lacan, and others call "a false self" leaves him more disconnected from himself and others than ever. Earlier Paul had avoided a difficult moral choice—postponing the Pittsburgh decision—by masking his true feelings about the system in public, pretending to be its faithful servant while secretly holding it in contempt. "Outwardly, as manager," he says, "he was unchanged; but inwardly he was burlesquing smaller, less free souls who would have taken the job seriously" (134). The burlesque is Paul's delusion that by dividing himself into a secret self and a false self, he can avoid engulfment and keep his ideals and his integrity intact. Tranquillity being more important to him than integrity, he will go on, unless checked, nourishing his secret voice forever, which is exactly his situation at the Meadows.[25] Pleased that he has resisted the orgy of group singing, marching, and sentimental fellowship geared to drown thought and spontaneous feeling, he reaffirms his determination to quit the system "if he felt like it. No hurry" (201). Laing observes that the danger of a split like Paul's is that it may create an "equivocal nature."[26] The two selves are pitted against each other, a will to live and a will to cease. The compulsion of the negative self is to negate any impulse of the aspiring self, resulting in interminable contradiction, impotence, and emptiness. The creation of a mask may also become compulsive, uncontrollable, and as with other forms of withdrawal, render the individual less and less able to participate in real life.

Paul asserts his pseudopersonality when asked to infiltrate the ranks of the discontented and inform on old friends. He pretends indignation, resolving never again to serve as an appendage to machines, institutions, or systems (297). But the moral alternatives are so clear that he admits "he was in excellent shape to afford integrity" (132). Paul receives the challenge with relief, but the resulting hollowness proves intolerable. Finding "reality disquieting at all points" (223), he heads for a saloon.

If Paul is incomplete as a blindly loyal corporation personality, he remains incomplete too as that fragmented person who has wanted so badly "to get the feel of the world as a whole" (170). For now, he merely renounces one master, one lobotomizing system, for another. As the proposed new Messiah for the Ghost Shirt Society, a society potentially as totalitarian as the one it seeks to replace,[27] Paul is used impersonally, as a mere name, a front for their organization, and his effort to resist assimilation into the collective will of the group is futile. Finnerty tells him he need only keep out of sight while everything is done for him. Now that he belongs to history, he does not matter as an individual, and he need accept responsibility for nothing (280).

Once again, Paul's identity is successfully neutralized, and he meets the problem in the same old way, drugging himself to reality and relinquishing his will to others. "His muscles were only faintly connected to his will, and his will, in turn, was a fuzzy, ineffectual thing" (272), he thinks. And Lasher notes: "He'll do nicely," suggesting that Paul is exactly pliant enough, suggestible enough, to serve the revolution's need for a robotlike figurehead (272). When Paul is described as dreaming only of pleasant things under the influence of the drug given him by the Ghost Shirt Society (270), the larger significance of the reference is obvious: he is once again choosing comfort over integrity. When he clowns around and Finnerty admonishes him that "this isn't a joke, Paul," Lasher remarks: "Everything's a joke until the drug wears off" (274).[28]

At the novel's end, Paul notes that Lasher was the only one who hadn't lost touch with reality, and, more portentously, that it was he, Paul, who had been the one most out of touch, having had little time for reflection and so "eager to join a large, confident organization with seeming answers to the problems that had made him sorry to be alive" (314). So by Paul's own test at the book's beginning, he is more insane than not, "disembodied, an insubstantial wisp, nothingness, a man who declined to be any more" (134). Yet while the outer revolution in *Player Piano* is as doomed as Paul's cat, culminating in a blind orgy of indiscriminate wreckage and the inclination to put the same old system back together again, there are hints that Paul may yet be able, with the proper awareness and courage, to put his distinguished self and world together again too. Observing that the most beautiful peonies he ever saw were grown in "almost pure cat excrement" (300), Paul displays a capacity for embracing life's ambiguities, for exploring his shadowy inner world, and for thus realizing the potential for change and growth implicit in his last name—Proteus. In Carl Rogers's terms, Paul's name represents the drive for self-actualization of all organic life—the urge "to expand, extend, become autonomous, develop, mature." [29] The denouement to Paul's psychodrama is still to come, but not until the dialectical struggle between hope and despair that begins with Paul is worked out through such extensions of the Vonnegut hero as Malachi Constant, Jonah, Howard Campbell, Eliot Rosewater, Billy Pilgrim, and Kilgore Trout.

Thomas Hoffman seems right in viewing the ending of this novel as affirmative in that it "reassures us that humans will continue to rebel against this prisonhouse of their own creation despite the failure of *this* rebellion, *this* man, or *this* period of history."[30] Yet while it is doubtlessly again a "political, economic, and technological" prisonhouse against which Proteus struggles for autonomy (a social conflict), the more immediate danger against which Vonnegut warns is profoundly psychological in nature. Paul will remain pent up in his private inner world, irresolute in his dualistic commitment to and against tyrannical systems of control ("split . . . right up the middle") as long as he masks Oedipal tensions, muffles the cry of conscience, and continues to relinquish his will to others. It is this personal crisis, the self-induced neutralization of Paul's ego, that seems best to account for the lack of resolution at the novel's end.

Sirens of Titan: Though This Be Madness, Yet There Is Method in It

Son—they say there isn't any royalty in this country, but do you want me to tell you how to be King of the United States of America? Just fall through a hole in a privy and come out smelling like a rose.

Sirens of Titan

We cannot unthink unless we are insane.

Arthur Koestler

Vonnegut informs us in *Sirens of Titan* that the action of the novel takes place at a time when "men did not know that the meaning of life was within themselves . . . mankind, ignorant of the truths that lie within every human being, looked outward—pushed ever outward" (7). They left inwardness unexplored while giving themselves over to the mad delusion that the quest for material acquisitions—for money, power, and fame—was the path to salvation. This belief in satisfying spiritual needs with outward attractions, an insanity fed by technology, allowed that nations might glorify themselves by "hurling some heavy object into nothingness." With our "crazy towers and rockets to heaven," we might approach paradise itself (32). But, Vonnegut tells us from a perspective a century later, "Everyone now knows how to find the meaning of life within himself. . . . Outwardness lost, at last, its imagined attractions. Only inwardness remained to be explored. . . . This was the beginning of goodness and wisdom" (7, 8).

This explains Vonnegut's essential use of fantasy in *Sirens*—to intensify our awareness of the madness of our present lives from a futuristic perspective, while preparing us for a world that might be if we learn to solve the "puzzle boxes" within ourselves.[1] To this end we look inward into the "uncharted terrain" and "bizarre flight patterns" (30) of the mind of Malachi Constant, who only seems to travel to Mars, Mercury, Titan via a supernatural force called the UWTB, to be caught in a superterrestial phenomenon called "chrono-synclastic-infundibula," and to encounter various space monsters, "hideous . . . and uniformly cataclysmic" (5, 6). If Malachi is to overcome the insanity that threatens him at the novel's opening, his challenge is to learn to direct such inward journeys himself—to improve upon Paul Proteus's ability to look within himself for the answer to his spiritual needs, to stop expecting divine intervention to give his life purpose, and to negotiate his own destiny if he is to go anywhere at all.

One key to Vonnegut's fantasy vision in this novel comes in the form of parallels to Lewis Carroll's *Alice in Wonderland* and *Through the Looking-Glass.* In addition to direct references to *Alice in Wonderland,* numerous references to glass, portholes, windows, mirrors, and crystals, and to doors, caves, tunnels, and chimneys indicate extensive similarities between the two Alice books and Vonnegut's novel. Carroll sends Alice down a rabbit hole to the center of the earth while Vonnegut sends Malachi Constant into outer space, flights of imagination with highly dangerous consequences. As we see, both are shitholes (65).[2] Symbolized by the pervasive garden imagery in the Alice stories and by spirallike fountains, staircases, and mind-numbing cocoons in *Sirens,* illusions of peace and harmony threaten to lead these twin space travelers straight to hell rather than to the paradise they are promised. Ultimately, however, as with Alice, *Sirens* is more the story of Malachi's growth, of his adoption of awareness and courage and his quest for psychic wholeness, than the story of his madness. For he finally realizes that the world of chaos and brutality he enters is a projection of his own spiritual potential for creating a heaven or a hell of life on earth. Like all Vonnegut's protagonists, Malachi holds the Alice-in-Wonderland key to the doors of bedlam inside his own mind. He learns that with a little imagination and heart, he can, like the perfect machine Salo, dismantle his self-imprisoning machinery and reconstitute his being.[3]

Evidence that it is not outer space but the "uncharted terrain" of Malachi's own mind and soul where the main action of the novel takes place comes through the image of the "Alice-in-Wonderland door" (10) that Malachi enters to the Rumford estate. Just as the lost and dazed Alice concludes, "Then it really has happened after all,"[4] so Malachi prefers to think that everything behind the door was real. "This was exactly the case" (46), he says. Before this revelation, Constant had looked upon his Newport adventure as "one more drug-induced hallucination," one more vivid and entertaining peyotl party but of no consequence (46). He applauds himself for discovering that it had all been real (47). The evidence is overwhelming, however, that his first guess had been right, that the little door had been a dreamy touch . . . the dry fountain another . . . and the chimneylike room under the spiral staircase . . . and the photograph of the three sirens of Titan . . . and Rumfoord's prophecies . . . and the discomfiture of Beatrice Rumfoord at the top of the stairs. (46)

Just as the dreaming Alice enters her imaginary worlds with the help of a key she finds on a glass table and with the help of a chimney-piece in the second story, so Malachi unlocks the door to his equally fabulous kingdom with a private key, slamming the door behind him with a clang; he later discovers another key in the bottom of a drinking glass that opens other mental corridors.

That the Rumfoord door is a psychical one with the characters and events behind it subjective extensions of Malachi's own dreaming or hallucinating mind is further indicated by references to Rumfoord's materialization from pure wave phenomena into human form as "magic lantern slides projected . . . on the blank stone walls . . . of morbid imaginations," and by the fact that the realities behind the walls of the Rumfoord estate are experienced by Malachi alone (8). The materialization is described as "strictly a private affair on private property"; the crowd outside "knew it wasn't going to see anything"; it could only imagine what was happening inside (8–9). In fact, the most respected and learned men in the world beg to see a materialization and are turned down cold (9). We are told that Malachi has been invited to a materialization because Winston Niles Rumfoord insists he knows Malachi well from having met him on Titan, yet we learn that Malachi had never been to Titan, had never, "so far as he knew, been outside the gaseous envelope of his native planet, the Earth" (16). Just as Rumfoord exists as "one node of a wave phenomenon extending all the way from the Sun to Betelegeuse," (21) we hear that his wife spoke to almost no one, that her voice comes to Malachi "like the wind in the treetops," that her face even is "like the face of Malachi Constant" (40). Despite the sign outside the iron door to the estate that warns of the dog Kazak, inside there is only a dog's skeleton, a cunning model of a "flesh-ripping machine" (11–12).

Still more evidence that Malachi is the only verifiable character in the novel comes in the fact that, as with Alice, all of his inventions, no matter how bizarre or supernatural, can be traced to experiences he has really known.[5] "What the blast would I go there for?" says Malachi, thinking of Titan. It takes him a moment to realize why he had used those particular words.[6] "Blast was what space cadets on television said when a meteorite carried away a control surface" (35). Malachi himself owns the magazine, supposedly given to him by Rumfoord, in which pictures of the Sirens of Titan are displayed. Even the building in which Malachi works, the home of Magnum Opus, the corporation whose sole purpose was to manage Malachi's financial affairs, bears a striking resemblance to Rumfoord's palace on Titan, stocked with Earthling food and Earthling liquor. The palace is also an extension of the Rumfoord estate in Newport

(66, 67). In the caves of Mercury, Malachi thinks he sees buildings where his jailers and the masters of all creation live, but legless furniture floating in the air in both sets of buildings shows that these "dumb, cold crystals" reflect Malachi's memory of Magnum Opus again (187). It is Magnum Opus too that makes the spaceship that presumably takes Malachi on his space journey and that produces hoists similar to ones that lift him off the ground during his stint as Space Wanderer.

In short, the seeds of all Malachi's illusions are present in his very real, very insane earthling environment. He is painfully aware of the potential in the world around him for the development of the military nightmare represented by the planet Mars, a society with a large military and industrial complex whose flag has "red and white stripes and many white stars on a field of blue" (106). Not only are the Martian guns all American makes, but the Martian war machine is made possible by "capital gains on investments in land securities, Broadway shows, and inventions on earth" (92). Contemplating the Martian inhumanity of breeding people as though they were farm animals, Rumfoord admits that the Martians are doing only what his own class had done. The future of his class depended cynically on carefully calculated marriages (27). As with Alice and her looking-glass experiences, Malachi's fantasies mirror a very bizarre but recognizable present.[7]

Late in the novel, then, supposedly on Titan, when Malachi hears the voices of others coming back to him as his own echo (291), we appreciate the metaphorical and psychological content of his experience. But if the source or meaning of Alice's psychological projections is innocent and playful in kind, these "echos" in *Sirens* are of a mind increasingly paranoid and seeking to hide in self-imprisoning fantasies of comfort and protection.[8] Not that Malachi's suffering—his fear of drowning in that "sea of raging flesh" (43) of lunatic humanity that crowds around the Rumfoord estate waiting for miracles—is purely delusional. His withdrawal is a natural reaction to very real terrors from which he does well to shrink. His crisis, that spoken of when Mrs. Rumfoord notes that the materialization is a "a tragic family affair" (10), is that the dubious wisdom that comes to him by way of his Martian and Tralfamadorian hallucinations may condemn him to the "existential gangrene" described by Laing in *The Divided Self*. Withdrawal from an outer world of people and things into one of phantom fulfillment may lead to a total inability to act and finally to a state of nonbeing and a desire for death.

As with Paul Proteus, Vonnegut's hero at the beginning of *Sirens of Titan* is in deep emotional trouble, his life a nightmare of void and meaninglessness, "not yet one of the lunatics but the nearly sane" in the crowd through which his limousine passes (43). As the inheritor of almost three million dollars and speculator in corporate securities for the giant business conglomerate he owns, Magnum Opus, Malachi Constant is outwardly America's richest human being

(56).[9] But years of hypocrisy and sharp business practice have created an emotional void he tries to fill with "a lewdness and lascivious questing" (160–61) that numbs his pain and leaves his heart and soul untouched. Malachi has used his fortune

> to finance an unending demonstration that man is a pig. He wallowed in sycophants. He wallowed in worthless women. He wallowed in lascivious entertainments and alcohol and drugs. He wallowed in every known form of voluptuous turpitude. At the height of his good luck, Malachi Constant was worth more than the states of Utah and North Dakota combined. Yet . . . his moral worth was not that of the most corrupt little fieldmouse in either state. . . . He was as benevolent as Marie Antoinette, as creative as a professor of cosmetology in an embalming college. (251, 252)

Looking for some small sign that his life has something of human value in it,

> Constant ransacked his memory like a thief going through another man's billfold. Constant found his memory stuffed with rumpled, overexposed snapshots of all the women he had had, with preposterous credentials testifying to his ownership of even more preposterous enterprises, with testimonials that attributed to him virtues and strengths that only three billion dollars could have. . . . All that remained to Constant were the husks of his memory—unstitched, flaccid flaps. (21, 22)

As with Proteus, the guilt and emotional void in Malachi's life has a deeper source than his disgust with corporate machinery. The degeneracy of his personal life is more a symptom than the cause of his unhappiness. Certainly he wishes to transcend the perversions of Magnum Opus, that engine of destruction that violates "thousands of laws without . . . running afoul of so much as a city ordinance" (78). But it is Malachi's obvious need for parental love and guidance that causes him to hallucinate a surrogate father figure like Niles Rumfoord who is going to tell him exactly what to do, and an escapist, mind-numbing philosophy in which he is promised entrance into a paradise of perfect peace, beauty, and understanding.

Late in the novel Malachi says that the central problem of his life had been to win the love of his wife and child, probably because he had come from a shattered family (163).[10] Malachi is the unloved byproduct of a loveless marriage, arranged solely to promote the coldly pragmatic interests of Magnum Opus, itself described as "a product of a complex of inabilities to love" (81).[11] We are told that Malachi spent his childhood daydreaming of seeing and loving a father who did not want to see Malachi or be loved by him (147). The first and only time Malachi ever sees his father is on his twenty-first birthday. His father, embarrassed by his son's presence, gives Malachi two pieces of advice: "Don't touch your principal and keep the liquor bottle out of the bedroom" (82). Noel writes in a letter that he has been long dead to life because

Nobody loved me and I wasn't very good at anything and I couldn't find any hobbies I liked
and I was sick and tired of selling pots and pans and watching television so I was as good as
dead and I was too far gone to ever come back. (90, 91)

For peace of mind, Noel pretends he has drawn his financial powers from the
advice of his Gideon Bible, but he is not terribly convinced. He suspects that,
rather than based upon merit of any kind, his enormous wealth has been a matter
of copious quantities of pure dumb luck, emanating from a capricious and
inscrutable universe, "a matter of the way the wind swirls and the dirt settles
eons after God has passed by" (252). He concludes his letter to his vulnerable,
love-starved son with the fatalistic advice that, since life is pointless, the world
insane, Malachi should latch onto the first person who comes by "with a crazy
proposition" (91).

It is not surprising then that, infected by his father's cynicism, Malachi's
lifestyle becomes aggressively wasteful and self-destructive, "making himself
and mankind look bad": "Constant bristled with courage—but it was anything
but un-neurotic. Every courageous thing he had ever done had been motivated
by spitefulness and by goads from childhood that made fear seem puny indeed"
(29). Malachi's feeling of worthlessness climaxes by the side of his swimming
pool in Hollywood, California, after a colossal fifty-six-day debauch. We find
him lying in the gutter of the pool in a drugged stupor, the pool looking "less
like a facility for sport than like a punchbowl in hell" (53). The pool is littered
with marijuana butts and contains an ominous hypodermic syringe. To a shocking degree Malachi achieves his aim of making himself "unworthy of any
destiny—incapable of any mission." A friend tells him he had put on quite a
show, climaxed by a big crying jag and confessions of a very unhappy childhood
(61).[12] Malachi finds further anonymity in the wearing of dark glasses and a
beard (11). Taking a hint from Winston Niles Rumfoord to "forget who you
are" (Rumfoord is the first person to come along with a "crazy proposition")
(22), Malachi even changes his name. As he speeds toward the Rumfoord estate
in a seeming date with destiny, we are told that no one knows where Constant
is, and that neither the chauffeur nor the pilot knows Malachi's true identify.
"Constant was Mr. Jonah K. Rowley to both" (45). Whether the character of
Winston Niles Rumfoord, like all the novel's other characters, exists in objective reality or whether he is the embodiment of a fatalistic philosophy existing
only in Malachi's mind is problematical. Rumfoord, for instance, exists mainly
as wave phenomena, and the voice of his wife Bea, the wife of Malachi as well,
comes to Malachi like "the wind in the treetops" (40); nevertheless, at his
father's advice, Malachi embraces Rumfoord's fatalistic worldview, signaling
his most dangerous withdrawal from reality. Emanating from a godlike figure
with seemingly omniscient answers and palliatives to the miserable riddle of
Malachi's life, the voice of Rumfoord informs him that the loveless, aggressive

spiral of his life has been a matter of historic inevitability, a kind of enormous roller-coaster ride Malachi is helpless to resist (57). From an omniscient point of view he calls "chrono-synclastic infundibulated" (14, 15), which provides an overview of human destiny,[13] Rumfoord explains not only that the events of Malachi's life are inevitably structured to be the way they are, but that submission to the view that "everything that ever was always will be, and everything that ever will be always was" (15) will bring him to paradise.

Malachi is predestined, goes Rumfoord's prophesy, to be shot into outer space to the far reaches of Mars, Mercury, and Titan on the biggest spaceship ever built, where along with his wife Bea and son Chrono, he will encounter true contentment (38). On Titan, he is told, he will find the most pleasant climate imaginable and women who "are the most beautiful creatures between the Sun and Betelgeuse" (36). About the photograph Rumfoord hands Malachi, we hear,

> The effect was much like that of a rectangular glass window in the surface of a clear, shallow, coral bay. At the bottom of that seeming coral bay were three women—one white, one gold, one brown. They looked up at Constant, begging him to come to them, to make them whole with love. Their beauty was to the beauty of Miss Canal Zone as the glory of the Sun was to the glory of a lightening bug. (38)

Nor is this would-be seduction a merely sensual one. Rumfoord tells Malachi he can expect aristocratic treatment on Titan without having to prove his worth, that his natural dignity and intelligence will come to the fore (63).

Cruelly unloving parents leave Constant so withdrawn that "hallucinations," usually drug-induced, were all that would surprise or entertain him anymore (19). Consequently he searches for comfort and wholeness in fictive mirrors and Alice-in-Wonderland rabbit holes. In *Through the Looking-Glass,* Alice believes that the world behind the Looking-Glass will be warm "with such beautiful things in it" and that no one from the real world will be able to get her there (149). In both stories, Alice longs to escape the dark hall from which she stumbles into the imagined sanctuary of "the loveliest garden you ever saw," one with "beds of bright flowers and . . . cool fountains" (16). In both cases, of course, this supposed Eden is more hellish than heavenly in nature. It is a world of terror and chaos in which everyone, according to Cheshire Puss, is mad. "You can't help going among mad people," he tells Alice. "We're all mad here. I'm mad. You're mad. . . . You must be," he says, "or you wouldn't have come here" (70). And Alice admits, "the way all the creatures argue, it is enough to drive one crazy" (162). Most of the creatures Alice meets are irrational and vindictive; miscommunication and injustice are commonplace; even violence (symbolized by the Tiger Lilies Alice finds in the garden) and death itself pursue Alice throughout her venture; "off with their heads" (88) is the

favorite cry of the demented Queen of Hearts. There is no womblike contentment for Alice at all, then, down the rabbit hole or, more portentously, down
the rat hole that leads to the garden. It is not surprising that one of the fabulous
monsters Alice encounters should suggest another famous Wonderland entered
by way of a hole in the earth, the Gryphon, with the head and wings of an eagle
and the lower body of a lion, from Dante's *Divine Comedy,* or that the Mock
Turtle's song about a whiting and a snail fleeing for their lives should suggest
that older song, "The Spider and the Fly," in which that pretty little parlor into
which the fly is lured at the top of the winding stair holds entrapment and death.
The garden, the fountain, the larger universe itself are for Alice what Malachi
calls in *Sirens* "a cruel and lovely illusion" (187), a "so-called bargain . . .
connected by fine wires to a dynamite bouquet" (290).

   In her search for the lovely garden, Alice is nearly drowned, trampled,
squeezed to death, poisoned, and decapitated. In her rashness to reach the
elusive Eden, suggestive of the central imagery of *Sirens,* she spins helplessly
out of control down the tunnellike shaft of the rabbit hole, into a seemingly
ever-deepening well. The well image is ominous because at the Mad Tea Party,
Alice learns of the three little sisters living at the bottom of a well, living only
on treacle, who were very ill indeed (79, 80). It is in a well of her own tears
that Alice nearly drowns. Consistent with the chimney image through which she
enters the world of the looking-glass and the tunnel image associated with her
fall, Alice takes a corkscrewlike path to the garden, saying, "I should see the
garden far better . . . if I could get to the top of that hill" (158). Thus it is that
Malachi Constant, seeking immunity from earth-bound problems, climbs impul-
sively to the top of the fountain of the Rumfoord estate to see "whence he had
come and whither he was bound" (17). But in seeming reference to the "slithy
toves" in Alice's dream, "cork-screw" looking lizards who make "nests under
sundials" (224), Malachi holds up his watch to sunlight "letting it drink in the
wherewithal that was to solar watches what money was to Earth men" (17) but
finding himself standing in the "ruins of birds'" nests. The suggestion is that
Malachi has given himself over to the relentless clockwork power of the solar
system, a mechanistic system of control like the one at Magnum Opus that he
hopes to escape, and that, thus entrapped, he like Alice will be sent spinning
helplessly to his doom. The fountain proves "bone dry," and he discovers that
the spirallike architecture of the interlocking bowls of the fountain move him
inexorably downward toward "the upturned mouth of the biggest bowl of them
all . . . a regular Beelzebub of a bowl" (19). As Alice is threatened by the
Gryphon, Malachi encounters the Cerberuslike Kazak, the flesh-eating hound
of space who he thinks will keep him treed on the fountain forever. Moments
later, trapped on the staircase of the Rumfoord estate, Malachi senses that the
spiral staircase "now swept down rather than up. Constant became the bottom-
most point in a whirlpool of fate" (42).

Even more forbodingly we see that, analogous to Alice's fear of decapitation, Malachi invites a beheading if his dangerous illusions of paradise persist. More than once he looks down the barrel of a rifle and thinks he sees paradise. "Unk," a pseudonym he is given on Mars,

> put his eye to the muzzle and was thrilled by perfect beauty. He could have stared happily at the immaculate spiral of the rifling for hours, dreaming of the happy land whose round gate he saw at the other end of the bore. The pink under his oily thumbnail at the far end of the barrel made that far end seem a rosy paradise indeed. Some day he was going to crawl down the barrel to that paradise. It would be warm there. . . . There were three beautiful women in that paradise. (108, 109)

Paul Proteus's search for substitute mothers has become more fanciful. Evidence that Malachi's Edenic illusions may blow up in his face comes in the form of the novel's pervasive looking-glass imagery. In the mirror world of fantasyland, nothing is what it seems to be—especially those enchanting visions of bliss and comfort, those devilishly disguised spirals, wombs, and mousetraps in which Malachi thinks he can hide. Clearly, then, it is Malachi's embracing of Rumfoord's fatalistic world view—the counterpart to Alice's suspicion that the figures behind the looking-glass are merely puppets moved by the hands of the invisible players of the game, that signals his most dangerous illusion.

If the moral were not clear from the novel's pervasive well and water imagery, the Lacanian looking-glass distortion vividly makes the case.[14] A victim of illusion while looking through her looking-glass, Alice had said, "you never can tell, you know, unless our fire smokes, and then smoke comes up in that room too—but that may be only pretence, just to make it look as if they had a fire" (149). Malachi is more deceived. Used to drugging himself to reality, searching for easy solutions to his suffering, he fails to heed the warning in the photograph—that escape into a world of phantom fulfillment may lead him directly to that "bottom-most point in a whirlpool of fate" he had experienced at the Rumfoord estate, into that "punchbowl in hell" of a swimming pool in the gutter of which he "drinks himself to sleep," or that "Beelzebub of a bowl" at the bottom of the Rumfoord fountain. Just as Alice nearly drowns in that pool of tears of her own making, Malachi or Jonah may well be swallowed up by the "Whale" (the name of his spaceship by which he escapes reality) if he continues his mad delusion of arriving at paradise at the end of a gun barrel or as the willing plaything of enormous systems of control he thinks himself helpless to resist.

The illusion represented by the Sirens at the bottom of the pool, offering erotic, probably Oedipal love, and at the end of the gun barrel, augers that displaced libidinal energy which drives men to quest for God through material means and for brotherhood through bloodshed. Thus deluded, Malachi's identity is thrice fragmented. First on Mars as the brain-washed, doped-up soldier called "Unk," he is led to murder his best friend in a test of loyalty to his Martian puppetmasters. Then as "Space Wanderer," sacrificial lamb for a mad religion called the "Church of God the Utterly Indifferent," he is used in a bloody suicidal invasion of earth in order to create martyrs for Rumfoord's religion, and as Rumfoord's mechanical Christ to pacify the earthling masses with obscene shows of spiritual sleight of hand (239, 244).[15] Malachi is convinced by Rumfoord that changing the world requires showmanship, a willingness to shed other people's blood, and a religion to help people atone for the horror and bloodshed (174).

It is not surprising that Magnum Opus, an institution that uses pictures of the Mona Lisa to advertise suppositories, should be made to represent through the materialistic lens of its architecture a purely spiritual reality. The Magnum Opus Building is a slender, prismatic, twelve-sided shaft, a spiral, as well as a looking-glass distortion, faced on all twelve sides with blue-green glass. The twelve sides are said by the architect to represent the twelve great religions of the world (66). Similarly, on Titan itself, Malachi confuses Rumfoord's pleasure palace—in reality the literally and spiritually bankrupt Magnum Opus—with Saint Augustine's City of God (291). And in the womblike caves of Saturn, Malachi presumes that the "big, beautiful buildings up above" contain the "masters of all creation" when in fact the buildings are "solid, dead, dumb-cold crystals" (207, 208).

Religion itself proves to be a looking-glass illusion, filled with dangerous escapist lures of mindless bliss and usually self-serving material answers to spiritual needs.[16] The windows to the Wilburhampton Hotel, where Noel Constant leafs through his Bible to discover tips to playing the stock market, are described as tiny and "diamond-shaped" (86). Again, in the caves of Mercury where Malachi's spaceship threads its way down a tortuous system of chimneys, Malachi looks out a porthole at the yellow and aquamarine diamonds the harmoniums made on the walls (190). The thin-skinned, surface beauty of the harmoniums, described as "obscenely unmotivated, insensitive, and dull" (197), appears to represent love and harmony. Their message, "We love you Boaz," spelled out in crystals on the wall of the caves, makes Unk's friend Boaz feel peaceful and holy (209, 210).[17] It is into a glistening ruby that Boaz looks when he says to Malachi, "Don't truth me . . . and I won't truth you" (202, 212). But Malachi identifies the "trap" for what it is—a "pathetic delusion," a "crazy appeal in the name of love" to keep them sedated and jailed in the caves forever (207, 209). Later, returning to Earth weary and dazed from too many years in the army of Mars and buried in the caves of Mercury, Malachi finds himself believed to be the long-promised space wanderer, Christ figure for a religion that delivers as well as promises miracles.

In a grotesquely carnival atmosphere replete with plastic sacrificial Malachi dolls with rhinestone eyes, mass-produced for the occasion and blessed by Malachi himself (231), Malachi finds the people of earth ready for the moment for which all true believers wait. Expressing "bedlam joy," his eyes on Malachi, the Reverend C. Horner Redwine speaks for the devout when he cries, "No Hell, No Hell, No Hell!" (222). Redwine's vision of salvation is as mad as the fanatical methods of self-handicapping by which his followers seek to solve the world's injustice (220, 221, 224).[18] His first view of Malachi is through glasses whose lenses are clouded from wetness from a fairy rain storm (225). The second time he sees his supposed savior, it is by pressing his adoring face against the glass of the porthole to Malachi's spaceship. Behind the porthole, in reality, is the hopeless and deeply wrinkled countenance of Malachi, "the face of an intelligent ape in a zoo" (225). Malachi wears a transparent plastic bag encrusted with semiprecious stones, designed, like the trashy religious symbols being sold at the concession stands inside the "twilit tunnel" (236, 238), to make him a credible Christ.

The machinery of religion fragments Malachi as much as the machinery of war; his capacity for self-determination is seriously eroded during his stint as Space Wanderer: "The Space Wanderer's mind did not teem with questions. . . . The Space Wanderer was not paying strict attention. His powers of concentration were feeble—possibly because he had been in the caves too long, or on goofballs too long, or in the army of Mars too long" (246, 252). Malachi has even taken to swallowing goofballs again and to practicing Schlieman breathing.[19] He tries to assert himself but can see "nothing he would have chosen of his own free will" (249). Beguiled by Rumfoord's notion that his church will make everyone so peaceful and kind that life will be perfect on Earth (247), the sedated, deluded Malachi prepares for his reward on Titan by walking again through an "Alice-in-Wonderland door" (239) where he allows himself to be "hoisted onto a gilded system of catwalks, ramps, ladders, pulpits and stages," spirals all. Then he moves up "the longest free-standing ladder in history," a ladder painted gold with gilded rungs, to the door of his spaceship (247).

Taken in all, rather than preparing him for paradise, rather than moving him closer to the life of dignity and purpose for which he feels his name has destined him, Malachi's space adventures have been exercises in madness—escape into lovelessness and brutality. The worst thing that has happened to him is that in believing he is the helpless pawn of fate, wired like a robot and aimed into space by Rumfoord, he has allowed himself to be fragmented into robotlike identities that distort and threaten the loss of his true self. It is precisely the form of schizophrenia experienced by Alice, the "curious child" who "was very fond of pretending to be two people." "Why there's hardly enough of me to make one respectable person," she says (19). "Who in the World am I . . . that's the great puzzle . . . I'm never sure what I'm going to be, from one minute to the other" (23). "Be what you would seem to be," the Duchess admonishes her (99). But Alice, like Malachi, is impulsive and too often intimidated by authority so that determining what is real in the world around her or about herself is usually left to others. Just as Malachi finds it difficult to challenge the apparent superiority of Rumfoord, so Alice, confronted with the sovereign will of the Queen and King of Hearts, wonders whether she "ought not to lie down on her face like the gardeners" (87). But Alice does resist the tyranny of the bloody queen and grows to be a queen herself. "Thinking again?" asks the Duchess, striking Alice with her chain. "I've a right to think," says Alice, courageously (100).

The wood behind Alice's looking-glass world in which things have no name, filled with nonsense objects and riddles that have no answers, is in fact the same chaotic, irrational, absurd universe inhabited by Malachi—a relativistic universe in which ultimate truths are unknowable and values have no objective or intrinsic meaning. Even the reality of one's own existence is called into question (181, 227). In such a world it is easy to go mad, to escape into visions of paradise, to lapse into will-lessness, surrendering one's identity to the authority of others. Thus a central metaphor in the work of both writers is the game of chess, in which the characters are ignorant of the game's purpose and cannot tell if they move of their own wills or are being pushed by unseen hands, "Punch and Judy knights at war" (295). On Mars, Malachi is one of the empty-eyed recruits ("eyes empty as the windows of abandoned textile mills") (150) scuffling for one of the squares painted on the floor of his barracks. On their assigned squares, arranged in rank and file, the recruits move only as their masters program them to move, controlled by horrible pain inflicted through antenna implants in their skulls. By letting "other people do the thinking and worrying," we read, Malachi (Unk) had "reduced himself to a cipher" (156).

If this were the end of Malachi's adventure, we might conclude with Alice that "there's no room to grow here any more" (41), or with critics Hendin and Goldsmith that *Sirens* is a pessimistic novel about the sense of helplessness life engenders, but the chess analogy leads us to the opposite conclusion—that growth through existential awareness and courage is the focus of both writers. Alice learns that lesson when Humpty Dumpty asserts that he uses language to mean just what *he* chooses it to mean (222). In other words, survival in an absurd universe may depend upon the ability to do what Malachi calls making universes out of nothingness, making nothingness insist on becoming somethingness (138). It is such a recognition that enables Alice to capture the bloody Red Queen and results in checkmate of the Red King. Significantly, Alice's only friend and the one to get her off her chessboard nightmares gives her a lesson in the creative possibilities of subjective reality by manipulating the words to a song, ignoring its conventions. "It's my own invention" he says (246). Malachi, too, learns that, rather than existing as the helpless pawn of Rumfoord, he himself "was one of fortune's cruelest agents" and must thus fight the pain from his antenna to reverse the destructive, self-created spirals of his life—lovelessness, narcissism, and moral escapism. It is this effort to resist the inhuman purposes of Rumfoord that compels our attention, or should, through the latter half of the novel.

Actually, Unk, the life-affirming voice of Malachi Constant, has been attempting to make his way up the spirallike prison walls of the caves of Mars for a long time; we read that soon after they had landed, he and Boaz moved in very different circles. The circles in which Boaz moves are small and at the bottom of the spiral; the circles in which Unk moves are vast and restless, suggestive of wider and higher consciousness.[20] On the lower level where Boaz lives, life is cozy and mindless, the harmoniums plentiful and fast-growing (198, 199). On the upper levels, life is forbidding and the harmoniums are stunted and few. It is only when Unk realizes that nobody is going to come and get him out (he waits for rescue the way he waits for destiny) that he determines to save himself, braving the colder upper levels by learning to pilot the space-ship buried at the bottom of the caves. He will blast upward and out of the spiral by virtue of a force known as UWTB, the Universal Will to Become (138), a phenomenon used to power spaceships but so great that it makes universes out of nothingness—that makes nothingness insist on becoming somethingness. Described as the most powerful conceivable source of energy (173), UWTB is of course merely brain power used to full capacity, which in this case provides Malachi with the grace and intelligence to get his stalled spaceship moving and headed up the spirallike system of chimneys (211, 212, 214).

Elsewhere in the novel the son of Bea and Malachi, Chrono, is similarly instructed in the art of resisting spirals. Taken on an educational tour of a flame thrower factory, Chrono watches the factory manager become ensnarled in a spiral of steel strapping, scratching his ankle and tearing his pants before he gets free of the spiral. Vonnegut writes, he "thereupon put on the first really comprehensible demonstration that the children had seen that day. Comprehensibly he blew up the spiral" (143). Chrono doesn't escape unscathed, however; a piece of the spiral he picks up "became as much a part of him as his right hand. His nervous system, so to speak, extended itself into the metal strap. Touch it and you touched Chrono" (142, 143). Chrono must deal with loveless mechanisms as much as his father.

Dazed and brainwashed, Rumfoord's mechanical Christ is sent to his promised reward in Heaven, or Titan, the supposed paradise. On Titan Malachi's quest for autonomy and for love fares better than it does as Rumfoord's automated boob of a savior for the Church of God the Utterly Indifferent. His attempt to reverse his fate, to resist entrapping mirrors and rabbit holes, draws him closer to his mate and child "than they had been on the gilded system of catwalks, ramps, ladders, pulpits, steps and stages in Newport" (245). His illusions are fewer. At first glance the Rumfoord palace on Titan shines to him

like St. Augustine's City of God, but the domed and minareted building ultimately shows itself as the city of the devil (267, 278), a spirallike replica of
Rumfoord's estate on earth. He sees too that those who think themselves "as
much above the beastly concerns of mankind as the harmoniums in the caves
of Mercury" (288) are turned to stone, or like Rumfoord, dematerialized.[21]

Whereas Malachi had once yearned for the Sirens in Rumfoord's photograph to "make him whole with love," an erotic attraction that through an
Alice-in-Wonderland "glass window" seems spiritual to him (38), it is the development of compassion and self-sufficiency and the turning away from the potentially petrifying image of the three beautiful, imaginary females that returns him
to himself. Not only does he grow close to his wife and child, announcing that
the "three great beauties didn't mean so much to him now, really" (309); he
works to drain the pool to expose the stone statues of the three women for what
they are (308, 309). The pool drains slowly, but drains. He even contemplates
digging up the pipes if necessary, an act of psychic excavation. In a forboding
image of averted schizophrenic impotence, he declares,

> The minute it looks like something or somebody wants me to act in some special way . . . if
> anybody ever expects to use me again in some tremendous scheme of his . . . he will be a lot
> better off trying to get a rise out of one of these statues. (289, 290)

Glancing up at the rings of Saturn, he announces, "Isn't that just too beautiful
for words," and spits in contempt (290). Stating that he has taken part for the
last time "in experiments and fights and festivals" he doesn't like or understand,
he hears the word "Understand" come back to him as an echo, and says to the
echo, "What happens next? . . . All the statues come to life?" When Beatrice
explains that the word "Life" is also an echo, Malachi says, "I know it's an
echo" (290).

Malachi realizes that the destiny he has been waiting for (his name means
faithful messenger) is nothing more than an echo of his own potential for living
a creative or destructive life on earth, an existential matter of harnassing the
power of the Universal Will to Become and realizing himself in the present.
Ultimately, all the novel's main characters denounce the mechanisms that have
warped their lives, "the claptrap that has so often enslaved us or driven us into
the madhouse" (215). In so doing, they achieve a humanness they have never
known before. Salo, a robot messenger from the planet Tralfamadore fated to
carry a nonsense message from "one rim of the Universe to the other" (269),
determines to "make war against the core of his being, against the very nature
of being a machine" (300). He dismantles himself not because of the futility of
his message, but because he has blindly carried it without questioning the sense
of his errand. Rumfoord learns that, rather than the omniscient seer he had taken

himself to be, he has been the grand dupe of the Tralfamadorians, who he says "reached into the Solar System, picked me up, and used me like a handy-dandy potato-peeler" (296); Rumfoord is surrounded and consumed by a huge electrical spiral that sends him "cracking off through space like buggywhips in the hands of a lunatic" (287). But he gains in humanness by considering the spiral with contempt; it spins "a continuous cocoon of green light," suggesting new life for him or for Malachi Constant. "Perhaps Earthlings will now be free to develop and follow their own inclinations," he says, as he passes on (298). Beatrice spends *her* last days, like Vonnegut, "spinning arguments against the importance of the forces of Tralfamadore,"[22] writing a book refuting Rumfoord's notion that earthlings have no free will and that the purpose of human life has been nothing more than the attempt to get a grounded messenger from Tralfamadore a missing part for his spacship and on his way again (308).[23]

On the one hand, it might appear that madness claims Malachi in the end. He dies under the posthypnotic illusion given him by Salo that he sees his best friend, Stony Stevenson, again and that a golden spaceship encrusted with diamonds carries him happily off to paradise.[24] But several actions before Malachi's death, and the novel's Alice-in-Wonderland dream structure, suggest that a double awakening is in store for Malachi. Returning to earth from Titan, Malachi resists Salo's suggestion that he be left off by a shuffleboard court in St. Petersburg, Florida. He insists instead on being taken to Indianapolis, Indiana, "a far from ideal place for a homeless old man" (314), because it was "the first place in the United States of America where a white man was hanged for the murder of an Indian" (315). Rather than physical comfort, he chooses a place where guilt and responsibility matter. In his last days on Titan, Malachi practices existential self-creation, moving "the elements of his own life about experimentally—but he did it in his head" (305). At such times we are told that Malachi acknowledges his greatest inner needs, to atone for the murder of Stony Stevenson and to win the love of Beatrice Rumfoord.

The overriding truth of this novel is that nearly everything Malachi has done has been done "in his head," the product of that "drug-induced hallucination" by which he enters the "Alice-in-Wonderland door" to the Rumfoord estate, a microcosm of his own mind. So he has no more died in actuality than he has left his native earth or been controlled by the infamous Tralfamadorians, alleged instigators of all suffering and meaninglessness in the universe. Malachi learns that the Tralfamadorians—defined as "all of us"—are we ourselves (268), perpetrators of our own soulless, mechanistic nightmare. Like Tweedledum and Tweedledee, mirror reflections of one another who do battle, Malachi must battle the Rumfoord madness within himself. His challenge, if he is to avoid the insanity that threatens him at the opening of the novel, is to awake from this Tralfamadorian nightmare (or fatal dream) and to negotiate his own destiny.

With awareness and courage he can become one of those who, as Vonnegut writes from a perspective a century later, now knows how to find the meaning of life within himself. The next Vonnegut hero will explore inwardness in a way that moves him to still greater goodness and self-wisdom.

3

Mother Night: Nations of Lunatics

> *The Second World War presented a mirror to the human condition which blinded anyone who looked into it. For if tens of millions were killed in concentration camps out of the inexorable agonies and contractions of superstates one was obliged . . . to see that no matter how crippled and perverted an image of man was the society he had created, it was nonetheless his creation, his collective creation . . . and if society was so murderous, then who could ignore the most hideous of questions about his own nature?*
>
> Norman Mailer, *Advertisements for Myself*

In Vonnegut's first two novels, we have seen the sometimes despairing, sometimes hopeful efforts of his fragmented protagonists to put their disintegrated selves together again—to resist various forms of escapism that paralyze the creative will of characters from Paul Proteus to Leon Trout. We should meanwhile hold in mind that we are watching Vonnegut's attempts to work out the schizophrenic dilemma which Howard Campbell calls "that wider separation of my several selves than even I can bear to think about" (136). In chapter 1 we began to observe various correspondences between Vonnegut's war experiences and those of his protagonists that run throughout his work. Suffice it to say that the preface to *Mother Night* alone is proof that when Campbell speaks of echoing "the soul's condition in a man at war" (117) in a monstrous picture he has drawn, he implicates the soul of his creator as well. Vonnegut writes not only that he had experienced firsthand the insane bigotry and paranoia behind the Nazi's persecution of the Jews, but that as an American prisoner of war he had been forced to witness the largest massacre in European history—or at least its immediate aftermath.[1]

And then hundreds of thousands of tiny incendiaries were scattered over the kindling, like seeds on freshly turned loam. More bombs were dropped to keep firemen in their holds, and all the little fires grew, joined one another, became one apocalyptic flame. Hey presto: fire storm. . . . We didn't get to see the fire storm. We were in a cool meat-locker under a slaughterhouse with our six guards and ranks and ranks of dressed cadavers of cattle, pigs, horses, and sheep. We heard the bombs walking around up there. . . . If we had gone above to take a look, we would have been turned into artifacts characteristic of fire storms: seeming pieces of charred firewood two or three feet long—ridiculously small human beings, or jumbo fried grasshoppers, if you will. . . . Everything was gone but the cellars where 135,000 Hansels and Gretels had been baked like gingerbread men. So we were put to work as corpse miners, breaking into shelters, bringing bodies out. And I got to see many German types of all ages as death had found them, usually with valuables in their laps. Sometimes relatives would come to watch us dig. They were interesting, too. (vi, vii)

Never mind that Campbell winds up a prisoner of war in a different town or that the horrors he witnesses are differently set; the atrocities they see are the same, a common legacy of endless human destruction, terror, brutality, injustice, warpedness, and indifference to human suffering. Campbell too is made to look at "the gutted, scabby, bugeyed, spavined dead heaps" in the Nazi death camps (33); "bombs walked and walked" over his head as well (175), and there is little doubt why Campbell, during one of his most demoralized moments, sees himself not in New York but "at the doors of cells in a jail in a burning city somewhere" (169) . The very fact that Vonnegut, in a fictional context, has taken on the task of editing Campbell's nightmarish confessions, that both are writers of mixed German and American heritage engaged in a struggle with guilt and pessimism, and that both write from a seemingly numb and detached point of view that masks a tortured conscience suggests their common identity and their common dilemma.[2] Most importantly, however, we find both men daring to venture into their own heart of darkness, their own "Mother Night" (xi), to expose the capacity for cruelty and moral blindness within the soul of every man and woman. It is that same spiritual journey into darkness made by Conrad and James, and by Hawthorne and Melville before them. It is a plea for the recognition of the Devil within and its power for distorting our humanity, and it is an act of expiation carrying with it a hope for renewal.[3]

When Howard Campbell tries to rationalize his affinity with universal darkness, mentioning that "it was my world rather than myself that was diseased" (185), we see that he is not entirely wrong. Campbell finds himself confronted with a world in which overwhelming madness—some perverted or pathological state of mind—is viewed as the norm rather than the exception. In "a period of insanity" among "nations of lunatics," Campbell's friend and ping-pong partner, Heinz Schildknecht, tells him, "All people are insane" (90). As an example, he cites the fact that much of the war is being fought by fifteen-and sixteen-year-old boys in fully armed death traps all their own. The people he sees as succeeding either in or out of the war are "specialists in slavery, destruction, and death" (91). Hence he is on his way to "smoking his brains out" (91). But Campbell doesn't require convincing. About his father-in-law, Campbell is told that Noth's principal offense as chief of police was that he had no conscience about introducing persons suspected of misdemeanors and crimes into a system of justice that "was insane" (86). Those to whom Noth hands over his prisoners find the distinction between the guilty and the innocent unimportant. Merely to be suspected is a crime, and prisoners are all to be "humiliated, exhausted and killed" (87). Noth himself becomes the victim of such insane, arbitrary justice.

> My father-in-law was stood on a footstool four inches high. The rope was put around his neck and drawn tight over the limb of a budding apple tree. The footstool was then kicked out from under him. He could dance on the ground while he strangled. . . . He was revived eight times, and hanged nine. Only after the eighth hanging did he act like a child being tortured. For that performance . . . he was rewarded with what he wanted most in all this world. He was rewarded with death. He died with an erection and his feet were bare. (87)

The use of organic life, the budding apple tree, as an instrument of death, symbolizes the perversion of Noth's own life instinct by the instinct of aggression and death. Death produces the erection that life could not.[4] When Resi tells Howard Campbell that "war must be a very sexy thing to Americans" (107), she implicates her father. Another time Campbell's guard Mengel tells about having played dead while a German soldier pulled out three of his teeth without suspecting that Mengel was not a corpse (24). Other instances of torture and hideous death that wear indelibly on Campbell's mind vary from his own execution of Resi's puppy, to the suicide of his garbage man who kills himself with the rope intended for Campbell, to the gassing of millions of Jews (111). The garbage man, Lazlo Szombathy, dies in "a final fandago of paranoia and masochism" (113), and Campbell hears this after shooting Resi's dog in the back of the neck.

> The old soldier came over, expressing a professional's interest in the sort of wound such a small pistol might make. He turned the dog over with his boot, found the bullet in the snow. . . . He now began to talk of all sorts of wounds he had seen or heard of, all sorts of holes in once living things. "You're going to bury it?" he said. "I suppose I'd better," I said. "If you don't," he said, "somebody will eat it." (84)[5]

Actually, the horrors Campbell encounters during the war stretch all the way back to childhood. We learn that his father kept books of World War I with "pictures of men hung on barbed wire, mutilated women, bodies stretched like accordians—all the usual furniture of world wars" (31). In turn, his mother, his principal companion until he turns ten, was a "morbid" person who drank most of the time and was preoccupied with death (32). He remembers that she once made them both look corpselike by creating a deathly light in the room.

"There—" she said, "that's what we'll look like when we're dead." "From that moment on," he says, "I ceased to be her companion. From that moment on she hardly spoke to me—cut me dead, I'm sure, out of fear of doing or saying something even crazier" (32).[6] Nor is the death of the body the only kind of death Campbell learned about. People with rent, agonized souls like that of his mother, or those who have been hollowed of emotional and spiritual substance like his father are everywhere around him, the victims of war or of other forms of totalitarian machinery that uses them for inhuman ends. Campbell says that the General Electric Company used up his father's energy and spirit so that "he had scant time and imagination left over for anything else" (31).[7] Campbell encounters other pitiful examples of machine dehumanization in his sister-in-law, Resi Noth, and in the maniacal superpatriot Bernard O'Hare, a dispatcher of frozen-custard trucks who, according to Campbell, felt just as pointless about his life as poor Resi did at her cigarette-making machine in Dresden (70).

Particularly wearing on Campbell—because it mirrors his own condition—is the way such mechanical processes, extensions of the killing machines of war, have left people feeling not only used up, but disembodied, will-less, and unable to feel. They become like those nameless, sexless, and shapeless female prisoners of war etched so deeply into Campbell's memory, "squinting, lumpy, hopeless, grubby ragbags . . . pretty as catfish wrapped in mattress ticking" (66, 86). Or they become like Resi and Campbell as they see themselves after the war, "ghostlike . . . God-awful old and starved and moth-eaten" (107). By the time Campbell has come through the war and spent fourteen years in a depressing attic purgatory of a New York apartment with rats in the walls,[8] he feels so totally used up by his multiple roles—as loathsome anti-Semite, Nazi radio propagandist, American intelligence agent whose broadcasts carried coded information out of Germany, and author of highly melodramatic plays—that he tells Frank Wirtanen, "You've wiped me out . . . alles Kaput" (47). He feels as much like war surplus as his underwear and socks. Resi explains that Campbell is too used up to love anymore. There is nothing left of him but "curiosity and a pair of eyes" (166). When Campbell discovers the sign on his gutted, ratty attic that reads "Nobody and nothing inside" (176), he knows how completely true that is.

After learning not only that his supposed best friend and his imagined true love are Russian agents, using him for their own political ends, but that his plays have been shamelessly bowdlerized and produced under another name in Russia, Campbell likens his condition to that of a dismembered pig in the stockyards of Chicago. He feels that experts have found a use for every part of him, including his squeal. The part of him that thirsted for truth got turned into an expert liar. The lover in him became a pornographer. And the artist in him was twisted into ugliness such as the world had rarely seen. Finally, he muses that every cherished memory was converted into "catfood, glue, and liverwurst" (150). No wonder that when Resi asks him if he writes anymore, Campbell replies that he no longer has anything to say. When Resi adds "After all you've seen, all you've been through darling?" Campbell says, "It's all I've seen, all I've been through . . . that makes it damn near impossible for me to say anything . . . I speak gibberish to the civilized world, and it replies in kind" (96). Unfortunately the poem Campbell had written that Resi hands him makes perfect sense about his present condition.

> Here lies Howard Campbell's essence
> Freed from his body's noisome nuisance.
> His body, empty, prowls the earth,
> Earning what a body's worth.
> If his body and his essence remain apart,
> Burn his body, but spare this, his heart. (96)

Campbell's disembodiment has left him unable to feel or express emotion, like the soldier Mengel who says "I was like almost everybody who came through that war . . . I got so I couldn't feel anything" (25). Mengel had explained to Campbell:

> Every job was a job to do, and no job was any better or any worse than any other. After we finished hanging Hoess . . . I packed up my clothes to go home. The catch on my suitcase was broken, so I buckled it shut with a big leather strap. Twice within an hour I did the very same job—once to Hoess and once to my suitcase. Both jobs felt about the same. (25)

In that frame of mind Campbell tells his friend Heinz that he was really very fond of him, to the extent that he was "capable of being fond of anybody" (92). When Resi grants us a peek into Campbell's infamous unpublished work entitled "Memoirs of a Monogamous Casanova," we see that the style in which the author has portrayed his erotic experiences with Helga is so utterly mechanical and clinically obsessed that some have called it "insane" (99). Campbell speaks as if far removed from his body, referring to their bodily parts with scientific detachment as "instruments of pleasure" (100, 101). In addition to feeling a separation of mind and body, Campbell has grown so lonely and anonymous in exile after the war that he wonders if he really exists at all. He wonders even if he has only dreamed or fantasized certain past experiences. Frank Wirtanen, his American espionage contact, tells him that, after his service as double agent, all records pertaining to his identity had been burned during the war (120). And later, that "you're already disappeared again . . . there'll be no records . . . to show that you ever arrived." (137). Campbell so distrusts the reality of his own being that he applies for a job as a teacher of German in a private school in New York not because he wants the job, but so as "to demonstrate to myself that there really was such a person as me" (54).

When we read that Campbell finally falls into a "state of catalepsis," a condition likened to that of "a friendly robot" who must be told where and when to move next (185), we are ready to believe that the words Campbell writes in a letter are mainly what this book is about—" what makes people go crazy," and "the different ways they go crazy" (191). In a chapter entitled "The Answer to Communism," Campbell encounters a man in a bar "who claimed he could satisfy, thoroughly satisfy, seven women in a night, provided they were all different. . . . I mean really different." Campbell thinks, "Oh, God—the lives people try to lead. Oh, God—what a world they try to lead them in!" (108). A decidedly more destructive and universal form of madness that describes the lives people try to lead is that which Campbell meets in barfly number two. The barfly tells Campbell that the answer to communism is "Moral Rearmament," a movement that believes in "absolute honesty, absolute purity, absolute un-selfishness, and absolute love" (108).

It is this habit of mind, which separates individuals, groups, and nations into single entities, all good or all evil, that Campbell finds operating perni-ciously in the character of his personal "Fury" Bernard B. O'Hare and in the Reverend Doctor Lional Jason David Jones, DDS, DD, publisher of *The White Christian Minuteman,* who was expelled from dental school for "what would now be diagnosed . . . as paranoia" (57). He was expelled for his political interpretations of teeth—for pursuing his theory that the teeth of Jews and Negroes proved beyond question that both groups were degenerate and, eventu-ally, that the degeneracy of Catholics and Unitarians could be proven in their teeth as well (58). Bernard B. O'Hare in turn believes that the "gathering darkness of the intellectual and moral climate in America during the Second World War" had come to a focus in Harold Campbell (58). Believing him pure evil, O'Hare seeks to destroy Campbell with vengeful crazed fantasies of "good triumphing over evil" (180). What Campbell finds most alarming about the Joneses and O'Hares of the world is that their maniacally self-righteous concern with pure good at war with pure evil creates in them the capacity for committing any amount of violence, any number of heinous acts of brutality or injustice, in the name of goodness (180). Campbell remarks, "I doubt if there has ever been a society that has been without strong and young people eager to experi-ment with homicide, provided no very awful penalties are attached to it" (120). It is no coincidence, of course, that at the time of the Reverend Jones's expul-sion from dental school, five loaded pistols and a bayonet were found under his mattress.

It is during Campbell's final confrontation with O'Hare, the man Campbell says "thought of himself as St. George and of me as the dragon,"[9] that Vonnegut leads us to see the kind of idiocy that motivates patriotic lunatics like Jones and O'Hare (177). Convinced that it has been his mission from birth to overcome pure evil in the world by destroying Campbell, O'Hare tells Campbell, "It's in the stars . . . you realize you are being aimed right straight at something . . . and neither one of us could have avoided it if we'd tried" (178–182). "By God," he says, "I was born just to take you apart" (180). But it is Campbell who takes apart O'Hare's absurdly heroic illusions by breaking his arm with fire-tongs and with the following words:

> I'm not your destiny, or the Devil either! Look at you! Come to kill evil with your bare hands, and now away you go with no more glory than a man sideswiped by a Greyhound bus! And that's all the glory you deserve! That's all that any man at war with pure evil deserves. There are plenty of good reasons for fighting, but no good reason ever to hate without reservation, to imagine that God Almighty Himself hates with you, too. Where's evil? It's that large part of every man that wants to hate without limit, that wants to hate with God on its side. It's that part of every man that finds all kinds of ugliness so attractive. It's that part of an imbecile that punishes and vilifies and makes war gladly. (181)

While O'Hare vomits from pain and humiliation, vowing nevertheless to get Campbell if it is the last thing he does, Campbell identifies the source of O'Hare's delusions—his attempt to amend a life of hopeless mediocrity and petty frustrations by concentrating his pent up fear and hatred on a single, undiluted, recognizable enemy. Campbell says that O'Hare's crusade may give his dreary life a sense of purpose and seeming importance, but that it will not change his destiny of "bankruptcies, frozen-custard, too many children, termites, and no cash." Campbell admonishes O'Hare to try the Salvation Army if he wants to be a soldier in the Legions of God (182).

Campbell recognizes that O'Hare's form of madness carries with it not only a homicidal capacity for inflicting pain and death but the proclivity to blind oneself to one's own "Mother Night," one's own cruel and destructive impulses hidden behind seemingly virtuous behavior. It enables one to maintain, when it suits one's purpose, perfectly contradictory states of mind, humane and cruel, creative and destructive, by willfully blocking one or the other out. Hence Campbell says about George Kraft, alias Iona Patapov, friend and enemy, devious spy and marvelous painter simultaneously, that

> it was typical of his schizophrenia as a spy that he would use an institution he so admired for purposes of espionage. It was typical of his schizophrenia as a spy that he should also be a true friend of mine, and that he should eventually think of a way to use me cruelly in advancing the Russian cause. (51)

The willful committing of crimes while ignoring whatever facts do not suit one's needs or ends at the moment, concludes Campbell, was how a household as divided as the one composed of Jones, Father Keeley, Vice-Bundesfuehrer Krapptauer, and the Black Fuehrer, a Jew, a Catholic, and a Negro, each devoted to racial purity and ready to die for the cause, could exist in relative harmony:

> That was how my father-in-law could contain in one mind an indifference toward slave women and love for a blue vase—That was how Rudolf Hoess, Commandant of Auschwitz could alternate over the loudspeakers of Auschwitz great music and calls for corpse-carriers—That was how Nazi Germany could sense no important differences between civilization and hydrophobia. That is the closest I can come to explaining the legions, the nations of lunatics I've seen in my time. (163)

When Jones asserts that a once-proud America was falling into wrong hands and that "to get it back on the right track" "some heads are going to roll" (162), Campbell is amazed that Father Keeley and the Black Fuehrer are oblivious to the fact that it is their heads that will be the first to roll:

> I have never seen a more sublime demonstration of the totalitarian mind, a mind which might be likened unto a system of gears whose teeth have been filed off at random. Such a snaggletoothed thought machine, driven by a standard or even a substandard libido, whirls with the jerky, noisy, gaudy pointlessness of a cuckoo clock in Hell. (162)

The totalitarian mind is explicitly schizophrenic, formed by paranoia, a repressed libido, and operating in accord with its own bizarre sense of reality and time. Concluding that there were no teeth in the gears in the mind of Jones and his companions, a G-man who comes to arrest them says more simply, "You're completely crazy" (162).

Campbell himself appears relatively sane on the subject of broken teeth as compared to those more demonstrably deranged people around him. In fact, he says about the teeth in his own "thought machine" that he knows some are missing, some he was born without, some will never grow, and others have been mangled by the "clutchless shifts of history" (163). But he insists that he has never knowingly destroyed a single tooth on his thinking machine or rationalized the importance of those that were gone: "Never have I said to myself, 'this fact I can do without' " (163). For instance, when Resi asks him if he hates America, Campbell replies that hating a country would be as silly as loving it. He deplores the paranoid habit of affixing moral qualities to geography. Boundaries, he says, are as imaginary to him "as elves and pixies." He refuses to believe that such lines mark the end or the beginning of anything that should really concern the souls of men and women—"Virtues and vices, pleasures and pains cross boundaries at will" (103). What Campbell himself has been too long unwilling or unable to admit, however, is that he too has been guilty of blurring distinctions between civilization and hydrophobia. When Campbell denies his own insanity, when he asserts that he is somehow exempt from those "nations of lunatics" around him, that "it was my world rather than myself that was diseased" (185), he is being less honest than when he admits to Resi, "I'm not a well man. . . . My judgment, my senses, my intuition obviously aren't all they should be" (105). It is Campbell's own brand of madness that has allowed him to survive the war, a madness which has become increasingly apparent to him during the course of his narrative. "I've always known what I did," he explains. "I've always been able to live with what I did. How? Through that simple and widespread boon to modern mankind—schizophrenia" (133).[10] Yet but a short time later he confesses that it is just such a defense that has caused him his greatest loss, the inability to mourn for his wife's death "as an agonized soul, indivisible." "It represented," he says, "a wider separation of my several selves than even I can bear to think about" (136). It is when Campbell ruminates upon Resi's remark that he is so used up he can't love any more ("There is nothing left of him but curiosity and a pair of eyes. . . .") that he recognizes what this schizophrenia has cost him in terms of his own battered, sinned-upon soul (166). "I froze," he said:

> It was not guilt that froze me. I had taught myself never to feel guilt. It was not a ghastly sense of loss that froze me. I had taught myself to covet nothing. It was not a loathing of death that froze me. I had taught myself to think of death as a friend. It was not heartbroken rage against injustice that froze me. I had taught myself that a human being might as well look for diamond tiaras in the gutter as for rewards and punishments that were fair. It was not the thought that I was so unloved that froze me. I had taught myself to do without love. It was not the thought that God was cruel that froze me. I had taught myself never to expect anything from Him. What froze me was the fact that I had absolutely no reason to move in any direction. What had made me move through so many dead and pointless years was curiosity. Now even that had flickered out. . . . If I was ever going to move again, someone else was going to have to furnish the reason for moving. (167)

There is no doubt that some of Campbell's missing moral teeth—those that have allowed him to survive by evading the truth about his own crimes against humanity—are the world's doing and not his own.[11] To a large extent, Wirtanen is correct when he indicates that the lifelong process of dehumanization that has turned Campbell into the lifeless, will-less, moribund creature described above was "pretty much out of your control" (150). Campbell's suffering—the shock of war, coupled with tragically disillusioning childhood experiences—has clearly crippled his ability to believe in the value of human aspiration, in the value of justice, love, or God, and led him consequently to develop a convenient form of schizophrenic amnesia. He is, as R. D. Laing says about the typical schizophrenic, a "desperate man . . . without hope." [12] As with Paul Proteus and Malachi Constant, however, the tendency of Campbell's defeatist self to rationalize his guilt and to retreat from difficult moral issues postpones the process of awareness, atonement, and moral growth that might return him to a wholeness of spirit. When Frank Wirtanen after the war offers to find Campbell "a false identity" (140) and "a few red herrings" to help him hide (59), it is no more than Campbell has done for himself all his life. When Wirtanen accuses him of having been one of the most vicious sons of bitches who ever lived, Campbell replies, "That wasn't me" (138). It is possible, in fact, that Campbell has invented Frank Wirtanen, his "blue Fairy Godmother," to further escape responsibility for his role as Nazi propagandist. Campbell's lawyer tells him that all he needs to be a free man is the barest proof that there ever was such a person as Wirtanen (189). Wirtanen speaks of Howard as one of his "dream children" (137). "Nobody believes in him but me," Campbell says (41). He is even uncomfortable talking about Wirtanen ("NEAR TWIN" by anagram), "alias God knows what" (48).

Campbell's paralysis is enforced by the same fatalism that besets Paul Proteus and Malachi Constant—a pose that renders him one of "those bland, pleasing, easily manipulated playthings" he condemns in children's toys (60). Before being recruited by Wirtanen, he had said about Hitler's treatment of the Jews, "it isn't anything I can combat . . . so I don't think about it" (38, 40). Campbell projects his fatalistic view of human experience in this poem about history as "a great steam roller."

> I saw a huge steam roller,
> It blotted out the sun.
> The people all lay down, lay down;
> They did not try to run.
> My love and I, we looked amazed
> Upon the gory mystery.
> "Lie down, lie down!" the people cried.
> "The great machine is history!"
> My love and I, we ran away,
> The engine did not find us.
> We ran up to a mountain top,
> Left history far behind us.
> Perhaps we should have stayed and died.
> But somehow we don't think so.
> We went to see where history'd been,
> And my, the dead did stink so. (62)

Believing history beyond their means to shape, Campbell and Helga Noth fail to see that there are alternatives other than escape into some kind of protective shell or womb.[13] Hence they retreat into what Campbell calls their "Nation of Two."[14] Running away with his love, Campbell withdraws into a self-spun cocoon in which his and Helga's feelings for each other become their only reason for being, the boundary of which is their bed (95). After the war, Campbell comes into possession of a quantity of morphine and says he is tempted to take it. Why not, he reflects, since he has the money to support it?

But he remembers, "I was already drugged" and "feeling no pain" (47). The narcotic that got him through the war was the habit of letting his emotions be stirred only by his love for his wife, Helga. By so completely concentrating his emotion and loyalty, he had developed a lover's "happy illusion" into "a device to keep me from going insane." It ultimately becomes "the permanent axis" about which his thoughts revolve. Identifying the "Nation of Two" as a function of Thanatos, Campbell observes that he "became a death worshiper" as oblivious to reality as any "narrow-minded religious being" (47). The "Nation of Two" reduces life for him to an endless game of hide-and-seek, reminding him of that mournful childhood cry, "Olly-ollyox-in-free" (30). Helga, it appears, is another Oedipal love, a dangerous mother substitute. It is a relationship from which Campbell must be "weaned" (106). Resi, who in turn substitutes for Helga, is, by anagram, a "HOT SIREN." The fate associated with such retreatism comes through Campbell's reflection that their cozy little family made him and Helga felt like Noah and his wife on Mount Ararat. The flood was far from being over, he says. With that thought, an air raid siren blows (173).

Just as Campbell retreats from the world's horrors into the shell of his love for Helga, so he attempts preservation of body and soul by burying and hiding an essential part of himself within the confines of his own mind and projecting another make-believe self to the outer world. As a writer, he has been used to creating romantic fantasies—insanely melodramatic portrayals of heroism and villainy. He even sees himself as Don Quixote (127). The problem becomes that both as writer and Nazi propagandist, he deludes himself that he can separate the fake from the real. "I knew full well what ignorant, destructive, obscenely jocular things I was saying," he claims, "all I can say is *I* didn't believe them" (133):

> I would fool everyone with my brilliant interpretation of a Nazi, inside and out. And I did fool everybody . . . I began to strut like Hitler's right-hand man, and nobody saw the honest me I hid so deep inside. (65)

What he learns is that despite his hope "to be merely ludicrous" (66), the distinction between playing Nazi and actually being one had broken down. He learns from numerous people who have heard his anti-Semitic broadcasts that he could never have served the allies as well as he served the Nazis (80). His German father-in-law tells him

> that almost all the ideas that I now hold, that make me unashamed of anything I may have felt or done as a Nazi, came not from Hitler, not from Goebbels, not from Himmler—but from you . . . you alone kept me from concluding that Germany had gone insane. (67)

Evidence that Campbell had become what he pretended to be—signaling the novel's moral—comes in his invention of "The Free American Corps," a Nazi "daydream"

> of a fighting unit composed mainly of American prisoners of war, a high-morale fighting machine, motivated by a love of Western civilization and a dread of the Mongol hordes. When I call this unit a Nazi daydream, incidentally, I am suffering an attack of schizophrenia— because that idea of the Free American Corps *began* with me. *I* suggested its creation, designed its uniforms and insignia, wrote its creed. (68)

Campbell understands that he has paid a dear price for his "moral and political idiocy" in the form of tragic alienation and schizophrenic splitting. Yet it is his ultimate willingness to confront the consequences of his previous moral blindness that proves his salvation, first through his confessions that bring him face to face with the homicidal maniac within. And then through the decision to take his own life as a final affirmative statement that in an amoral world, one without absolute moral sanctions, the moral man must take responsibility for his actions. Sick to death of having lived so long without a conscience, he will create order and meaning and justice where none seems to exist.

It is through a contrast between himself and Adolph Eichman, the architect of Auschwitz and murderer of six million Jews, that we can pronounce Campbell not only sane but, perhaps for the first time in his life, fully in possession of his own soul. Oblivious to his crimes, Eichman tells Campbell during their first meeting to "relax" (122). Campbell says, "That is how I got here" (72). Having faced his crimes, he is able to say too, "My case is different. . . . This [convenient amnesia] cannot be said of me now" (124). *Now,* in contrast to Eichman's schizophrenic inability to distinguish between right and wrong, Campbell says he is "capable of imagining the cruel consequences of anybody's believing my lies," and of knowing "cruelty is wrong" (74, 123). It is this distinction, he says, that should send Eichman to a hospital, but for which punishments for people such as himself are conceived (75). In *Cat's Cradle,* the hero learns more about the dangers of schizophrenic reality avoidance—missing moral teeth that freeze or petrify the human soul.

4

Cat's Cradle: **Jonah and the Whale**

Too much sanity may be madness, and the maddest of all is to see life as it is and not as it should be.

Man of La Mancha

I realize today that nothing in the world is more distasteful to a man than to take the path that leads to himself.

Herman Hesse, *Demian*

Cat's Cradle, a novel Vonnegut himself awards an A +, shows a world so devastated by forms of mechanistic insanity that only a cynical religion like "Bokononism" will serve to make existence tolerable. Frustrated in the attempt to achieve meaningful social reforms in a society that has become unmanageable and eventually doomed by technological horrors such as "Ice-9," an ultimate doomsday device, Bokonon offers a solution based upon "a bitter disappointment for which no remedy exists unless laughter can be said to remedy anything" (134). Proposing that "everything happens as it is meant to happen," Bokonon encourages the population of San Lorenzo to turn away from thinking about things as they are and to live in harmony with seemingly harmless, comforting lies or illusions that make their remaining, darkening moments less terrifying. The challenge awaiting the protagonist on San Lorenzo is to discover that the moral advantages of lying about reality and surrendering to Bokononist fatalism are tragically mistaken.[1] Relieved of having to deal with complex experience, the protagonist is threatened by the moral and physical petrification that has turned San Lorenzans into puppetlike creatures who expedite their own demise. To be true to the courage and conscience of his predecessor Howard Campbell, Jonah must reject defensive self-deceptions and act against the totalitarian machinery that threatens to engulf him.

To understand the narrator called "Jonah," whose psychic drama comes to the fore in the second half of *Cat's Cradle,* we must backtrack briefly to the fictional city of Ilium,[2] New York, and a particularly hellish caldron called the General Forge and Foundry Company, birthplace of the atomic bomb and an equally deadly substance called "Ice-9" that threatens the end of life on earth. At General Forge science is worshiped as the strongest and most beneficial force in the life of mankind; its practitioners, especially pure researchers like Nobel Prize winning Felix Hoenikker, are viewed practically as gods. Felix is the father of the atomic bomb and of "Ice-9" but also of three very strange children whom Jonah, collecting material for a book to be called "The Day the World Ended," has come to interview. It is in the course of these interviews that a less charitable image of the saints of pure science begins to form in Jonah's mind.

Suggesting the perversion of natural, life-directed processes by such mechanistic activities as characterize Felix's so-called pure research, the brother of the research director at General Forge explains to Jonah,

> I know all about how harmless and gentle and dreamy he was supposed to be . . . how he was so innocent he was practically a Jesus . . . but how the hell innocent is a man who helps make a thing like an atomic bomb? And how can you say a man had a good mind when he couldn't even bother to do anything when the best-hearted, most beautiful woman in the world, his own wife, was dying for lack of love and understanding. . . . Sometimes I wonder if he wasn't born dead. I never met a man who was less interested in the living. (52, 53)

Felix and Thanatos are directly related. Felix's lack of interest in his wife (he once leaves her a tip for preparing his breakfast) indirectly causes her death and Newt's deformity. She dies in an accident caused when she picks up the car Felix abandons in a "glacier" of automobiles. Her grave marker is an "alabaster phallus . . . plastered with sleet" (48). Ice-9, a device that once set in motion can turn the world into a solid glacier and its inhabitants into statues of ice, proves a compelling symbol for the coldness and lovelessness bred into Felix Hoenikker who, caring only for his work, passes the effects of his coldness to all those around him. The impersonal processes at General Forge have rendered the workers there so vacant and dull-witted that they almost welcome the mindless, robotlike functions assigned to them by "faceless voices of scientists on dictaphone records" (34). One secretary decides that she will go crazy on the spot if anybody asks her to do any thinking (31). In effect, the black elevator operator named Lyman Enders Knowles, who grabs his own behind and cries, "Yes, yes!" whenever he feels that he's made a point, has made a point indeed when he asks, "How come they got to build a building like this . . . and fill it with all these crazy people?" (47).

Suggestive of the novel's pervasive water imagery, the souls of the women in the foundry's "girl pool" (31–34) have been drowned in the loveless, mechanized swirl of their "deathlike jobs" (136). So the three Hoenikker children, grotesquely victimized by parental lovelessness and likened to "babies full of rabies" (47), turn into ice-chips off the family block of ice represented by Felix.[3] The youngest son Newt is a four-foot-tall midget to whom his father has hardly ever spoken. Equally misshapen, Angela is a giantess worn out by age twenty-two from having to mother Felix as well as her two brothers. Frank Hoenikker is so hollowed of identity that he is referred to as "a man with a paper rectum," a man with almost no experience of talking to anyone because of a totally furtive existence (25). All in all, what has been done to the Hoenikker children is described by the plastic picture folder in which Angela keeps "all the people I love." They have been trapped in plexiglass like fossil beetles in amber, frozen or petrified into objects incapable of growth (82).

The emotional and physical deformity of the Hoenikker offspring is even more tragic because of thwarted artistic potential. Newt, described as "shrewdly watchful" and capable of "amiable grace," is a talented artist who can paint only morbid pictures; Frank's architectural genius, which he finally realizes only as a puppet-sycophant to a dictator, is diverted into years of masturbating and building model airplanes. And Angela plays the clarinet so beautifully but with such pain that the narrator senses "the depth, the violence, and the almost intolerable beauty" of her "disease." "Such music from such a woman," says Jonah, "could only be a case of schizophrenia or demonic possession" (123, 124). A form of schizophrenia is doubtlessly the correct diagnosis of the disease that has claimed the Hoenikker children and the workers at General Forge, and that stalks the narrator throughout the course of the novel. Eros, the instinct to love and create, has been petrified in the Hoenikker children by such unfeeling, mechanized forces as represented by Felix, Asa Breed, Ice-9, and the deathly, impersonal life at General Forge, which spreads like proliferating Ice-9 to the Hoenikker home. In effect, Newt, Frank, and Angela have been caught up in the dehumanizing mechanism of a "cat's cradle," symbolized in this novel and throughout Vonnegut's work by insidious spirals, tunnels, clocks, caves, staircases, and mountain rims, which appear to entrap unwary individuals and send them spinning toward certain doom. Whether these mechanistic traps represent structures of control that are economic, religious, philosophic, militaristic, environmental, psychic, or biological, their chief evil is that they offer the kind of illusory protection and security that lure Paul Proteus, Malachi Constant, and Howard Campbell, while locking them into cycles of action indifferent to individual will or aspiration. Such is the spiral of lovelessness that reproduces itself in the Hoenikker family, or that of Ice-9 or the nuclear arms race that assumes a deadly momentum toward global destruction. Notably, Jonah is in a tombstone salesroom, a room of death, when he first hears of the labyrinthine miseries of the Hoenikker children. Feeling himself drawn into the spiraling mechanisms that have destroyed them, Jonah senses the room tipping and its walls and ceiling transforming into "the mouths of many tunnels" (55). Frank Hoenikker has a wiry pompadour, "a sort of cube of hair" (60) that rises to an incredible height.

Laing's paradigm for schizophrenic loss of self becomes the central expression of Jonah's plight—engulfment in the form of drowning or petrification. Hence it is that Jonah feels strongly drawn toward the girls in the girl pool. As he contemplates the devouring mechanisms at work in the foundry, he sees his own fate reflected by that "sea of pale faces" into which Dr. Breed benignly peers (30). Felix himself is "facing the sea" when he dies from Ice-9 poisoning (82). What Vonnegut is telling us about cat's cradles is conveyed by the fact that such drowning imagery occurs in this novel whenever individuals lend themselves passively to mechanistic systems, entrapping spirals that they believe themselves helpless to resist, or when they believe themselves to be mysterious agents in the working out of destinies they are not to question. In short, those who out of moral inertia rationalize cat's cradles are as responsible for such apocalyptic nightmares as Hiroshima, or that which befalls ill-fated San Lorenzo in this novel, as are the amoral scientists who dissociate themselves from the potential horror of their playful creations. The sea of futility in which they drown is one they themselves have made. The fact that Felix was found constructing a cat's cradle with a piece of string the day the atom bomb was dropped on Hiroshima suggests that, while both activities originate from an impulse more playful than devious, cat's cradles like atom bombs can become the deadliest of adult realities, especially if their use is determined by such warped and childishly irresponsible people as the Hoenikker children prove to be.

The precise nature of the challenge facing the novel's narrator comes in the image of poor Frank Hoenikker, wanted by the Florida police, the FBI, and the Treasury Department for running stolen cars to Cuba, washed up onto the shores of the Republic of San Lorenzo in the Caribbean after his pleasure craft has sunk. Heedless of the man-eating sharks that make ominous spirallike circles in the water around him, Frank observes, "I raised my eyes to my Maker, willing to accept whatever His decision might be. And my eyes alit on a glorious mountain peak above the clouds. Was this Fata Morgana—the cruel deception of a mirage?" (62). That Frank should consider Mount McCabe or his deliverance to the rocky shores of diseased, poverty-ridden San Lorenzo as an act of God, as something glorious, is a mirage more deceitfully cruel than this spiritual ostrich will ever know. The fact is that in his pathetic need to believe that he is finally to play an important role in an experiment that is humanly meaningful—helping to build a utopian society as Minister of Science and Progress in San Lorenzo—Frank comes to the destitute banana republic unwittingly to complete the process of moral petrification his father had begun in Ilium. By relinquishing what is left of his frozen soul to the totalitarian forces on San Lorenzo, he becomes transformed into a totally subservient, puppetlike creature who expedites his own doom while initiating global destruction. Linking the cat's cradle of scientific progress in Ilium with the cat's cradle of totalitarianism in San Lorenzo, he brings with him to this second Ilium the Trojan horse of Ice-9.

Following his journalistic instincts that all is *not* as promised in the ad in the New York Sunday *Times* about the "healthy, happy, progressive, freedom-loving, beautiful nation" of San Lorenzo (60), Jonah looks up Fata Morgana and learns that it *was* in fact a "mirage" named after Morgan le Fay, a fairy who lived at the *bottom* of a lake. "It was famous for appearing in the Strait of Messina, between Calabria and Sicily. Fata Morgana was poetic crap, in short" (62). On the one hand, Jonah's realism reveals to us his determination at the beginning of the story to tell about "the human rather than the technical side of the making and dropping of the bomb on Hiroshima" (14), the human costs of irresponsible technology. To be true to his purpose he must above all else remain free from the defeatism and the self-imprisoning fantasies of paradise on San Lorenzo that have swallowed up Frank Hoenikker. The problem is that for reasons of moral comfort Jonah is tempted by the same pain-killing, womblike illusions of contentment and security that shipwreck Frank. Coming from a past as wasteful and degenerate as that which demoralizes Malachi Constant, Jonah describes himself early in the novel as feeling "bristly, diseased, cynical," his soul seeming "as foul as smoke from burning cat fur" (27). Too much involvement with cat's cradles has evidently taken its psychological toll. It has been "two wives . . . 250,000 cigarettes . . . 3,000 quarts of booze ago" that he had begun his book (136).[4] His second wife had left him "on the ground that I was too pessimistic for an optimist to live with" (58). When he attempts to put his thoughts in order to conduct his interviews, he finds, he says, "that my mental health had not improved. . . . I found that the public-relations centers of my brain had been suffocated by booze and burning cat fur" (34). It is not surprising then that Jonah's commitment to truth should be so compromised by a potentially incapacitating pessimism that he should state his intentions as examining "all *strong* hints as to what on Earth we, collectively, have been up to," as if in his dazed condition to look carefully at more subtle hints is more than he is capable of (13). We wonder too at the lassitude behind his statement that "when a man becomes a writer, I think he takes on a sacred obligation to produce beauty and enlightenment and comfort at top speed" (156). The comfort may only be Jonah's if the truths he tells are superficial. When asked on San Lorenzo if a writer may not be a drug salesman, Jonah answers, "I'll accept that. Guilty as charged." When further asked if he has written anything like that, Jonah says, "Not yet" (106).

Both *Mother Night* and *Cat's Cradle* focus Vonnegut's concern with fiction as a form of play that can be constructive or destructive. In the editor's note to *Mother Night*, Vonnegut writes that lies told for the sake of artistic effect can be the most beguiling form of truth (94). Kraft tells Howard Campbell that future civilizations will be judged by the strength of their artistic will, and by the quality of their creations (52, 53). Whether Jonah is to be as a writer and a human being a drug salesman, a dispenser of quick and easy answers to complex questions, an evader of painful realities like the spurious prophet Bokonon, rather than the honest writer we feel he would like to be, is a main conflict in Jonah as well as in all Vonnegut's artist-protagonists. His essential challenge is to learn to distinguish good or bad "lies" or fictions that, as David Ketterer says, either encourage the forces of aggression and death or abet the forces of life—of hope, compassion, and engagement.[5] The writer (or prophet) who lies to escape pain or to encourage others to do so is as mad as the scientist who blithely engages in research designed to make doomsday weapons. When a character by the name of H. Lowe Crosby refers to caricatures used for target practice by the San Lorenzan Air Force, saying, "They got practically every enemy that freedom ever had out there" (155), the truth, for Jonah at least, is that the enemy is the one within, the agonizing split in his soul represented by the voice of fatalism on the one hand and the voice of affirmation on the other. By the start of the story, we see that Jonah has already embraced the will-sapping philosophy of the bogus holy man Bokonon, whose religion, though outlawed, constitutes the pervasive faith of all those on San Lorenzo. "I am a Bokononist now," he tells us on page 1, which in effect means one who believes in "the folly of pretending to discover, to understand" (13), hardly a fitting prerequisite for a reality seeker. Rather than truth, the cynical Bokonon, whose social utopianism had failed to alleviate the suffering of San Lorenzans, encourages the population to turn away from thinking about things as they are and to live in harmony with *seemingly* harmless, comforting lies called "foma" that make their remaining, darkening moments less terrifying. The Bokononist faithful do not have to worry about reality because reality is too terrible to contemplate, and because, says Bokonon, "everything happens as it was meant to happen" (24, 63, 158), because "it is impossible to make a mistake" (138), and because "each of us has to be what he or she is" (178). What no one on San Lorenzo seems to notice is that this supposed holy man (Felix has been identified as a modern "holy" man too) and his hide-from-it-if-it-hurts philosophy has turned San Lorenzans into hopelessly conforming, petrified statues as effectively as Ice-9 could have done. In the meantime Bokonon lives a cozy existence in the jungle, where he writes all day and eats the good things his disciples bring him (53). Not as Edenic for Bokonon as it sounds, however, since his corrosive pessimism and the mask of gentle holy man behind which has been hidden a complex and fragmented spirit have driven him insane (118.)[6]

Because Jonah is a Bokononist, one who "would have agreed gaily to go anywhere anyone suggested" (50), who believes that "somebody or something . . . has compelled me to be certain places at certain times without fail" (55),[7] his susceptibility to cat's cradles on San Lorenzo may put him into a deep spiritual sleep and produce the fate of his biblical namesake. The narrator captures his penchant for the easy way in his very first words to us: "Call me Jonah. My parents did, or nearly did. They called me John. Jonah—John—if I had been a Sam, I would have been a Jonah still" (11). Jonah receives his first "very personal shove" in the direction of Bokononism by imagining that "God Almighty knew all about me . . . that God . . . had some pretty elaborate plans for me" (53). But if his religious delusions, his belief that his thoughts or actions are controlled by others, may lead him straight into the mouth of the whale of moral oblivion, John, his real self, the voice of conscience, his anti-Bokononist voice, is still sufficiently alive and alarmed over the dubious consolations of Bokononist fatalism to fight for the narrator's divided soul. The key to the novel's ultimate moral affirmation is that Jonah's story, like Howard Campbell's, is told in retrospect, and though the narrator is still under the influence of Bokononist thought, we get the feeling that, as the story unfolds, the drug has begun to wear off, that John has come increasingly to suspect that the benefits of Bokononism are as dubious as those of technological progress offered by Felix Hoenikker. In less than reverent tones, Jonah's narrative is an imaginative reconstruction of events that led to Jonah's Bokononist conversion with a chance to reexplore their meaning. This defies the deathly stasis of Bokonon's own view of human and societal structures. When Jonah suggests an improvisation of Bokonon's Twenty-Third Psalm, Bokonon cannot change a single word. That a growth in awareness has indeed taken place is indicated by the narrator's observation near the close of the story that "I turned to the Books of Bokonon, still sufficiently unfamiliar with them to believe they contained spiritual comfort somewhere" (177). Evidently he has learned better.

The nature of Jonah's particular brand of schizophrenia is that his spiritual self, that affirmative voice that wants to tell the truth, is so effectively counterbalanced by the voice of futility that a kind of stasis results, reflected in "the cruel paradox of Bokononist thought" about the heartbreaking necessity of lying about reality (189). The part of him that prefers foma to reality interviews the demented Julian Castle with the view, "I knew I wasn't going to have an easy time writing a popular article about him. I was going to have to concentrate on his saintly deeds and ignore entirely the satanic things he thought and said" (116). It is also the part that allows him to be used as a puppet-president of San Lorenzo by Minister of Science and Progress Frank Hoenikker and threatens, so to speak, to put the *ice*ing on the cake of his schizophrenic dilemma, making him as morally dead as Frank or Felix Hoenikker or Bokonon. As a machine, he experiences no libidinal energy, hence no creativity, at all. He mourns that he has no "sex urge left," thus "no dreams . . . nothing" (188). At first, when the cancer-ridden dictator of San Lorenzo decides to commit suicide with the Ice-9 Frank has given him and to take the rest of the world into the frozen sea with him, and Jonah is asked to rule the doomed island, his resistance is firm.

"Nuts," he tells Frank. When Frank says "You haven't really thought about it," Jonah answers, "Enough to know it's crazy" (134). Frank knows Jonah's moral evasiveness and pleads, "Come on. Be president of San Lorenzo. You'd be real good at it, with *your* personality" (136). Suggestive of the soulless political machinery to which Frank wants Jonah to be a mindless accomplice, "Frank made his fingers into gears again. 'We'd work together,' " he says. " 'I'd be backing you all the time'" (134). In effect Frank invites Jonah to become the public side of himself so that each is but half a human being—a mechanical being at that. When Franks tells him they could really hit it off, that they "mesh," Jonah notes: "I was grateful when he took his hand from my shoulder. He meshed the fingers of his hands like gear teeth. One hand represented him, I suppose, and the other represented me." "We need each other," Frank continues, wiggling his fingers to show how the gear worked. Frank explains that Jonah is a worldly person good for public show and he himself is a technical person who works best behind the scenes (133). Jonah feels that watery oblivion threatening him as his will weakens, aided by the bribe of a hundred thousand dollars a year and a palace of his own where he will drink out of gold goblets every night and eat off of gold plates. Jonah observes, "Frank was frantic for me to complete his thought, to do it enthusiastically, but I was still at sea" (133). Increasingly powerless to resist, Jonah says that Frank has made Jonah's will as irrelevant as the free will "of a piggy-wig arriving at the Chicago stockyard" (128). Jonah then sums up the combined forces that have depleted his will for years and made him a prime candidate for Bokononism (136).

> And the time of night and the cave and the waterfall—and the stone angel in Ilium. . . . And 250,000 cigarettes and 3,000 quarts of booze, and two wives and no wife. . . . And no love waiting for me anywhere. . . . And the listless life of an ink-stained hack. . . . And Pabu, the moon, and Borasisi, the sun, their children . . . [Bokononist cosmology]. . . . All things conspired to form one cosmic vin-dit, one mighty shove into Bokononism, into the belief that God was running my life and that He had work for me to do. And, inwardly, I sarooned, which is to say that I acquiesced to the seeming demands of my vin-dit. Inwardly, I agreed to become the next President of San Lorenzo. Outwardly, I was still guarded, suspicious. (137)

Jonah has adopted the same false self system of previous heroes, resulting in an increasingly depleted inner being. When Frank dissociates himself from the pending destruction of San Lorenzo, making Jonah the new president with the words, "You're the boss, sir," Jonah reflects: "each time he said those words they seemed to come from farther away, as though Frank were descending the rungs of a ladder into a deep shaft, while I was obliged to remain above." Jonah realizes with chagrin that agreeing to be boss, secretly withdrawing his true self, he has freed Frank to do what his father had done: to receive honors and creative comforts while escaping human responsibilities. Frank was accomplishing this by going down a "spiritual oubliette" (151).[8] While Jonah is appalled at Frank's

sudden abdication from human affairs, he himself escapes into a spiritual oubliette both literally and figuratively by becoming a Bokononist stooge, a "stuppa,"
a "fogbound child" (135). Literally he flees down the manhole cover of an
oubliette into the "rock-womb" (176) of his castle's cozy bomb shelter to escape
the gnashing, gobbling mouths of tornadoes spewing the poisonous bluewhite
frost of Ice-9 (175). Repeatedly, as Jonah allows himself to be carried along
by the mindless momentum of what he assumes is his unmistakable destiny,
we see him headed toward a watery grave at the end of entrapping tunnels,
staircases, caves, shafts, mountains, some form of devouring cat's cradle. When
he accepts the puppet role of president, it is in "a cave that was curtained by a
waterfall"; he experiences "the ragged rim of oblivion . . . now inches from my
curling toes" (173). "I looked down," he says. "My lukewarm sea had swallowed all." Ominously he notes, "I was a respectful stranger to my own voice.
My voice had a metallic authority that was new. I was already starting to rule"
(173).

It is of course the Frank Hoenikker or Bokonon part of his personality that
has started to rule, rule *him* as well as the island, abetted by a golden-haired
creature named Mona Aamons, the adopted daughter of the island's dictator
who automatically belongs to Jonah as the island's new leader. Jonah's diffused
will is no match for this latest siren. Says Jonah,

> While I didn't feel that purposeful seas were wafting me to San Lorenzo, I did feel that love
> was doing the job. The Fata Morgana, the mirage of what it would be like to be loved by
> Mona Aamons Monzano, had become a tremendous force in my meaningless life. I imagined
> that she could make me far happier than any woman had so far succeeded in doing. (64)

Jonah fantasizes that Mona is not only the most heartbreakingly beautiful girl
he can ever hope to see, but also "luminously compassionate and wise" (60).
He is more than willing to trade his writer's integrity for Mona's "warm and
creamy soul . . . peace and plenty forever" (98). After all, he reasons, "She was
all there was to understand. Mona was the simplicity of the All" (98).

Jonah is thrilled, heartbroken, hilarious, and most significantly, "insane,"
over Mona, immune to reality while enjoying the catatonic, orgiastic rigidity
of boko-maru with her—the kissing of souls by mingling the bottoms of their
feet together. Under her anesthetizing influence he is less likely than ever to
know what is real. But it is the discovery that she is as false a mother as she is
a lover that engenders a moral awakening and delivers Jonah from the mouth
of the whale. He recognizes not only that her love is promiscuously mechanical
but that, as with Felix, Frank, or Bokonon, compassion is unknown to her. After
the "pool pah," the shit storm, has struck, after Ice-9 has left nearly everyone
dead or threatened by eternal winter, Mona looks down from Mt. McCabe at
thousands upon thousands of dead San Lorenzans who, at Bokonon's command,

had gathered themselves together first to practice boko-maru and then to commit suicide by Ice-9 poisoning. The transition from mechanical love, a form of death-in-life, to literal death is simply achieved. Not only does she not cry; in fact, says Jonah, "she seemed to verge on laughter" (183). Then, with an actual laugh that strikes Jonah as "startlingly deep and raw," "strolling down among the petrified thousands," still laughing, she says, raising her arms lazily, "It's all so simple, that's all. It solves so much for so many so simply" (182).

While Mona finishes up as insane as Bokonon, Jonah's new self-assertiveness suggests *his* sanity may be returning, his splintered soul on the mend. He announces that, in case anyone was interested, he was willing to answer tough questions about what had gone wrong—"where and how" (181). Telling his story about the human rather than the technical side of the bomb, one exactly like that in which he appears, provides the therapy and self-discovery he needs to resist the cat's cradle that had always been his personal nemesis—overwhelming pessimism. The fact that Jonah's mysterious last name may be "Vonnegut" suggests that this story is Vonnegut's too. A German immigrant had once ordered an angel to mark the grave of his diseased wife. Marvin Breed says that the last name on the marker, "a screwy name," was probably Americanized to Jones or Black or Thompson. "There you're wrong," Jonah assures him. When Marvin asks if Jonah knows some people by that name, Jonah says, "The name was my last name, too" (55, 56). The book by Jonah and the one by Vonnegut, or the one by Jonah Vonnegut, are incomplete . . . directing our attention to "what might yet be, if the world would thaw" (189). If John and Jonah remain split, the John and Jonah in Vonnegut are closer to whole, closer to fulfilling Jonah's ancient role of warning the world against self-destruction. Jonah's battle for awareness and self-possession continues in what is Vonnegut's prototypal schizoid hero, Eliot Rosewater.

5

God Bless You, Mr. Rosewater:
The Saga of Vonnegut's Sanest Lunatic

Much madness is divinest sense—
To a discerning eye. . . .
Assent—and you are sane—
Demur—you're straightway dangerous—
And handled with a chain—

Emily Dickinson

Insanity—a perfectly rational adjustment to an insane world.
R. D. Laing

While most critics stress the sociological aspects of this novel,[1] it is its psychological dimension that constitutes the story's complexity and special poignancy. The question posed to the reader-turned-psychoanalyst is whether Eliot is the "flamboyantly sick man" envisioned by most of the people around him, "crazy as a loon" (10), "irrevocably bananas" (33), or whether he is one of the sanest characters in Vonnegut's fiction—according to his wife's father, the sanest man in America (64), and, according to Kilgore Trout, instigator of one of the most important social experiments of his time—learning to treasure people who have no use (183). Or is Eliot some whacky, fluctuating combination of the two, losing and regaining his mental equilibrium at intervals? Sometimes Eliot's tormentors themselves are undecided:

> It was common gossip in the office that the very first president of the Foundation, Eliot Rosewater, the Senator's son, was a lunatic. This characterization was a somewhat playful one . . . Eliot was spoken of by Mushari's co-workers as "The Nut," "The Saint," "The Holy Roller," "John the Baptist," and so on. (10)

The interpretive challenge is complicated by the fact that Vonnegut denies us easy answers, preferring we form our own. And by the fact that Eliot Rosewater is so fundamentally decent, his antagonists so formidably evil that we are likely to confuse Eliot's dangerous tendency toward withdrawal and passivity with kindness and restraint. Complicating the issue further is the fact that Eliot, with Hamlet as his favorite literary character (19), plays with madness as a strategy to expose the viciousness of his adversaries, which invites us to wonder if a deliberate split with reality does not become something Eliot eventually cannot control, bringing on real psychosis. But if Eliot is judged insane, Vonnegut is telling us that the world of lovelessness and materialistic lusts that Eliot can no longer inhabit is far sicker than the world of his own mind in which he seeks escape.

Early passages in *God Bless You, Mr. Rosewater* show that notions of sanity are inescapably tied to the ideological assumptions of the speaker and say as much about the values of the accuser as the accused. Just as Senator Rosewater is horrified that Eliot should object to a system in which honest, industrious, peaceful citizens are classified as bloodsuckers if they asked for a living wage (12), Eliot is aghast at the violently cruel and repressive system of justice his father advocates in a speech delivered on the floor of the Senate. Stressing "those two sex maniacs Anthony and Cleopatra" as a negative example for modern times, Lister argues the importance of stamping out modern degeneracy through the same measures used in ancient Rome by Caesar Augustus (25, 26). He calls for a police force as cruel and unsmiling in treating law breakers as Caesar's, stringing offenders up by their thumbs, throwing them down wells, feeding them to the lions, among other undesirable experiences sure to make people good citizens. His motto? "Let's force Americans to be as good as they should be" (26).[2]

According at least to the definition of sanity provided by Eliot's psychiatrist Dr. Brown, the senator is right about himself when he declares, "this family never produced and never will produce a chronic drunk or a chronic lunatic" (24). Both ideologically and linguistically, the doctor's thinking is determined by "language with ... slow narrow meanings" (173). To justify the brutal economic system he serves, he uses what J. H. Van den Berg calls the "vocabulary of denigration."[3] A normal person, says the doctor, is one who functions well in the upper levels of a prosperous industrialized society, hardly ever hearing his conscience at all (43). Eliot tells us that his father has left the manipulation of his assets to lawyers and banks and spent nearly the whole of his adult life in the Congress of the United States "teaching morals" and successfully ignoring thoughts about the effects and implications of his inherited wealth (14).

So the senator's dictim, "The hell with you Jack, I've got mine" (42), is to him normal, while Eliot's humanitarianism is lunacy. Taking your place guiltlessly at the "slurping machine" is sane; believing in kindness, generosity, and concern for others is not (88–89). The doctor explains that Eliot's instability comes from the fact that he has inherited his mother's sincere anxieties about the condition of the poor and is therefore among those rare individuals who reach maturity still loving and wanting to help their fellow men (43). We are told that Eliot's commitment to compassion is so deep that if he were to come down with the disease suffered by his wife, called Samaritrophia, he would probably kill himself, or perhaps a hundred others, and then be shot down like a mad dog before he could be treated (43). Samaritrophia, defined as "hysterical indifference to the troubles of those less fortunate than oneself," attacks only those with an overactive conscience (41–42).

In the case of Eliot's wife, the doctor makes it the goal of his treatment to make her superficially content with her lot rather than attempting to revitalize her conscience. With the help of chemotherapy and electroshock treatments Sylvia's conscience is silenced, but the process renders her near-schizophrenic and she subsequently repudiates her life with Eliot. She fantasizes fainting in the gaity of Paris into the arms of a tall dark stranger, hopefully a double spy, and refers to Eliot as "my dirty, drunk uncle down south" (44). The doctor insists that, while Sylvia is not schizophrenic, she manifests all the symptoms of paranoia when Eliot visits her (44). Ultimately Sylvia assumes a third personality—a feeling of worthlessness, shame, and "a suicidal wish to ignore her revulsions"—and withdraws into polite indifference (52). "She was content," says Eliot, "with being a splash pool three feet across, four inches deep, chlorinated, and painted blue." "Some doctor! Some cure!" (43). The formal question of Eliot Rosewater's sanity arises because a clause in the charter of the foundation of which he is president calls for the immediate expulsion of any officer adjudged insane (8–10). As the closest and oldest heir of Senator Lister Rosewater, Eliot inherits the presidency of the Rosewater Foundation, a supposedly charitable and cultural foundation constructed in 1947, under the expectation that he will pursue its hypocritical aims of protecting the family's sizable financial interests from tax collectors and other predators not named Rosewater (7). The foundation's specific task is to spend the copious profits earned by the more businesslike "Rosewater Corporation," which manages the foundation's capital and business enterprises and is solely dedicated to profit (8).

The family's problem is that the new Harvard Ph.D. in law determines to take his philanthropic role seriously, setting out with an office in the Empire State Building to accomplish "all the beautiful, compassionate and scientific things he hoped to do" (16–17). For six utopian years he spends the foundation's funds fighting countless human miseries—cancer, race prejudice, police brutality, and, ironically, mental illness. We are told Eliot was willing to pay any price for beauty, and even encouraged college professors to search for truth (17). A further embarrassment to the family is that in addition to distributing the family fortune on humanitarian grounds, Eliot spends his time openly denouncing the cruelty of free enterprise and the vicious class system he believes it creates.

In a direct confrontation with his father, Eliot excoriates heartless governments that let some babies be born owning a big piece of the country, the way he was, while letting others be born without owning anything. At least, Eliot says, the government could "divide things up fairly among the babies" (88). It is when Eliot springs his favorite metaphor of "the money river" on his father that their respective views of sanity clash openly. "People born close to the river slurp to their hearts' content," says Eliot, "even taking slurping lessons from lawyers and tax consultants." It is by proximity to the money river, he says, that he is allowed to make ten thousand dollars a day just by snoozing and scratching himself and occasionally answering the phone (87, 89). "It's insane," Eliot declares, that the money and power of an earthling millionaire should allow him to do such a thing (21). His father counters that people would stop feeling so miserable if they ceased believing in "crazy things" like the money river and got to work (89–90).

Initially, in contrast to the greed and brutality of people like his father and his lawyer, Norman Mushari, an embodiment of corporate legal viciousness, Eliot's humanity suggests that it is they alone who need to be removed from society. The first piece of so-called solid evidence that Eliot is crazy indicts the accuser rather than the accused. Norman Mushari, "an envious ass, which was luminous when bare" (9), plots the violent overthrow of the Rosewater Foundation when he learns that the Rosewater fortune was the largest money package represented by his law firm. He decides to make good the main lesson he had learned from his favorite professor, Leonard Leech, about getting ahead in law.

> There's a magic moment during which a man has surrendered a treasure, and during which the man who is due to receive it has not done so. . . . If the man who is to receive the treasure is unused to wealth, has an inferiority complex and shapeless feelings of guilt, as most people do, the lawyer can often take as much as half the bundle and still receive the recipient's blubbering thanks. (9)

Mushari knows that the magic moment could be brought about by proving Eliot insane, forcing Eliot to relinquish the presidency of the Rosewater Foundation to the next person in line, a cousin in Rhode Island who was inferior in all respects.[4] Mushari sets out to embarrass and humiliate Eliot in every way he can. He starts by producing a confidential document locked inside the family's vault, supposed to be delivered unopened to whomever took over the foundation when Eliot was dead.

What Mushari sees in the letter as clear indication of Eliot's insanity is an unwillingness to be a good capitalist who lines his own pockets at the expense of others. The reader sees an exposé and repudiation of moral ruthlessness and criminal exploitation underlying the Rosewater family fortune, first accumulated by a "humorless, constipated Christian farm boy" turned speculator and briber during and after the Civil War (11). "Noah Rosewater," Eliot has written, "my great-grandfather, who was born in Rosewater County, Indiana, opportunistically seized on the national tragedy to sell at top dollar swords and bayonets and livestock whose quality was never questioned with a well-placed bribe" (12). With the help of venal office holders and with a carefully plotted marriage to one of the ugliest but richest women in Indiana, Noah expanded into all related markets, eventually peddling watered stocks and bonds. Discovering that nothing was too sacred for his money to buy, Noah thus became one "of a handful of rapacious citizens coming to control all that was worth controlling in America" (12). Ultimately Eliot denounces the family's vicious grab for money and power as part of the force that turned the American dream belly up, "turned green, bobbled to the scummy surface of cupidity unlimited, filled with gas, went bang in the noonday sun" (13).

A closer look reveals that despite the rational if comic exposure of his family's sins, Eliot's emotional problems may be far more serious than he or his antagonists suspect, so serious, in fact, that "no amount of booze seemed to make him drunk" (17). Despite his doctor's obtuseness, he is probably on target when he observes that Eliot "has the most massively defended neurosis I've ever attempted to treat" (28). "In over a solid year of work," says the doctor, "I have not succeeded in even scratching its armor plate" (28). "Do you know what we talk about?" he asks Eliot's wife:

> American history! Here is a very sick man, who among other things, killed his mother, who has a terrifying tyrant for a father. And what does he talk about when I invite him to let his mind wander where it will? American history. (28)

Eliot acknowledges that the statement that he had killed his beloved mother was crudely true. When he was nineteen, sailing in Cotuit Harbor, the slashing boom knocked his mother overboard and "Eunice Morgan Rosewater sank like a stone" (28).[5] "I ask him what he dreams about," the doctor continues:

> And he tells me, "Samuel Gompers, Mark Twain, and Alexander Hamilton." I ask him if his father ever appears in his dreams, and he says, "No, but Thorstein Veblen often does." . . . Mrs. Rosewater, I'm defeated. I resign. (28)

The doctor sees no relevance among the anal constriction of Eliot's great-grandfather, Eliot's relationship with his parents, and the legacy of guilt left to him by American history; for Eliot, the sins of one are inseparable from the sins of the other. While it is obviously easier for Eliot to contemplate the remoter sins of his country, he suspects that a direct line of culpability leads from childhood fears and insecurities to his present instability. "You have some doubts as to your own sanity?" his father asks. "Certainly," says Eliot. "Since I was ten maybe" (153). Like Eliot, the senator prefers not to examine his early relationship with his son too closely. "I seem to get around to everything about Eliot twenty years too late. I've never been able to get through my head that such a splendid animal could ever go so much to hell" (71). He attributes Eliot's compulsions to "the whoop-dee-doo" about Eliot's being mascot for the fire department when he was a child. They spoiled him, he says, letting him ring the bell. "Booze and fire engines," he concludes, "a happy childhood regained" (62).

A more likely source of Eliot's problems is his father's lifelong hysteria over nudity. In recalling that the doctor wanted to know about his childhood and his feelings about bodily hair, the senator winces and asks the doctor to please get off the subject, insisting that his revulsions are shared so far as he knows by decent men everywhere (72). The difference between pornography and art, the senator declares, "is bodily hair!" (72), a difference he writes into law, his legislative masterpiece, that makes publication or possession of obscene materials a federal offense carrying penalties of up to fifty thousand dollars and ten years in prison, without hope of parole. The law defines obscenity as categorically as the senator defines insanity: "any picture or phonograph record or any written matter calling attention to reproductive organs, bodily discharges or bodily hair" (71).

In a moment of desperation, however, admitting to the doctor "I ran out of ideas about my boy . . . years ago," the senator says to him, "Stick your stainless steel spoon in this unhappy old man's brains, Doctor, and stir" (72). The doctor explains nervously that his thoughts will necessarily touch upon matters of sexual perversion:

> Let's assume that a healthy young man is supposed to be sexually aroused by an attractive woman not his mother or sister. If he's aroused by other things, another man, say, or an umbrella, or the ostrich boa of the Empress Josephine, or a sheep, or a corpse, or his mother, or a stolen garterbelt, he is what we call a pervert. (72, 73)

Explaining that such perversion is essentially a case of crossed wires, he says that Eliot's case has led him "to bring his sexual energies" to an inappropriate object. "Eliot is bringing his sexual energies to what?" asks the senator. "To Utopia," says the doctor (73). This identifies the basic psychic disturbance of protagonists from Paul Proteus to Eugene Debs Hartke—"libidinal displacement, the perversion of vital creative energy into abstract, mechanistic, or grandiose schemes."

Sylvia indicates that Eliot's sexual energies have indeed gone somewhere else. She explains that while Eliot was never interested in producing children, he went from being "a sweet fanatic for love-making" to sexual indifference near the end of their marriage (71). At least as responsible for Eliot's failed marriage and obsession with utopian reform are his traumatic experiences as a soldier, which led to emotional collapse. Eliot had led a platoon in an assault on a clarinet factory in Bavaria, supposedly infested with S.S. troops. After pitching a grenade through the window, he enters the room, stumbles over dead German bodies, and finds himself facing a helmeted German in a gas mask. Whereas he had never stuck a bayonet into anybody before in years of carnage, "Eliot, like a good soldier, jammed his knee into the man's groin, drove his bayonet into his throat, withdrew the bayonet, smashed the man's jaw with his rifle butt" (63). At which point he hears an American sergeant yelling to cease fire, that they have mistakenly assaulted a group of firemen (64). Eliot had killed three unarmed firemen, ordinary villagers—one a fourteen-year-old boy. The immediate effect on him, before being sent to a mental ward of the American hospital, is that he lies down in front of a moving truck, remorseful and rigid with fear (64).

Visiting Eliot at the hospital, Sylvia's father finds him "the sanest American he had ever met" because he has reacted appropriately to the horror of war (64). His assessment is flattering and understandable but hardly an accurate measure of Eliot's condition. More likely, memories of war have deepened Eliot's guilt and crippled his ability to function in a way that a head filled with idealistic hopes, a doctorate in international law from Harvard, and presidency of the Rosewater Foundation cannot hope to cure. From 1947 to 1953, Eliot at the helm, the Rosewater Foundation spends fourteen million dollars in a veritable orgy of social reform. While his mission is heartfelt, Eliot's motives are suspect and his actions become increasingly compulsive and antisocial. Friendless, he spends his time driving away his rich friends by telling them that whatever they had was based on dumb luck, alienating his artist friends by telling them they failed to reach the poor, his scholarly friends by insisting they wrote only boring crap, and his scientific friends by telling them they were responsible for all the dubious scientific advances he had read about in recent newspapers and magazines (27).

Eliot's grip on reality is increasingly tenuous. Promising his wife that he doesn't hear voices (31), he yet insists that he is meant for a special destiny far away from the shallow and preposterous posing that is life in New York. "And I roam, and I roam," he says (31). His will grows increasingly diffuse. Longing for definite instructions from someone stronger and wiser, he scurries anxiously about the country like a whirling dervish, a compulsive drunk and wanderer delivering rambling tirades against the rich and their exploitation of the promised land. He especially attacks the "all-American family named Rosewater" (34)—even speaking of a revolution led by infantry veterans and volunteer firemen (32). He frequently poses as a volunteer fireman, once writing Sylvia a letter describing the fire apparatus of Elsinore, California, "as though Sylvia would be avid for such details," addressing his wife as Ophelia and signing off as Hamlet (31, 32). Among other signs that he is indeed going, in his wife's words, "irrevocably bananas" (33), Eliot gets drunk and breaks in on a science-fiction writers' conference in Milford, Pennsylvania, praising them for being the only ones crazy enough to care about the future, "really noticing what machines do to us, what wars do to us, what cities do to us, what big, simple ideas do to us, what tremendous misunderstandings, mistakes, accidents and catastrophes do to us" (18). From Milford Eliot goes to Swarthmore and makes a drunken, impassioned speech in a bar on the dangers of breathing oxygen and, in the midst of a crying jag, praises the fidelity of volunteer firefighters (22). He then heads across the country drinking with firemen and trading away his expensive clothes for surplus jackets.[6]

When Eliot finally stumbles home, wondering what in the hell people are for, he enters psychoanalysis, swears off drinking, takes pride in his appearance again, and seems to be recovering. It is then that he and Sylvia go to the Metropolitan Opera for the opening of a new staging of *Aida,* Eliot wearing a friendly face and his blue eyes "glittering with mental hygiene" (29). Everything goes fine until the last scene of the opera, during which the hero and heroine are placed in an airtight chamber to suffocate. As the doomed pair fill their lungs, Eliot calls out to them, "You will last a lot longer, if you don't try to sing." Then he stands, leans out of his box and tells the singers, "Maybe you don't know anything about oxygen, but I do. Believe me, you must not sing" (29). He permits Sylvia "to lead him away as easily as she might have led a toy balloon" (29).

At this point Eliot makes a kind of last ditch effort to save his sanity as well as to settle the problem of guilt and moral responsibility created by family history. Determined to make the ten-thousand-dollar-a-day foundation money do some concrete good, he moves into the town of Rosewater in Rosewater County, Indiana, with the idea of relating to the poor on a personal rather than institutional level. He will abandon his grand humanitarian dreams and simply give the money away directly to the "plain, dumb, ordinary people of poor old Rosewater County" (60). "I'm going to love these discarded Americans," he asserts, "even though they are useless and unattractive. That's going to be my work of art" (36).

At first glance Eliot's attempts to return feelings of self-respect to these people seem sane and useful. From his mildewed office on Main Street across the street from the firehouse, he talks to lonely people, listens tirelessly to misshapen fears and dreams, cheers people up by stroking sagging egos, and gives out sums of money large and small (40). He tempers his charity with humor and common sense. He tells a potential suicide that instead of enumerating wonderful reasons to want to go on living, he will ask the caller to name a rock-bottom price for living for just one more week (76). When the caller says he might not want to live through the next week even for a million dollars, Eliot says, "Try a thousand." "A thousand," the man agrees. "Try a hundred," Eliot counters again. "A hundred," the caller agrees. "Now you're making sense," says Eliot. "Come on over and talk. . . . Don't be afraid of the dogs in front of the firehouse. . . . They only bite when the fire horn goes off" (76, 77).

Typical of Eliot's extreme compassion, he gives a suicidal tool-and-die maker a Rosewater Fellowship of three hundred dollars (77, 78). The recipient has been laid off work, is a veteran of the Second World War, and has a wife and three children, the second child suffering from cerebral palsy. Typical of Eliot's determination to make this an exercise in indiscriminate love, he helps those who are so dumb and weak that when it came time for their sons to go into the armed forces, the sons were generally rejected as mentally, morally, and physically undesirable. "God Bless you, Mr. Rosewater" (61), says ugly, stupid, and boring Diana Moon Glampers, whom no one has ever loved (56), "for forsaking money, position, and power to help the little people of Rosewater County." She tells Eliot that his medicine has been more powerful than that of all the doctors in Indiana put together (60).[7]

While some of the town's people are said to have the pride and guts to stay away from Eliot and his uncritical love, most like Diana Moon Glampers are ready to deify him. Diana says,

> Dawn Leonard had boils for ten years, and you cured 'em. Ned Calvin had the twitch in his eye since he was a little boy, and you made it stop. Pearl Fleming came and saw you, and she threw her crutch away. And now my kidneys have stopped hurting, just hearing your sweet voice. (60)

As a preacher, Eliot bears an ominous resemblance to Bokonon in *Cat's Cradle*, who lies to make people feel better. When Eliot is pressed by someone who insists that he is an organized religion, he replies that he is a Two-Seed-in-the-Spirit Predestinarian Baptist. Actually there was such a sect, which broke off from Baptist orthodoxy in the early 1800s. They were conspicuously Bokononist, embracing a dualistic relationship between good and evil, and believing that destiny is set at birth.

Messiah complex or not, Eliot is deluded about the personal motives underlying his altruistic adventure, and the amount of good Eliot actually does in Rosewater as opposed to potential harm is seriously in question. Eliot's general prescription for most of his clients, regardless of the problem, is "to take an aspirin tablet, and wash it down with a glass of wine" (78). Such flamboyant gestures as snubbing the petit bourgeois of Rosewater by getting out the family crystal, silver, and gold to throw lavish banquets for morons, perverts, starvelings, and the unemployed seem hollow in light of the real suffering of his guests (40). On one occasion Eliot makes a last payment on a client's motor scooter, and immediately afterward the client kills himself and a girlfriend in a crash (85). Eliot's method of dealing with a poet he meets at a cocktail party suggests not only the futility of his gestures but his habit of using money as a quick and simple fix to very complex problems. When the poet tells him he wants to be free to tell the truth, regardless of economic consequences, Eliot writes the alleged poet a check for ten thousand dollars on the spot and tells him, "You go tell the truth, by God. It's about time somebody did" (66). The dazed artist begs Eliot to tell him what to write about and later on sends him an eight-hundred-page book and a letter of thanks that reads, "This book could not have been created by me without you. . . . I mean your insistence that the truth be told about this sick, sick society of ours" (69). Later, Eliot opens the book and reads, "I twisted her arm until she opened her legs, and she gave a little scream, half joy, half pain (how do you figure a woman?), as I rammed the old avenger home" (70). Eliot found himself with an erection.

Even if Eliot's smattering of money and pity does a few people a little good, the long-range results are negative to himself and to others who depend upon him for everything and cannot function without him. When Eliot decides to leave Rosewater, Diana Moon Glampers becomes hysterical because she says Eliot is her only friend. When Eliot tells her she can join some church group, she answers, "You're my church group. You're my friends" (172). The greatest harm of Eliot's supposed beneficence, however, may be to Eliot himself—to that fragile stability which after his experience in Rosewater appears more strained than ever (175). David Goldsmith notes that Eliot's rescue service in Rosewater obviously parallels a volunteer fire brigade through which he hopes, if only unconsciously, to atone for the crimes of his inherited wealth and his accidental murder of the three German firemen during the war.[8] In truth, Eliot's cajolings and bribes can be seen as a form of moral prostitution, trading money for peace of mind, suggested by a client who calls and describes what someone has written in the phone booth he is calling from. "Eliot Rosewater is a Saint. He'll give you love and money. If you'd rather have the best piece of tail in southern Indiana, call Melissa" (75).

The fact that Eliot has deluded himself and others as to his clients' virtues indicates the importance to him of his mission. He argues that the people he was trying to help had in past generations cleared the forests, drained the swamps, built the bridges, and that their sons had given themselves freely in time of war (56). That these people who lean on him regularly are in fact grotesques—moral, mental, and physical deficients—adds to Eliot's mounting feelings of sorrow, failure, and exhaustion. Eventually we see: "Eliot revealed here that he had no illusions about the people to whom he was devoting his life . . . firebugs, too, no doubt, no doubt" (91). The fact is that serving as Rosewater's sole dispenser of comfort leaves Eliot, at best, emotionally drained, at worst, dangerously withdrawn and will-less. When Sylvia, in the process of adding to Eliot's despair by divorcing him, asks him why he has not been to see the baby twins of Mary Moody as is his usual practice, we read: "Eliot sounded sick of doing it" (92). Eliot's sickness suggests that his attempts at uncritical love are something other than "sentimental," as Tony Tanner believes.[9] That Eliot seeks to make such indiscriminate love his "art" is particularly revealing. It masks his deeper psychic needs, diffusing his ego and defusing real creative effort, leaving him "no sex at all" (157). In Freudian terms, Eliot "displaces" what he "mainly values from being loved." He protects himself

> against the loss of the object by directing . . . love, not to single objects but to all men alike [avoiding] . . . the uncertainties and disappointments of genital love by turning away from its sexual aims and transforming the instinct into an impulse with an inhibited aim . . . a love that does not discriminate seems to me to forfeit a part of its own value . . . and, not all men are worthy of love.[10]

During Eliot's rambles about the country a fireman had said to him, "You must be crazy," and Eliot had answered, "I don't want to look like me" (23). Trying to lose himself, to hide from his past while pretending to come to grips with it in the guise of utopian reform is what Eliot's Rosewater experience has been mainly about. Aside from the telephone, the only sign of contact with the outside world in Eliot's Rosewater office is the yellow slicker and red helmet of a volunteer fireman which hangs on pegs by the door. Eliot has become fire lieutenant and has imported a seven-hundred horsepower Messerschmitt engine that has a thirty horsepower electric starter to run the fire horn—the main air-raid siren of Berlin in World War II. We are told that Eliot almost never leaves his office except to fight fires (55). Paying a visit to him, his father notes painfully that his six-foot-three athletic son has gone to lard; the once purposeful, much-decorated captain of the Infantry has grown "puffy and pasty." He sleeps in his underwear, eats a balanced diet of potato chips, Southern Comfort, and Rosewater Golden Lager Ambrosia Beer (47). He swigs at a bottle of booze while dealing with clients and regularly narcotizes himself with the headache remedies, hemorrhoid salves, laxatives, and sedatives that overflow his medicine cabinet. Eliot sleeps like a baby, but with obvious help (50). Even during a violent thunderstorm that sends a dog scrambling out of the firehouse with psychosomatic rabies, "Eliot slept on" (54).

In one of numerous drowning images that pervade the novel, we read that the toilet in the foul little office lavatory had all the bad dreams; "it gurgled that it was drowning" (54). Eliot feels that if he leaves his cozy Rosewater womb to try to live a normal, conventional life again, drowning, or dissolution of soul, would be his fate. "You know what would happen to me?" he says. "The minute

I got near any navigable body of water, a bolt of lightning would knock me into the water, a whale would swallow me up, and the whale would swim down the Gulf of Mexico . . . up Lost River, up Rosewater Creek . . . and spit me out" (149). The truth is that unless Eliot stops drugging himself to pain and learns to deal with the more personal problems of love and identity that have been haunting him and Vonnegut's previous protagonists since early childhood, he will invite the very drowning he hopes to avoid. Several times we find him hiding his head under a blanket—likened to a shroud and suggestive of the moral or spiritual death that awaits if he continues playing the ostrich. Eliot must do what the protagonist does in the unfinished novel he keeps in his desk—renounce the illusory peace and comfort of fantasy utopias and despite the agonies of life on earth be courageous enough to be reborn into the real world. "I am going to have to cease to be dead," the literary character concludes (82). Eliot's unfinished novel is the counterpart to his own incomplete and fragmented self, symbolized by the "stagnant canal" that divides Rosewater County. His creative energy will remain stifled or displaced until he stops writing and living fictions as romantic as those practiced by the founders of Rosewater County, who sought "absolute truthfulness . . . cleanliness . . . and love"; "they were now scattered to the winds" (37, 38). The main architectural ornamentation in Rosewater County? Spires and clocks (38)! Ironically, once the public, godlike mask Eliot has worn for the people of Rosewater begins to slip, his personal suffering is shown to be greater than ever. The image of Eliot's sickly translucent drip-dry shirt hanging from a ceiling fixture like a ghost is an appropriate picture of Eliot himself at the end of his Rosewater experience, wrung out and hollowed of identity (54).

At this point in the novel we see that the real insanity that looms before Eliot has little to do with opposing the capitalistic madness of his father; rather it is Eliot's lifelong unwillingness to deal with the more painful and immediate hostilities between himself and his father that keeps him seeking an illusory peace in various fantasy utopias. Clearly Eliot and his father want desperately to love each other, but their mutual habit of masking true feelings—the father behind illusions of the importance of power and money, Eliot behind illusions of Messianic goodness—proves too strong a barrier. In the novel's most poignant scene between them, when they are desperately trying to connect, the senator expresses their mutual defense: "Get away. You'll only hurt me more, and I can't stand any more pain" (160). What the senator particularly flees is a threat from Eliot that is partly valid, partly not. On the one hand, he confuses Eliot's lack of love with opposition to his social ideals. "You certainly loved me, didn't you?" he says. "Loved me so much you smashed up every hope or ideal I ever had" (160). On the other hand, the senator is probably right in describing Eliot's philosophy of uncritical love as a retreat from the more demanding problem of loving people in the particular. "You're the man," his father tells him, "who stands on a street corner with a roll of toilet paper, and written on each square are the words, 'I love you,' and each passerby, no matter who, gets a square all of his or her own. I don't want *my* square of toilet paper." "I didn't realize it was toilet paper," says Eliot (90). The scatological reference suggests the corruption of love between the two men—Eros converted to anal aggression. The senator informs Eliot that until he stops drinking, he is not going to realize anything (90). Eliot's actual attempt at showing affection to his father is as superficial and irrelevant as his father's fear that Eliot's enthusiasm for science fiction—"all that Buck Rogers stuff"—will prove him unbalanced (156). "I just wish there didn't have to be this acrimony, this tension, every time we talk. I love you so," Eliot says sweetly (90). His greeting to his father, however, is mechanical and perfunctory. "What a pleasant surprise," he says. "You look wonderful" (152).

When the senator asks Eliot if he realizes how insane Eliot's living conditions are in Rosewater, Eliot answers, "You'd be surprised what I don't know, Father" (154). The reply seems almost a rebuke—a suggestion that what Eliot doesn't know or understand about his father explains their mutual unlovingness and Eliot's dangerous tendency to withdraw. When the senator comes to tell Eliot that Mushari and the Rhode Island Rosewaters are going to try to prove he is insane in court, the subject of the senator's anal fixation with nudity and physical disorder and his constrictive obsession with purity is introduced for the second time in the novel. We are told the conversation was a highly dangerous one between two highly vulnerable men, a conversation of which they are both afraid (155). This time it seems clear that the father's almost violent aversion to the physical is the source of the vicious cycle of lovelessness passed down from grandfather to father to son. The bottled up feelings of the senator, whose libidinal energies have been diverted to the quest for money and power, have in turn created an inability to love in Eliot so that now neither can do anything but push the other way.

Appalled by the uncleanliness of Eliot's office, the senator announces importantly, "I shower every morning and night. . . . Soap and water are the important things" (155). Averting his eyes from what appear to him to be Eliot's obscene and ineffectual ablutions, the senator reads a love poem Eliot had written to Sylvia several years earlier, and it leaves him shocked. "If I were there with you / I might ask you to bare your belly / In order that I might take my left thumbnail / And draw a straight line five inches long / Above your pubic hair" (157). It was the mention of "pubic hair," we are told, that really appalled him. He has seen few naked bodies in his time, perhaps five or six, and pubic hair was to him the most unmentionable, unthinkable of all materials (158). Ironically, the senator ponders Eliot's "unnatural sexlessness along with the other evidences of insanity" (157). When Eliot comes out of the lavatory naked and hairy, drying himself with a tea towel, "The Senator was petrified, felt beset by overwhelming forces of filth and obscenity on all sides" (158).

At first Eliot finishes drying himself unaware of his father's discomfort. He throws the tea towel into the wastebasket and begins playing unconsciously with his pubic hair. Finding a hair that was a "lulu," he keeps pulling at it until it becomes one foot long. He looks down at it, then glances at his father "incredulously proud of . . . such a thing" (158, 159). The exasperated senator cries, "Why do you hate me so?" (159). Despite Eliot's protests—"Hate you? Father—I don't hate you. I don't hate anybody"—we wonder if this Hamlet doth not protest too much, whether there isn't a significant truth in his father's assertion:

> "Your every act and word is aimed at hurting me as much as you possibly can . . . I have no idea what I ever did to you that you're paying me back for now, but the debt must surely be settled by now." (160).

The suggestion is strong that herein lies the source of that buried neurosis Eliot's doctor couldn't reach, which the prosecutor at Paul Proteus' trial calls Oedipal.

As the senator continues berating Eliot with the story of how Eliot has ruined the life and health of his wife, his father, and himself, Eliot covers his ears. He finishes dressing as though nothing had happened. He sits down to tie his shoelaces, and straightening up, "froze as still as any corpse" (160). This is the beginning of Eliot's descent into real madness, the point at which he crosses the borderline from a schizoid condition to psychosis and actually requires treatment in a mental hospital. It is the onset of "the big click," as described by Eliot's former client, Noyes Finnerty. Anxious that Eliot's memory has gone completely blank (we're told Eliot neither remembers the fight with his father nor recognizes the voices of any of his friends), Finnerty looks closely into Eliot's vacant eyes and observes, "He heard that *click,* man. Man, did he ever hear that click" (161). In fact the whole town of Rosewater hears the click, "as clearly as they would have heard a cannon shot" (164).

"You get to know a man," says Finnerty,

> "and down deep there's something bothering him bad, and maybe you never find out what it is, but it's what makes him do like he does, it's what makes him look like he's got secrets in his eyes . . . you ask him 'How come you keep doing the same crazy things over and over again, when you know they're just going to get you in trouble again?' Only you know there's no sense arguing with him. . . . And all of a sudden you hear this click from him. You turn to look at him. . . . He's all calmed down. He looks real dumb. He looks real sweet. . . . He can't even tell you his own name right then. He goes back to work, but he'll never be the same. The thing that bothered him so will never click on again. It's dead, it's dead. And that part of that man's life where he had to be a certain crazy way, that's done." (165)

Does this mean Eliot has transcended his lifelong Oedipal/utopian compulsions? When a suddenly rabid Finnerty tries to snap the handle of a broom, cursing Eliot and saying, "Motherfucker won't break!" (166), is this meant for Eliot? Will he have been so grotesquely bent yet not break? Preparing to leave on the bus, he announces that he has never felt better in his life, as though "some marvelous new phase of my life were about to begin" (166). "It was too fine a day for sad things anyway," Eliot says (167). Several incidents occur on Eliot's way out of town, however, that suggest the spooks are not only closing in on him, as he earlier feared, but that they have him (154). The "click" leaves Eliot experiencing a generalized indifference to anything and everything, inside and out; he is as empty and hollow as the tapped out flagpole he says he feels captured by in the Rosewater schoolyard (169).

When on Eliot's way out of town a former Nazi sympathizer and spy during World War II greets him with a "Heil Hitler," Eliot smilingly answers, "And Heil Hitler to you, sir, and good-bye" (168). Eliot's condition is epitomized by a poem handed him by Roland Barry, a client who has never recovered from a nervous breakdown ten minutes after being inducted into the army. The poem was occasioned when Barry was asked to take a shower with one hundred other men. Eliot, he said, had been the only one who didn't think what happened to him was funny. Eliot has seen Barry once a week for a year but doesn't recognize him (170). The poem abounds with water imagery—lakes, pools, wells, rivers, streams, geysers, lagoons, juxtaposed with bells, harps, flutes, trumpets, chimes. "Drink the water," it says, "As we poor lambs / All go to slaughter" (170). Is Vonnegut's protagonist on his way to drowning again in still another false identity? Are the bells the equivalent of a fire alarm?

On the bus Eliot is ominously enchanted by a story he reads about a man on a space age expedition that had reached what appeared to be "the absolute and final rim of the universe" (173), only to learn from his Tralfamadorian commanding officer that there was very bad news from home, a death, in fact. "What's dead?" the spaceman asks. "What's died," he's told, "is the Milky Way." When Eliot looks up from his reading, "Rosewater County was gone. He did not miss it" (174). It is when Eliot's bus reaches the outskirts of Indianapolis that we see the extent of his deterioration. When he looks up, "he was astonished to see that the entire city was being consumed by a firestorm. He had never seen a firestorm, but he had certainly read and dreamed about many of them" (175). The phantom firestorm is an image planted in Eliot's mind not through direct contact with the infamous firestorm in Dresden, Germany, which haunts the minds of so many other Vonnegut protagonists, but through a book on the subject that Eliot keeps guiltily hidden in his office. It was a mystery to him, he says, why he should hide it and feel guilty every time he got it out (175). Evidently the pent-up guilt of shooting innocent firemen has not been close to expunged from Eliot's ailing brain; rather now it threatens to consume him.

Appropriate to the schizophrenic's fear of engulfment by fire or petrification, we learn that everything went black for Eliot, "as black as what lay beyond the ultimate rim of the universe" (177), and it is an entire year later that he regains anything like normal consciousness. He awakes to find himself "sitting on the flat rim of a dry fountain" in the garden of Dr. Brown's private mental hospital in Indianapolis, to which he had brought Sylvia many years before. A bird sings in the sycamore tree, "Poo-tweet? Weet, weet, weet" (177). Eliot wishes that he were that dickey bird so that he could fly up into the treetop and never come down. "He wanted to fly up so high because there was something going on at ground zero that did not make him feel good" (178).

The four men in dark business suits sitting across from Eliot expect something significant from him because for the past year they have been pouring Eliot's shattered identity into a plastic mold that satisfies *their* concept of sanity. He has been dressed *all* in snowy white for tennis as if for a department store display; as Eliot bounds off the court, his father is delighted to see that he is trim and lean, "back to fighting weight," and because Eliot has just "killed" an opponent at tennis, "murdered," him in fact, his father rejoices that "this is the man . . . who has to prove tomorrow that he's not insane! Ha!" (180).

Despite the fact that Eliot has been dressed respectably and taught to speak clichés, his new mental health makes him a robot. Typical of catatonic schizophrenics, his movements are fixed and jerky, he feels detached from his body, and he knows his identity is not his own. "He closed his hand around the rocket handle experimentally to discover whether it was real and whether he was real . . . he had no idea what he looked like" (177). Ominously, he looks for insight into his new personality as it is reflected in the water of the birdbath in the fountain's pool, "a bitter broth of soot and leaves" (180). As his inquisitors await sounds from him that will confirm his normalcy, the disembodied Eliot feels "he had nothing of significance to say or give" (178).

Though Eliot is more desperately in trouble than any previous hero, the testimony of the writer Kilgore Trout is that Eliot is both sane and one of the world's greatest humanitarians. "What you did in Rosewater County," Trout intones,

> "was far from insane. It was quite possibly the most important social experiment of our time, for it dealt on a very small scale with a problem whose queasy horrors will eventually be made worldwide by the sophistication of machines. The problem is this: How to love people who have no use?" (183)

Trout tells Eliot that his devotion to volunteer fire departments was *also* very sane, since they are the only examples of "enthusiastic unselfishness to be seen in the land" (184). Finally he explains,

> "It seems to me that the main lesson Eliot learned is that people can use all the uncritical love they can get. . . . Thanks to the example of Eliot Rosewater, millions upon millions of people may learn to love and help whomever they see." (187)

As Trout speaks his last word ("the word was joy"), Eliot hears only, "Poo-tee-weet?" and wonders what his ideas about Rosewater had been.

Trout's integrity is not in question, despite the senator's declaration that "by God, you're great, you should have been a public relations man. You could make lockjaw sound good for the country" (185). Trout speaks the truth as he knows it to be. But regardless of the degree to which his words are valid, his speech is abstract, rhetorically pompous, and therefore ludicrous in contrast to Eliot's personal and immediate suffering. Eliot feels no joy; he feels nothing; and Trout's general condemnation of the cruelty and insensitivity of America would be better directed at Eliot's immediate tormentors—those trying to transform him from a robot saint into a robot figurehead who will preserve the family's fortune. It is again on the fountain's rim, foreshadowing engulfment, that Eliot is sitting when he agrees to parrot Trout's instructions at his sanity hearing. When the senator orders Eliot to say what Trout tells him, Eliot responds mechanically:

> "I will certainly say what Mr. Trout says I should say, and not change one detail of my make-up. I would appreciate, though, a last run-through of what Mr. Trout says I should say."

"It's so simple," says Trout. (183)

The *seeming* end to this novel is as simplistic as Trout's or the senator's one-dimensional view of Eliot's sanity. Most readers see it as categorical proof of Eliot's return to mental health.[11] To support his case against Eliot, Norman Mushari had gone around Rosewater County bribing women to say that Eliot had fathered their babies. That, says legal counselor McAllister, touched off a kind of female mania. Women all over the county started claiming their children were Eliot's (188). Mania or not, we have no proof except Eliot's word that he did not in fact secretly father some of the children as a way of undermining Mushari's plans to disinherit him. Regardless, Eliot, at least for the moment, regains his balance, becoming more canny and lucid than he has been in years. He remembers the scheme that had earlier come to him by which to defeat the greed of Mushari and his father both. He writes a check for one hundred thousand dollars to give to the Pisquontuit Rosewaters, and he has legal counsel draw up papers that acknowledge that every child in Rosewater County *"said* to be mine *is* mine. Let them all have rights of inheritance as my sons and daughters" (190). In tones of elated benevolence, Eliot declares: "Let their names be Rosewater from this moment on. And tell them that their father loves them, no matter what they may turn out to be. And tell them . . . to be fruitful and multiply" (190). By assuring an unbreakable chain to the control of the Rosewater Foundation, Eliot has thwarted Mushari and solved his immediate legal problems. But what long-range view of his mental health are we to take?

A partial answer—the most Vonnegut will offer—lies in the maxim cut into the rim of the fountain in the hospital courtyard: "Pretend to be good always, and even God will be fooled" (177). Vonnegut uses the recurring rim image here, as in other novels, to adumbrate alluring spirallike mechanistic systems of control that promise peace and harmony but lead instead to moral oblivion. Pretending to be good "always" *is* what Eliot has done for so long that its rigors have not only drained him emotionally but moved him further and further away from dealing honestly with feelings about his father. Before embarking on further moral reforms or before becoming anyone else's doctor or messiah, Eliot must cure himself by learning to eschew simple remedies to the tragic alienation and guilt of his life.

6

Slaughterhouse-Five: Pilgrim's Progress

*This is a novel somewhat in the telegraphic schizophrenic man-
ner of Tales of the Planet Tralfamadore, where the flying saucers
came from.*

Slaughterhouse-Five

*In the middle of the journey of our life I came to myself in a dark
wood where the straight way was lost.*

*Ah! how hard a thing it is to tell what a wild, and rough,
and stubborn wood this was, which in my thought renews the
fear.*

Dante, *The Divine Comedy*

From *Player Piano* to *Slaughterhouse-Five* Vonnegut describes the "collisions"[1]
of people and machinery without apparent resolution—an expression of the
author's own state of mind as he attempts to work out the schizophrenic dilemma
of his major characters. In *Breakfast of Champions* (1973) Vonnegut tells us
that the idea of schizophrenia had fascinated him for years. "I did not and do
not know for certain that I have that disease," he says. "I was sick for awhile,
though. I am better now. Word of honor—I am better now" (210). In a lighter
vein, Vonnegut portrays his personal disequilibrium in reference to what he calls
"Hunter Thompson's disease"—the affliction of "all those who feel that Americans can be as easily led to beauty as to ugliness, to truth as to public relations,
to joy as to bitterness. . . . I don't have it this morning. It comes and it goes."[2]
So come and go the efforts of Malachi Constant, Howard Campbell, Jonah, and
Eliot Rosewater to overcome that fear, cynicism, and will-lessness which im-
pedes the spiritual growth of Vonnegut's hero.

Each of these characters is more successful, however, than Paul Proteus
in achieving moral awareness and combining this awareness with existential
responsibility for his actions. Each confronts the dark side of his personality and

attempts to practice the moral imperative described by Malachi's spiritual twin, Unk, in *Sirens of Titan* as, "making war against the core of his being, against the very nature of being a machine" (300). Yet, tormented by the fear that he is no better than a robot in a machine-dominated world, each moves back from the threshold of complete moral awakening. The lingering pessimism that is Kilgore Trout, or Billy Pilgrim, remains. No resolutions are possible for Vonnegut or his protagonists until Vonnegut has found some way to achieve an "equilibrium" based on the belief that people can successfully resist becoming appendages to machines or, as is said of Billy Pilgrim and people in general in *Slaughterhouse-Five,* "the listless playthings of enormous forces" (164).

In opposing the standard view of Vonnegut as fatalist, Kathryn Hume objects as well to the notion that Vonnegut's work is static or repetitious—repeating rather then developing, as Charles Samuels says.[3] Hume sees that Vonnegut's "heavy reliance upon projection makes his books unusually interdependent," "a single tapestry."[4] She infers the spiritual progress of Paul Proteus by noting "the artistic and personal problems he [Vonnegut] takes up in one story are directly affected by those he did or did not solve in the previous story." Nowhere is Hume's insistence upon the intensely personal nature of Vonnegut's work and upon continuity and progress at the heart of Vonnegut's vision more pertinent than in the case of *Slaughterhouse-Five* and *Breakfast of Champions*—novels that Vonnegut says were conceived as one book and that Peter Reed identifies as the "central traumatic, revelatory, and symbolic moment" of Vonnegut's career.[5]

A striking paradox of *Slaughterhouse-Five* is that it presents us with Vonnegut's most completely demoralized protagonist while making what is to this point the most affirmative statement of Vonnegut's career. The former heroes' gains in awareness and moral courage fail Billy Pilgrim entirely—by design—for Billy like Kilgore Trout in *Breakfast of Champions* becomes Vonnegut's scapegoat, carrying the author's heaviest burden of trauma and despair, but his sacrifice makes possible Vonnegut's own "rebirth." Vonnegut is careful to dissociate himself from Billy as from no character before—signaled by the fact that the author speaks to us directly in the important first chapter about the impact of the war on him, and that with references such as "I was there," and "that was me," he personally turns up in the narrative four times.[6]

To understand that personal catharsis is central to Vonnegut's intentions, one must appreciate Thomas Wymer's view of those ludicrous-looking extraterrestrials in *Sirens of Titan* and *Slaughterhouse-Five* who kidnap Billy Pilgrim and appear to teach him wonderful ways to cope with suffering and death.[7] Disputing the usual interpretation that the Tralfamadorians speak for the author, Wymer shows that Vonnegut warns *against* the perils of fatalism rather than affirms such a philosophy. Those who confuse Vonnegut with Billy Pilgrim or mistake the author as a defeatist, believing that the insidiously addictive ideas that come to invade Billy's mind are Vonnegut's miss the predominantly affirmative thrust of *Slaughterhouse-Five* and Vonnegut's career as a whole. Billy Pilgrim's conversion to Tralfamadorian fatalism, OR FATAL DREAM, which is Tralfamadore by anagram, assures his schizophrenic descent into madness.

It is not surprising that readers typically confuse Tralfamadorian pessimism with the author's own thinking. Doubtlessly the author breathes some of his own despair into the dazed, impotent, and demoralized Billy Pilgrim. In an address at Bennington College in 1970, the author said:

> I thought scientists were going to find out exactly how everything worked and then make it work better. I fully expected that by the time I was twenty-one, some scientists, maybe my brother, would have taken a color photograph of God Almighty and sold it to *Popular Mechanics* magazine. What actually happened when I was twenty-one was that we dropped scientific truth on Hiroshima.[8]

At the end of World War II, while serving as a prisoner of war in Dresden, Germany, Kurt Vonnegut had scientific truth of this kind dropped on him as well, a truth that killed one hundred thirty-five thousand people and metamorphosed the loveliest city he had ever seen, "intricate and voluptuous and enchanted . . . into a blackened, smoldering hole" (148). In fact it is to pour out his personal pessimism about the massacre machinery of war and about the lasting traumatic effects of the war on his nerves that Vonnegut writes the important autobiographical first chapter of *Slaughterhouse-Five*.[9]

While Vonnegut comments about the ineffectiveness of war protests, the antiwar element in this novel is direct and powerful. Vonnegut tells his sons not to work for companies that make war machinery (19) and to express contempt for people who think we need machinery like that. Vonnegut makes clear that it is *O'Hare*'s view that antiwar books are like antiglacier books (3–4). True to his promise to O'Hare's wife, Vonnegut demonstrates that wars are fought by children, subtitling his novel "The Children's Crusade"; characters who glorify war like Colonel Wild Bob and Bertram Copeland Rumfoord are made to appear absolutely ridiculous. In one telling image, a war movie run in reverse, Vonnegut demonstrates the power of art to subvert the destructive process of war. Fires go out; dead or wounded soldiers are made whole; bombs fly back into planes which fly backwards to friendly cities; the bombers are dismantled and minerals used for bombs are returned to the earth (73–75). Unfortunately, Billy uses fantasy not to reconstruct his own robotic personality, but to escape the present. His vision transports him to an Edenic world of "two perfect people named Adam and Eve." He seeks a condition of "pre-birth" (43).

Billy Pilgrim's gentleness and subsequent refusal to participate in the world's destructiveness elicits our sympathy. Richard Erlich notes that even Billy's virtue as a "fool among knaves" [from Swift's *Tale of a Tub*] is a laudable ideal.[10] We see Billy as a latterday Christ who spends three days entombed in a slaughterhouse/bomb shelter. On the way to his Dresden prison camp, Billy suffers a sleepless agony, clinging to a "cross-brace" (78); he is found "lying at an angle on the corner-brace, self crucified" (80). Yet Billy is every bit as "flamboyantly sick" as Eliot Rosewater, who joins Billy in a mental ward. What passes for gentleness indicates the lobotomy performed on Billy by the cruel conditions around him. Billy is so crippled by the psychologically damaging blows he receives before, during, and after the war that he increasingly withdraws from reality and ultimately loses his sanity. Suggesting the spiritual death that awaits him, he arises from his underground tomb to find a green coffin and an old man pushing a baby carriage.[11] Billy's retreat from pain into the "morphine paradise" of Tralfamadore (whose inhabitants are green) will cancel any hope of new life.

The horrors of Dresden, Hiroshima, Nagasaki, and the Nazi concentration camps focus the panorama of violence and inhumanity that defines Pilgrim's world. Death, senseless cruelty, and absurd injustice are Vonnegut's main subject, prompting him to say that, "I believe . . . even if wars didn't keep coming like glaciers, there would still be plain old death" (4). Thus the slaughterhouse where Billy is kept as a prisoner in Dresden becomes more than a grotesque naturalistic image of human beings dehumanized by war, hanging like butchered animals on hooks. It becomes an all-encompassing metaphor for human existence in which suffering and death are commonplace. "So it goes," says Billy Pilgrim, without relief, cessation, or sense, now as always.

If one counts deaths that are predicted or imagined as well as those that occur, there may be a greater proliferation of corpses in *Slaughterhouse-Five* than in any other twentieth-century novel. We encounter death by starvation, rotting, incineration, squashing, gassing, shooting, poisoning, bombing, torturing, hanging, and relatively routine death by disease. We get the deaths of dogs, horses, pigs, Vietnamese soldiers, crusaders, hunters, priests, officers, hobos, actresses, prison guards, a slave laborer, a suffragette, Jesus Christ, Robert Kennedy, Martin Luther King, Billy Pilgrim's mother and father, his wife, Edgar Derby, Roland Weary, the regimental chaplain's assistant, Paul Lazzaro, Colonel Wild Bob; we get the deaths of a bottle of champagne, billions of body lice, bacteria, and fleas; the novel; entire towns, and finally the universe; we encounter individual deaths; the death of groups en masse; accidental, calculated, and vengeful deaths; recent and historical deaths. So it goes, says Billy Pilgrim, in a world of senseless suffering and meaningless death.[12]

There may be hundreds of "corpse mines" (214) operating in Dresden, but through Billy's time travelling we see that his entire life is like a corpse mine—a continuity of terror stretching all the way back to childhood when his hairy father threw him in the pool at the Y.M.C.A. and told him to sink or swim (which he says was "like an execution"—Derby's? (44)) and forward in time to his death when Paul Lazzaro makes good his promise to have Billy killed after the war.[13] At age twelve Billy wets his pants when from the "rim of Bright Angel Point," his parents make him peer into the cavernous depths of the Grand Canyon (89). The place is notorious for suicidal leaps. The vortex of Carlsbad Caverns, whose "darkness . . . was total" (90) proves equally frightening. We hear that Billy's parents have placed a particularly gruesome crucifix on the wall of his bedroom, hence that Billy "had contemplated torture and hideous wounds at the beginning and the end of nearly every day of his childhood" (38). Billy responds to childhood trauma as much as to the horrors of war when he commits himself to a mental hospital during his senior year at the Ilium School of Optometry. Billy feels that his mother's presence at his hospital bedside is particularly threatening. He feels himself get "much sicker" and pulls the covers over his head until she goes away. He experiences schizophrenic disorientation at the sight of her lipstick-smeared cigarettes and the "dead water" on the bedside table. Billy recoils from his mother because she is insipid, materialistic, and morally obtuse, but he is mystified that his aversion, his embarrassment and weakness in her presence, should be so strong simply because she gave him life (102).

Billy fails to associate fears of his father's aggression (throwing him into the deep end of the Y.M.C.A. swimming pool, then taking him to the rim of the Grand Canyon) with Oedipal desire for his mother conveyed by the womb/vortex imagery of rims and dark, foreboding holes. It is notably at his mother's touch that Billy wets himself. Montana Wildhack, a surrogate mother in Billy's Tralfamadorian fantasy, later causes Billy to have wet dreams (134). Billy and Eliot Rosewater share a mental ward partly because of what they had seen in war (101), but also because neither has yet penetrated that Oedipal screen Eliot's doctor describes as "the most massively defended neurosis I've ever attempted to treat." In the most direct and intimate Oedipal fantasy in all Vonnegut's fiction, Billy longs for the peace and security he felt during infant bathings:

> Billy zoomed back in time to his infancy. He was a baby who had just been bathed by his mother. Now his mother wrapped him in a towel, carried him into a rosy room that was filled with sunshine. She unwrapped him, laid him on the tickling towel, powdered him between the legs, joked with him, patted his little jelly belly. Her palm on his little jelly belly made potching sounds.
> Billy gurgled and cooed. (84–85)

Eliot is right when he comments to Billy's mother, "a boy *needs* a father" (103). But Billy's father is dead and the alienation between Eliot and Senator Rosewater appears irremediable. Only when Vonnegut's repressed persona begins to deal with buried Oedipal tensions and asserts a creative, independent identity will he stop being "dead to the world" (105), masking his fears with escapist fantasies or drugging himself to reality. John Tilton rightly observes that life against death-in-life is the psychic conflict at the core of this novel.[14] In Billy, the conflict between Eros and Thanatos significantly intensifies. The inability to bring repressed fear and guilt to consciousness causes Billy to pervert that which is organic and procreative (the vagina) into that which is mechanical and destructive, an entrapping mechanistic spiral. Not only must Billy deal with normal Oedipal longings; he must reconcile himself to a mother whose coldness and insensitivity to his feelings deepens his guilt and insecurity.

Vonnegut's omnipresent "clock" effectively merges Billy's childhood nightmare with that of his war experience—"the greatest massacre in European history, which was the fire-bombing of Dresden" (101). In the darkness (literal and metaphorical) of Carlsbad Caverns, the sudden glare of his father's pocket watch transports Billy forward in time to World War II. According to the Tralfamadorians, the two "clumps" of time bear no connection—"no moral, no causes, no effects" (88). Not only is time meaningless; they say the universal clock is fixed, immutable, and immune to human intervention. Events are inevitably structured to be the way they are and hence do not lend themselves to warnings or explanations (86). Only on earth is freedom of will a subject to be taken seriously. Lulled by the Tralfamadorian "anesthetic" (77) of fatalism, Billy remains a "bug trapped in amber" (77), a moral sleep walker who substitutes forms of "morphine paradise" (99) for necessary self-analysis. Billy's moral paralysis makes him feel as if he is "frozen" (81), turned to "stone" (81), entrapped by the spirallike ladder that leads into the Tralfamadorian spaceship. Will-less and unaware, he fails to see that his father's unconscious hostility, the violence of lunatic nations at war, Tralfamadorian aggression, and his own passivity represent the same universal will to destruction.[15]

Nothing really prepares Billy Pilgrim for the momentous horrors of Dresden and the unimaginable displays of human cruelty and injustice offered by the war. It is not long after Billy is sent overseas that he develops a vivid sense of the monstrous torture instruments, the killing machines of war, that tear and mutilate the body and create such sadistic creatures as the revenge-crazed Paul Lazzaro, who carries a list in his head of people he is going to have killed after the war (140), and the equally rabid Roland Weary.[16] Billy learns from Weary about wounds that won't heal, about "blood gutters" and such tortures as having your head drilled through with a dentist's drill and being staked to an anthill in the desert (36–37).

Billy's natural gentleness and innocence, appropriate to his role as a chaplain's assistant, hardly prepare him for the idiocy of battle. Vonnegut writes,

> Weary was as new to war as Billy. He was a replacement, too. As a part of a gun crew, he had helped to fire one shot in anger—from a 57-millimeter antitank gun. The gun made a ripping sound like the opening of the zipper on the fly of God Almighty. The gun lapped up snow and

vegetation with a blowtorch thirty feet long. . . . It killed everybody on the gun crew but Weary. (34–35)

In Billy's mind, war has converted the creative potency of God Almighty, along with his own, to aggression and death. Billy is loath to discover that his wife associates sex and glamor with war (121). In the opening chapter, Vonnegut jokes that the war has made his own phallus inoperable—a "tool" that "won't pee anymore" (2, 3).[17] Billy's prisoner-of-war experience becomes an "acrimonious madrigal" (79), a nightmare of victimization and madness. He and everyone around him exhibit some form of insane, mechanically conditioned behavior, that which is overtly aggressive, or that which allows aggression to happen. On the one hand, we encounter the mindless hating and killing, superpatriot machines of Howard Campbell, Colonel Wild Bob, and Bertram Copeland Rumfoord, whose glorifications of war and exhortations to battle appear ludicrous alongside the pitiful suffering of Billy and his comrades (67). Billy himself looks like "a broken kite" (97). Billy's absorption in the prison-camp production of Cinderella confirms his schizophrenic deterioration. He can relate only to imaginary scenes and people. "Theatrical grief" (125) becomes more real to him than anything in the outside world. Cinderella's silver boots, he discovers, fit him perfectly—"Billy Pilgrim was Cinderella, and Cinderella was Billy Pilgrim" (145). Billy even has to be told that he has caught fire standing too close to a prison-camp stove (91), an alarm as foreboding as the "enormous clock" (96) that presides over the Cinderella set and the "sea" of dying Russian prisoners in which Billy finds himself "dead-center" (93). No wonder, then, that Billy's self-protective delusions lead him to dream, like Eliot Rosewater, of floating up "among the treetops" (48), or, like Malachi Constant, to hallucinate a "morphine paradise" such as Tralfamadore (49, 99). Either prospect leaves him as disembodied as Winston Niles Rumfoord in *Sirens of Titan*. Notably, the Hound of Space, Kazak, barks in a voice "like a big bronze gong" (48).

We encounter the equally mindless cheerfulness of the British prisoners of war, whose obsessive pretense of order and cleanliness causes them to put up a sign that reads, "Please leave this latrine as tidy as you found it" (125), a madness of its own. This form of hopeless programming includes illusions of peace and harmony of people like Billy's wife and mother, who are blind to the more sordid and desperate aspects of existence, and the awkward sentimentality and automatic loyalty to God and country of Edgar Derby. All are fully automated boobs, ready to conform to the most convenient mold, whether in the mistaken interests of survival or friendliness or out of the lack of imagination to do anything better; thus, they become the ready slaves of whatever anonymous bureaucracies, computers, or authoritarian institutions take hold of their minds.

The horrors of war that prove most traumatic of all to Billy are the destruction of Dresden and the death of his best friend, Edgar Derby. Billy had been told by the English prisoners of war that, "You needn't worry about bombs, by the way . . . Dresden is an open city. It is undefended, and contains no war industries or troop concentrations of any importance" (146). Despite his manly bluff and awkward sentimentality, Derby seems a symbolic human extension of Dresden (83). He is a teacher of Contemporary Civilization who enters the war out of pure motives, who takes care of his body, and who with utter sincerity, over the rude suggestion of Paul Lazzaro that he "go take a flying fuck at the moon" (147), tries to provide helpful leadership to Billy and his fellow prisoners. Derby's loyalty to the sacred, civilized graces of family, love, God, country, leads Billy to believe that Derby must be the greatest father in the world. Yet none of this exempts Derby from the stupidity and absurdity of death, which Vonnegut himself comments upon in the first chapter of the book:

> I think the climax of the book will be the execution of poor old Edgar Derby. . . . The irony is so great. A whole city gets burned down, and thousands and thousands of people are killed. And then this one American foot soldier is arrested in the ruins for taking a teapot. And he's given a regular trial, and then shot by a firing squad. (5)

Other pitiful ironies of war that wear indelibly on Billy are the execution of Private Eddie Slovik, shot for challenging authority, and the fact that despite all the popular movies that glorify war and soldiering starring manly figures like John Wayne or Frank Sinatra, it is usually the nation's young and innocent who are first sent to be slaughtered.

Life for Billy after the war seems no less brutal or pointless; like glaciers, death keeps right on coming. All the members of Billy's family suffer hideous deaths, his wife by carbon monoxide poisoning (25), his father in a hunting accident (32), and everybody on the plane flying to an optometrists' convention is killed in a crash, except Billy and the copilot (25). Linking the horrors of war with the horrors of civilian life, Billy mistakes the Austrian ski instructors who come to rescue him for German soldiers. He whispers to them his address: "Slaughterhouse Five" (156). Billy's life at home is filled with the same pain and warpedness, the same maddening contrasts between sanity and insanity that went with war. He turns on the television set only to find that all the shows are about silliness or murder. He looks into the window of a tawdry bookstore only to find hundreds of books about sexual perversion and murder. He looks up at the news of the day being written across the top of a building and finds it to be about power, anger, and death (200).

Vonnegut protests the literal holes machines put in people, but it is the more subtle, spiritually corrosive effects of technological progress that destroy Billy's equilibrium for good. Surrounded by the soulless junk of middle-class suburbia and saddled with an inane wife who can't believe anyone has married her, Billy leads a sterile, machine-ridden life. In robot fashion, all sixty-eight thousand employees of General Forge and Foundry Company in Ilium are required to wear safety glasses manufactured by their own firm. "Frames are where the money is," Vonnegut remarks (24). Billy lives in an all-electric home, sleeps in a bed with Magic Fingers (62), owns a fifth of a Holiday Inn, and half of three Tastee-Freeze stands (61). In a perfectly chosen image of the debasement of spiritual realities by machinery, Vonnegut has Billy playing hymns on an organ and sermonizing from a portable alter made by a vacuum cleaner company in Camden, New Jersey (31). Not only has Billy's mechanical world despiritualized his environment and traumatized him with its awesome power for physical destruction; it has depleted his imagination and his will to be something better than a machine himself.

Is it really any wonder that Billy Pilgrim learns to experience death as merely a "violet light and a hum" (43), and that he invents a pain-killing philosophy of life for refuge? Whether it is the horrors of the Dresden holocaust or the nightmare of Billy's vapid civilian life at home with a fat and inane wife, what finally destroys Billy's equilibrium is the irreconcilable contrast in his life between an ideal world of beauty, justice, mercy, and peace, and that of the psychologically devastating accumulation of horrors that turn him into a dazed and disembodied scarecrow. This principle of ironic contrast—between Dresden and holocaust, justice and the arbitrary death of Edgar Derby—separates Billy from his sanity, inducing that state of "catalepsis" that lands Eliot Rosewater in an asylum.

Billy's final unbalancing, equal to Eliot Rosewater's "big click," comes at Billy's and Valencia's anniversary party when Billy listens to a barbershop quartet. Vonnegut writes:

> As the quartet made slow, agonized experiments with chords—chords intentionally sour, sourer still, unbearably sour, and then a chord that was suffocatingly sweet, and then some sour ones again . . . Billy had powerful psychosomatic responses to the changing chords. His mouth filled with the taste of lemonade, and his face became grotesque, as thought he really were being stretched on the torture engine called the rack. (172, 173)

Psychosomatic responses, indeed. Life, with its torturous vacillation between sweet and sour, sublimity and pathos, has become so unendurable for Billy that he becomes stuporous, his actions somnambulistic, and in an act of total disengagement, he retreats "upstairs in his nice white house" (176), which gives every appearance of being an asylum. Billy struggles momentarily to understand "the big secret somewhere inside" (173). He remembers the night Dresden was destroyed—the firestorm that "ate everything . . . that would burn" (178), that turned the city into a desert and people into little petrified human

beings. But Billy is again incapable of bringing his nightmare into full consciousness; rather he calls upon the consolations and alleged wisdom of his
outer-space, or inner-space, friends, the Tralfamadorians, who cause him to
believe that death does not matter since no one really dies, hence to resign
himself to his own death at the hands of Paul Lazzaro (143). The reality of
Billy's death is problematical, more a death-wish produced by unloving parents
and the horrors of war. After learning that Billy's "will" is "locked" up with the
tape on which he sees his death enacted, we are told that nobody else was
there—indeed, "not even Billy Pilgrim is there" (143). Perhaps Billy is merely
hallucinating again—his death no more real than those Tralfamadorian flying
saucers that "come from nowhere" (75).

According to Patrick Shaw, the key to understanding the Tralfamadorians
resides in their physical attributes, described thus:

> They were two feet high, and green, and shaped like plumber's friends. Their suction cups
> were on the ground, and their shafts, which were extremely flexible, usually pointed to the
> sky. At the top of each shaft was a little hand with a green eye in its palm. (26)

"A plumber's friend," Shaw explains,

> is the common household implement consisting of a rubber suction cup attached to a broom-
> stick-like handle. It is a gadget used for unclogging drains, for quite literally loosening
> excrement and accumulated filth from sewage pipes.[18]

Therefore Shaw concludes that the Tralfamadorians perform the symbolic function for Pilgrim of cleansing the pipes of his perception, unclogging his vision
and imagination by disabusing him of historical, sociological fixations. One
assumes that Shaw means the belief that human beings can have a meaningful
impact upon future events, that they can influence their own lives. Says Shaw,
"Roland Weary tries quite literally to 'beat the living shit' out of Pilgrim, but
only the Tralfamadorians, through unsentimental, sardonic logic, succeed in
removing the waste from Pilgrim's mind. Himself a bit of human waste sticking
in the cosmological pipes, Pilgrim comes 'unstuck in time' and simultaneously
unclogs his own perceptions so that he realizes the 'negligibility of death, and
the true nature of time.' "[19]

Shaw agrees with David Goldsmith that the superior vision provided by the
cycloptic Tralfamadorian eye atop the phallic, shaftlike periscope contrasts with
Pilgrim's own failure as an earthly optometrist to improve the way in which
people see. Billy falls asleep fitting his patients (56). Shaw says, "As his own
vision is progressively cleared by his experiences with the spacemen, as he
realizes more and more the defectiveness of his earthly 'eyes' and the fallacies
of history and earth time, Pilgrim is less able to function as an eye doctor." As

"one who is taught by extraterrestrial powers how to see into the past, the present, and the future," he becomes in a sense a kind of "contemporary, spastic Tiresias."[20] Goldsmith argues that as a projection of the author's own condition, this cleansing of Billy's pipes marks Vonnegut's "mature acceptance" of the horrors of life as something it does no good to worry about. Such a perspective, says Goldsmith, "simply provides the comforts which have enabled Vonnegut to live with his wartime nightmare."[21] Death, from the Tralfamadorian view, no matter how horrible, can have no significance. Thus Goldsmith says Vonnegut has finally washed the horror and guilt of Dresden from his mind and has come to accept the previously unacceptable—man's capacity for evil and his helplessness to do much better, as if he were controlled by some exterior force. To wit, "Billy the optometrist who fits people with glasses has fitted Vonnegut with a pair which, if not exactly rose colored, have enabled him to see things in their proper perspective."[22]

Because of the seeming inevitability of those forces that enfeeble Billy Pilgrim's will to survive, most critics agree with Shaw and Goldsmith that Billy's weary lament, "So it goes," projects the author's own sense of futility. Yet nothing seems further from the point of Vonnegut's novel than to believe that the Tralfamadorians speak for the author—that what Stanley Kauffmann and Jack Richardson join in calling the wisdom of "a higher order of life"[23] is in fact a revelation of the author's own sense of hopelessness in the face of those enormous deterministic forces that make playthings of all the novel's characters. Those who argue that the fatalistic philosophy offered by the Tralfamadorians makes *Slaughterhouse-Five* seem full of danger are right.[24] The consolations of Tralfamadorian fatalism are hideously bobby trapped—leading to a form of moral paralysis that precludes responsibility or action. Billy's flight from the responsibilities of "wakeful humanity"[25] leads directly into what John Tilton calls "a spiritual oubliette."[26]

Not only do the Tralfamadorians, with their "earthly combination of ferocity and spectacular weaponry and talent for horror" (115) not improve Billy's vision, they eventually blow up the universe while experimenting with new fuels for flying saucers. Caged in a zoo, turned into a puppet and made to do the bidding of mechanical creatures whose own world is both physically and morally sterile, Billy in his tranquilized existence becomes the very embodiment of what Vonnegut has warned against for years. Insulated from pain, Billy has simply abdicated his humanity, trading his dignity and self-integrity for an illusion of comfort and security, and becoming himself a machine.

If settling into his womblike Tralfamadorian environment,[27] closing his eyes to any unpleasantness in the world, Billy Pilgrim becomes more than ever the plaything of those enormous forces at work on him throughout his life, Kurt Vonnegut may have saved his own sanity through the therapeutic processes of art, climaxed by an act of symbolic amputation: the severing of the Billy Pilgrim within himself, poisoned with existential gangrene. That this is as much Kurt Vonnegut's baptism by fire as it is the story of Billy's madness may be the overriding truth of *Slaughterhouse-Five;* hence, the revelation in *Breakfast of Champions* that, "I see a man who is terribly wounded, because he has dared to pass through the fires of truth to the other side, which we have never seen. And then he has come back again to tell us about the other side" (180). Billy's regress is Vonnegut's progress. Not only has Vonnegut shored up his own sanity by facing directly into the fires of Dresden, making his long-deferred "dance with death," without which he says no art is possible (21), but like Lot's wife he has asserted his inviolable humanity and freed himself from the self-imprisoning fatalism of Tralfamadore. Vonnegut knows that the Tralfamadorians are merely ourselves—an appropriate symbol for the mechanistic insanity of our own planet, an extension into the future of our own warlike globe. He knows too that with sufficient imagination and heart, we can, like Salo in *Sirens of Titan,* dismantle our own self-imprisoning machinery and become whatever we choose to become.

No wonder after completing this process of cleansing and renewal Vonnegut said,

> Well, I felt after I finished *Slaughterhouse-Five* that I didn't have to write at all anymore if I didn't want to. . . . I suppose that flowers, when they're through blooming, have some sort of awareness of some purpose having been served. . . . At the end of *Slaughterhouse-Five* I had the feeling that I had produced this blossom. . . . that I had done what I was supposed to do and everything was O.K.[28]

If Vonnegut's "therapy" culminates in *Slaughterhouse-Five,* the full meaning of that therapy becomes clear in a novel that not only incorporates all the essential machine themes of his previous works but which serves as nothing less than the spiritual climax to his life and career, *Breakfast of Champions.*

7

Breakfast of Champions:
Spiritual Crossroads

He was awake a long time before he remembered his heart was broken.

Ernest Hemingway

The gratitude for this release of the Unconscious (the so-called "catharsis" or psychic house-cleaning), is the poet's main reward.

Dr. Hans Sachs, *The Creative Unconscious*

At age fifty, Vonnegut informs us that *Breakfast of Champions* represents the "crossing the spine of a roof—having ascended one slope" (4), and that he is thus writing as an act of "cleansing" and renewal "for the very different sorts of years to come" (293). The result is a startlingly revealing pinnacle from which to view the major crises in the author's spiritual evolution, his own Pilgrim's Progress, and to measure the spiritual and artistic consequences of his tortuous, uphill struggle to win the world back from machines. The first advantage this pinnacle affords us is a panoramic view of the massive critical human problems that have resulted from the promiscuous overdevelopment and overemployment of machines before we have comprehended their social effects or learned to deal with their wastes. We then take in an alarming picture of the pessimism that Vonnegut says overwhelmed him in later life—of his more embittered and cynical self that grew out of his fear that human beings were no better than robots in a machine-dominated world (3). But the final view from Vonnegut's metaphorical rooftop is more profoundly startling and revealing than any we will have glimpsed from this or any other vantage point in the author's work: that of spiritual transformation, of rebirth, in which the wearied author attempts to cleanse himself of the poisons that had accumulated in his system from his battle with technology—his own system and that of his work—by turning his fictional world on its head, dismantling the familiar trappings of his literary cosmos, including waving good-bye forever to all his old characters, "setting them free."

In the story of Kago near the beginning of *Breakfast of Champions,* Vonnegut makes his most devastating statement about the destructive effects of machines upon men and nature. Replete with sobering doses of apocalypse and gallows humor, the world that Vonnegut envisions through Kilgore Trout is a dying, nearly uninhabitable civilization of rusting junkers out of gas, which has turned the surface of the earth into an asphalt prairie, the atmosphere into poison gas, and the streams, rivers, and seas into sludge. Now even the automobiles, along with every form of animal and plant life, are threatened with extinction (26–29). Kilgore Trout learns that the river in Midland City (whose art festival he is headed toward throughout the novel for a fateful meeting with his creator, Kurt Vonnegut) contains, along with a washing machine, a couple of refrigerators, several stoves, and an infinity of Pepsi-Cola bottles, a 1968 Cadillac.

Dwayne Hoover reads in Trout's *Now It Can Be Told* that the Creator of the universe has programmed robots to abuse our planet for millions of years, so that it will be "a poisonous festering cheese" when he arrives (254). Vonnegut's readers get a similar message from the driver of the truck that takes Kilgore Trout to Midland City. From his perspective as an exhunter and fisherman, the truck driver embraces the fatalistic view of Kilgore Trout about the nation's depleted environment. He thinks of the marshes and meadows of a hundred years earlier and laments that his truck is poisoning the atmosphere and that in effect, he is committing suicide (84–86).

Perhaps the most dramatic visual effects of the machine's power for despoliation are the planet's ravaged land surfaces. Vonnegut observes that the surface of West Virginia, "demolished by men and machinery and explosives in order to make it yield up its coal," is sinking into the holes dug into it. He suggests that human beings often perpetuate their own destruction, commenting that the destruction of West Virginia took place with the approval of all branches of the state government, "which drew their power from the people" (119).

As in *Player Piano,* it is part of Vonnegut's purpose in *Breakfast of Champions* to show that the cost of a machine-dominated world is as disastrous to the human spirit as it is to the environment. Like D. H. Lawrence before him, Vonnegut demonstrates with remarkable persuasiveness the connection between the modern world with its inhuman industrial empire and the impotent, hopeless, and neurotic life of its citizens. Such a deathly connection is dramatically evinced in the example of Midland City's primary spiritual attraction, the cathedrallike "Sacred Miracle Cave," the symbolization of which is obvious but nonetheless foreboding. The cave is a microcosm of a world whose emotional and spiritual realities have been grotesquely perverted by industrial pollutions.

The Sacred Miracle is nearly invisible now, we are told, though "it was never easy to see" (117). The Sacred Miracle, a cross on the ceiling of the cathedral, is a traditional, unifying, and humanizing symbol for humanity. But the cave's pollution has engulfed the cross and turned its natural auras a sickly yellow, just as the spiritual reality represented by the statue of Moby Dick has been engulfed and debased. The underground stream passing through the Sacred Miracle Cave is polluted by industrial waste, which has formed "bubbles as tough as ping-pong balls." Soon these bubbles will engulf Moby Dick and invade the Cathedral of Whispers, where thousands of people have been married, including Dwayne and other characters in the story (116). The fact that the lives of those married in the cave have become horribly despiritualized, drab, and meaningless and that these people have lost their will to live and love speaks profoundly of the blighting effect of industrial civilization on the human spirit.

As in *Player Piano,* machines have literally taken over human functions, rendering people obsolete and purposeless; but worse, gadgets and mechanical processes have come to intercede in otherwise humanizing and emotionally nourishing sexual interaction, further sterilizing and alienating individuals from one another. One character in the novel performs an amazing act of biological perversion, learning how to reproduce himself by putting some of his cells into chicken soup. Society's solution to that perversion is to keep chicken soup out of the hands of unmarried people. Dwayne Hoover and Kilgore Trout learn dejectedly that they can now get sexual satisfaction, sans human partner, through mechanical, artificial devices. Trout is intrigued by the ease with which pornographic movie machines serve to satisfy baser human appetites (68, 69). For his part, Dwayne Hoover once saw a mail-order ad for a penis-extender and, in the same brochure, "a lifelike rubber vagina for when he was lonesome" (147). It is little wonder that just as the decision is made to close out the despiritualized life of Sacred Miracle Cave by cementing it over, suicide should prove a tragically tempting solution to their poisoned lives for nearly everyone in the novel, including Kurt Vonnegut. The cave winds up smelling like athlete's foot, we are told; the characters fare no better.

Vonnegut sees that the corrupting processes of a machine world are circular and unending. A ravaged, automated, and polluted environment sterilizes and demoralizes the minds of the citizenry, which in turn instills soulless and regimented values into its institutions and cultural pursuits. These institutions in turn continue to exploit the land and to subvert the individuality and emotional life of the people. Kilgore Trout observes ruefully that with no more ability to feel or think on their own than "grandfather clocks" (254),[1] the people of Midland City occupy themselves with the most mundane, brainless, and materialistic subjects and cultivate, in the name of culture, a reverence for the insipid and soulless junk of mass production that clutters their lives. Such programmed mindlessness serves to disfigure the land with garish billboards, pink flamingos, no trespassing signs, motion picture theatres that show nothing but dirty movies, and such bland aesthetic fungoids as Colonel Sanders Kentucky Fried Chicken franchises, Burger Chefs, MacDonald's Hamburger stands, and Holiday Inns.

What Vonnegut deplores about the people in Midland City even more than their soulless preoccupation with money, structures, travel, machinery, and other measurable things is that they all have a clearly defined part to play, and that they are almost passionately ready to relinquish their free will and human identity (hence to assume a machinelike existence) in order to satisfy those roles (142).[2] Such was the limitation of their imaginations, Vonnegut tells us, that they automatically imitated the thinking of their neighbors (136). They would become agreeable, fully automated boobs, ready to conform to the most convenient mold, embrace the most cuckoo ideas, and adopt the most militant, antihumanistic poses, whether in the mistaken interests of survival or friendliness, or sometimes simply out of the lack of imagination to do anything better. Ignorant of and incurious about what designs, ends, or masters they were programmed to serve, the "robots" of Midland City—like the characters in Trout's *Now It Can Be Told*—became instant money-making machines, consuming machines, housekeeping machines, self-pitying machines, butchering machines, weeping machines, loving or hating machines, killing machines, and breeding machines. Like Trout's character, they would adore infants and sex despite the fact that the planet was already desperately crowded with other programmed robots (254–55). Kilgore Trout learns that Midland City's plasticized citizens are so perfectly conditioned to serving as cogs in the greater social machine of the community that even if someone stopped playing his or her role for a time—a clear indication of insanity—everybody went on imagining that he or she was living up to expectations.

Vonnegut becomes aware that it is the amazing ease with which even the most monstrous ideas infiltrate and take hold in the human mind and the frenzied energy people are willing to spend on behalf of those ideas that allow them to become enslaved so quickly by anonymous bureaucracies, computers, and authoritarian institutions. It is this knowledge, as we will see later, that becomes first the author's undoing and then his making as a writer devoted primarily to mental health. A case in point concerns the somewhat innocent but nonetheless insidiously addictive ideas that invade Dwayne Hoover's mind as he sits listening to the social propaganda on the radio of his Plymouth Fury. He learns about cheap health insurance, better performance for his car, and constipation. He is even offered a Bible in which the speeches of God or Jesus are printed in red capital letters and a plant that eats disease-carrying insects. All this information is stored in Dwayne's memory "in case he should need it later on. He had all kinds of stuff in there" (62). It is programming of a more ominous sort—that which shapes and controls our proclivities for hating and killing—that appalls Vonnegut the most and against which he directs the brunt of his moral indignation. He speaks with humorous contempt, for instance, of those "robots" who act violently in the quest of such artificial and arbitrary lusts as gold, little girl's underpants, and wide-open beavers. But he reserves his ultimate condemnation for the most cuckoo ideas of all, those spurious ideals of national unity that convince people to turn themselves into meat machines to do the robot work of a few fabulously well-to-do people; or into homicidal maniacs, war machines, guaranteed to shoot rockets at and drop explosives on other human beings. It is the tragic susceptibility of people to antihumanitarian proposals, argues Vonnegut, that has perpetuated the misery of those "who couldn't get their hands on doodly squat," and that has been responsible for the worst of America's sins, slavery, genocide, criminal neglect (37, 293).

This returns us to the thematic center of Vonnegut's work—the message he has urged upon us for years. He sees as the great moral imperative of our age the need to combat the mindless conditioning processes that control and shape our more aggressive, self-destructive drives, drives which have put us on a collision path with Armageddon. He combats these processes first through massive resistance in the form of open displays of contempt and, second, by constantly asking painful questions about the nature of the information that is fed into us. We must guard ourselves, he asserts, not only against the organizational machines of political, economic, and military power structures (which attempt to subvert free will and individual autonomy) but also against any totalitarian entity or theory that undermines the individual's sense of control over and responsibility for his own destiny and that of the planet, including all theories of philosophic or religious determinism, historical determinism, and psychological, genetic, or chemical determinism.

We should notice that Vonnegut's solution to a dehumanized machine world differs significantly from that of such other antitechnology writers as D. H. Lawrence, Hemingway, Faulkner, Steinbeck, and Norman Mailer, all of whom believe, as ardent primitivists, that the machine's corruption of man's individuality, spontaneity, and general emotional wellbeing should be reversed by throwing off the trappings of civilization and retreating to a golden age in the past, particularly by getting back into a natural, organic, nonmechanical relationship with the land. Conversely, Vonnegut admonishes us that our only hope for salvation is intelligently and humanely directing our course into the future. He would have us move *up* the evolutionary ladder, not *down,* questioning though not always condemning mechanical and material change, using our brains to determine when such change is humanly valuable, when destructive, and to learn to act more compassionately toward one another.[3]

Vonnegut knows only too well the uphill nature of his struggle to move us along the evolutionary ladder to more sane and rational behavior, and has to battle his own despair along the way. The problem, he says in *Breakfast of Champions,* is that we humans train ourselves to be "agreeing" machines instead of "thinking" machines. The women in Midland City do not use their minds very much because they fear making their friends uncomfortable. Safety and comfort come first for them (136). They are like the female rabbit in Trout's *The Smart Bunny,* who becomes so convinced that her mind is useless that she views it as some kind of tumor (232). Another woman is satirized for her blind, mechanical loyalty to her lover. When she protests "You're my man" repeatedly, we are told that means she was willing "to agree about anything" with Dwayne, and to do anything for him . . . to die for him, and so forth (160). Trout, in one of his own sardonic tales of humanity's suicidal tendencies, registers his despair in the face of seemingly unending human stupidity by portraying earthlings who value friendship over thought, who are designed not for wisdom but for friendliness (28).

I mentioned earlier that the view from Vonnegut's metaphorical rooftop in *Breakfast of Champions* takes in far more than his panoramic portrayal of the machine's abuses of men and nature or his proposals for reform. Vonnegut also invites us to contemplate a portrait of his more embittered and cynical Trout-self—that "unhappy failure" who represents all the artists who searched for truth and beauty without finding "doodly-squat!" (37).[4] Although Vonnegut happens to be describing his fictional counterpart Kilgore Trout in this instance, their lives are in many ways so similar as depicted in this novel that what is said about the one often applies to the other. Trout is given an iron will to live but a life not worth living (71, 72). He is given Vonnegut's social conscience and artistic goals but a pessimism so great that it negates his artistic mission and vitiates his moral zeal. The most unsettling of these parallels in a commonly shared fate is that Trout is given the knowledge that he is a programmed writing machine whose miserable life is controlled solely by his author and who has succeeded only in wreaking psychological and emotional violence upon his readers rather than reforming or uplifting them. Trout certainly has harmed some of his readers by infusing them with his own pessimistic belief that human beings were no better than robots in a meaningless world; Vonnegut seems to fear having done similar evil.[5]

We learn that Trout's idea of the purpose of human life and, presumably, of his own artistic mission has been to be the eyes and ears and conscience of God, but that years of neglect and a growing sense of a life not worth living have made him temperamentally unfit for the task (67). He has given up caring seriously about what he writes because the world pays so little attention to him; he had even come to considering himself invisible and his ideas harmless, mere bulk for pornographic books and magazines put out by hardcore publishers who consequently paid him doodly-squat. He laughs now at attempts to reform the world, believing the whole mess futile. Kilgore Trout, Vonnegut says, would have sneered when he was a younger man at a "brotherhood" sign posted on the rim of a bomb crater, but his mind no longer harbors ideas about how things should be on Earth, as compared to how they are (103). Trout, in fact, has been turned into a proper Tralfamadorian, believing there is only one way for Earth to be—the way it is. Hence Trout reacts with bitter irony to the coordinator of the Midland City Arts Festival who implores him to bring humanizing new truths and hopeful songs to awake and restore the spiritually dead of his town. "Open your eyes!" exclaims Trout. "Do I look like a dancer, a singer, a man of joy?" (233). One is compelled to think of the cartoon drawing of Vonnegut at the end of the novel, a Vonnegut whose baleful countenance sheds a lonely tear.

Trout documents his lost faith and lost utopian zeal to the truck driver who gives him a lift in his truck to the Arts Festival. He says that he used to be a conservationist who bemoaned the killing of eagles from helicopters "and all that," but that he gave it up. Now when a tanker fouls the ocean, killing millions of birds and fish, he laughs and says, "More power to Standard Oil," or who-ever. He realized, he tells the driver, that since God wasn't any conservationist, it was a sacrilegious waste of time for anyone else to be one. "Ever see one of his volcanoes . . . tornadoes . . . tidal waves?" asks Trout. "That's God, not man" (84, 85).

The unavoidable fact is that Trout knows he has been transformed by his eternal disappointment into a harbinger of doom and that he has brought only suffering and desolation to those around him and to his readers. Vonnegut's narrator tells us that the pessimism that overwhelmed Trout in later life "de-stroyed his three marriages, and drove Leo, his son, away from home" (31). (A reading of Mark Vonnegut's autobiographical account of his own severe emotional illness, diagnosed as acute schizophrenia, in *The Eden Express,* sug-gests more than a casual relationship between his father's work and his particu-lar emotional dilemma.) But just as catastrophic is Trout's awareness that his inability to write about anything other than the triumphs of the machine over the human spirit has poisoned the minds of his readers by infecting them with his own disillusionment and cynicism.

It is through the character of Dwayne Hoover that Trout discovers that his pessimism has been turning his readers into monsters. It is true that Hoover had been in bad shape due to bad chemicals before he wandered into the demoraliz-ing sphere of Trout's influence by reading a science fiction novel entitled *Now It Can Be Told.* He was already a soulless victim of Midland City's machine-ridden culture, owner not only of the Pontiac agency and a piece of the Holiday Inn, but of three Burger Chefs and five coin-operated car washes. That in itself causes incipient insanity. But it is nevertheless Trout's book that gives Dwayne's craziness "shape and direction"—that turns him into a homicidal maniac, in fact, by planting the idea in his head that people are nothing more than machines, incapable of thinking, feeling, making choices, worrying and planning, and so on, but that perhaps he alone of all human beings has free will and hence the need to figure things out (14, 15).[6] The prospect of being the only nonmachine on the planet is so unbalancing that the only thing Hoover figures out is that if everyone around him is an unfeeling machine, he might as well treat them as inhumanely as he pleases. He subsequently embarks on a rampage that sends eleven people to the hospital.[7]

It seems unmistakable that, through the example of poor Dwayne Hoover, Vonnegut is dramatizing his own fears about the negative spiritual repercussions of his work on his readers. Trout's inadvertent mind poisoning of Hoover surely measures the degree of demoralization the author feels his own often despairing vision of a robot-populated world has inflicted on those who read his books.[8] But more personally revealing of the damaging consequences that have resulted from his long and enervating battle with machines is Vonnegut's use of Trout's dilemma to depict the effect of his work on his own mind. Just as Trout's crippling pessimism seemed to vitiate his moral energy and humanistic zeal and thus to negate his artistic mission, Vonnegut suggests that a similarly incapacitating despair had prevented him from carrying out with sufficient vigor his own guiding purpose as an artist, to serve as an alarm system to warn society of its technological abuses and dangers to man and nature.

If we had not gotten the message of Vonnegut's troubled, dual orientation through previous novels or through obvious parallels to Trout, the author tells us directly that his mounting fear and despair actually made him ill—that his machine-induced nightmares were dreadful enough, in fact, to result in a state of suppressed schizophrenia that led him to contemplate suicide (his mother's fate) as a solution. He was driven into a void, "my hiding place when I dematerialize," to distance himself from potentially overwhelming horrors (294).[9] Twin forces, which we may assume are those of optimism and pessimism struggling for control of his creative imagination, were at work in his soul, he says. But they balanced each other and canceled each other out, creating a kind of sterile ambivalence, or spiritual stalemate, out of which either irresolution or nihilism emerged as the dominant effect (219–20). He went to Midland City, Vonnegut says, "to be born again. And Chaos announced that it was about to give birth to a new me" (218).[10]

One force in what Vonnegut chooses to call his "pre-earthquake condition" was the conclusion that there is nothing sacred about himself or others, that all people are essentially machines fated to suffer endless collisions with one another, and hence that his life might be regarded as ridiculous (219). This force, Vonnegut concludes, turned him into a writing machine (225), which wrote about these hapless collisions, which were no more sacred than a Pontiac, mousetrap, or South Bend Lathe (220). It is this oppressive force, he indicates, that, placing him on a par with his own robotlike creator programmed him to be a mindless instigator of a world of suffering and despair in which he had been compelled to fashion the character of Kilgore Trout to bear the brunt of his own cosmic misery and futility. He has fractured his own mind, the character Vonnegut tells Trout, and he observes with self-deprecation that he has been caught up in an endlessly circular process of demoralization. As his creator has passed bad ideas and chemicals down to him, he had passed them on to Trout and Trout transferred them to Hoover. Trout's situation, Vonnegut's narrator concludes, to the extent that he was a machine, was "complex, tragic, and laughable" (225, 292).

While this recognition that a large part of him is dead machinery casts a huge pall over the author's sense of himself as a writer in control of his life and work, it also ironically proves his salvation. For the very act of recognition itself suggests the presence of an imaginative faculty capable of resisting subversion by the machine within and machines without. Vonnegut comes to see this awareness according to the vision of Rabo Karabekian as an "unwavering band of light," a sacred, irreducible living force at the core of every animal (221). This epiphany sets in motion the essential drama of this book and perhaps of all Vonnegut's work, his spiritual rebirth, in which he determines to repudiate his former pessimism and in which the tragically repressed voice of hope in his work gains ascendancy over its negative counterpart.[11] It is on such a healthy note that the "pre-earthquake condition" in his soul—the precarious balance between the forces of optimism and pessimism paralleling the "spiritual matrix" of the cocktail lounge—is resolved, and Vonnegut tells of his transformation beginning as "a grain of sand crumbled," the process continuing until "spiritual continents began to shrug and heave" (219).

So the final view we are afforded of Vonnegut's arduous climb to his rooftop, the spiritual climax to his "first" career, is his achievement of faith in the inviolability of awareness, especially human awareness, which, if properly cherished and cultivated, may yet redeem us and our planet from the technological horrors of the twentieth century. From this faith came his decision to cleanse and renew himself for the years ahead by performing the most daring and rebellious act of his writing life, the setting free of all his literary characters, including the omnipresent Kilgore Trout. The symbolic liberation of Trout, which amounts to the author's repudiation of his most pessimistic voice, is a necessary act of exorcism that both prepares for and explains the author's rebirth. It liberates him from the pessimistic and cynical strain in his work that had constituted the critical emotional malady of his main characters, and it signifies his determination to disengage himself from a mechanical relationship with his own creator, who programmed him to write as he has (4).[12] Vonnegut is connected to his creator in the same way that the characters he has created are connected to him: "stale rubberbands," not "steel wires" (202). Only moral inertia had to be overcome before he could steer his fictional course, as well as his own life, in a more sane and vital direction. Whatever happens, he vows that he will serve no longer as anyone's puppet, nor put on any more puppet shows of his own (5).

Does this mean that Kurt Vonnegut is winning his war with machines—a struggle both sociological and psychological in nature—that, as the quotation from Job in front of *Breakfast of Champions* would seem to inform us, he has been tried and "come forth as gold"? I think that we can take the author at his word that if he was sick—if he had indeed felt like that syphilitic machine standing underneath the "overhanging clock" that his "father designed . . . eaten alive by corkscrews" and unable to fit together the world of self and the world of society (3, 5)—he is "better now" and positively transformed by what he has been through. With the help of Phoebe Hurty, that mother surrogate who at the spiritual crossroads of his life at age sixteen helped him develop the necessary moral sense and faith in human improvement to survive the Great Depression, and with the help of his fiction as therapy, he has created for us and for himself that "humane harmony" lacking in the world around him. It is perhaps the great *personal* depression that Vonnegut has survived that *Breakfast of Champions* is most about—depression based upon a legacy of parental unhappiness, suicide, and the horrors of war, depression that turned him into a writing machine, writing as he was seemingly "programmed" to write.

We might well see the author now in the light shed upon Kilgore Trout by the director of the Midland City Arts Festival, who sees him as a "terribly wounded" man because he passed through the "fires of truth" and returned to tell us of them (234). If Kurt Vonnegut has successfully negotiated his personal and artistic freedom from machinelike forces of control, he is not so naive as to suggest that freedom is ever absolute or that it solves all life's problems. Recall that the author wants to make his "head as empty as it was when I was born onto this damaged planet fifty years ago"—an effort to regain lost innocence. But life's ultimate clock, time itself, does not cooperate. Thus Kilgore Trout calls out twice at the novel's end, "Make me young!" Nor has Vonnegut exorcised totally the image of that saddened, worn-out father (whose voice becomes Trout's) or that of his "suicide mother who babbled of love, peace, wars, evil, and desperation" (181). These two presences he associates with death and void to the very end of the book. Nevertheless the Phoebe Hurty in him has prevailed over the Philboyd Studge, the voice of hope over the voice of despair.[13] And we experience the first fruit of the author's spiritual rebirth in his novel *Slapstick: Or Lonesome No More* (1976). His subject here is the same—the damaging excesses of the machine upon the human spirit—and he writes of desolated cities and the depletion of nature, of loneliness and spiritual death—but he writes in a voice that is more persistently affirmative than ever before. Dreaming up numerous improvements for mankind, and putting great emphasis on his old idea of the karass from *Cat's Cradle*—bringing together in *Slapstick* people without great wealth or powerful friends into membership in extended families whose spiritual core is common decency, Vonnegut confirms in this book his optimistic faith that human beings can be anything we want to be. Because people are just families rather than nations, even wars become tolerable; the machines no longer fight and there are no massacres. As Kilgore Trout says in *Breakfast of Champions*, we are free now to build an unselfish society by devoting "to unselfishness the frenzy we once devoted to gold and to underpants" (25).

Part II

Resolution: The Second Fifty Years

Every creative possibility is contained in the "stuff dreams are made of." Out of it unfolds the most marvelous pageant the world has ever seen of fantastic figures, some of them scurrilous, others charming, some venerable, others terrifying, occasionally speaking wisdom and at other times talking gibberish. They are the dreams of our nights and the halfdreams of our days with many in-between forms.

Dr. Hans Sachs, *The Creative Unconscious*

And how did we then face the odds,
Of swan's rude slapstick, yes, and God's?
Quite at home and unafraid,
Thank you,
In a game our dreams remade.

Slapstick

8

Slapstick:
The Meaning of the Dizygotic Twins

If name be needed, wonder names them both;
From wonder into wonder
Existence opens.

Lao Tzu

Utopians are like people who've been disappointed in love all
their lives but keep on writing love poems.

Anatole Broyard

Despite Vonnegut's declaration in *Breakfast of Champions* that he has become "better now," it is likely that his attempts to work out in fictional form the schizophrenic dilemma mentioned in that novel required one more purge: the summoning up of deeply repressed childhood experiences which needed to be faced as he faced the traumatic experiences of war in *Slaughterhouse-Five* (1969). Critic Mark Shechner has said that Joyce needed to create Stephen Dedalus's character in order to forge some tenable sense of himself from the brittle and painful fragments of childhood."[1] It is precisely this that Vonnegut seems to have done in *Slapstick* (1976), *Jailbird* (1979), *Deadeye Dick* (1982), and *Galápagos* (1985)—the final catharsis in the author's career-long process of fictional cleansing and renewal.

In *Slapstick* and *Jailbird* the protagonist literally ascends into the family's mausoleum in a ritualized attempt to raise and face haunting parental ghosts. The collective weight of traumatic family history in these novels is in fact so great, so shockingly personal that Vonnegut says in a letter to me, "It was easy for me to describe each of my novels briefly until I got past *Slaughterhouse-Five*. After that I found the novels too personal to sketch—I became thick of speech."[2] Vonnegut says in the prologue to *Slapstick* that "the museums in children's minds, I think, automatically empty themselves in times of utmost horror——to protect the children from eternal grief" (15). If something like this happened to Vonnegut, revisiting that museum, descent into the family crypt as he had formerly descended into the fires of Dresden wins him the grace of the novel's opening inscription: "Call me but love, and I'll be new baptized."

The ghost of immediate concern in *Slapstick,* described in the prologue, is Vonnegut's sister Alice, who had recently died among strangers in New Jersey of cancer at the age of forty-one (11). Discussing her impending death with a kind of quiet acceptance and dignity, Alice comments to Vonnegut, "Soap Opera . . . Slapstick." Her death is projected into the novel in the form of Wilbur Swain's twin sister Eliza, killed in a bizarre accident, an avalanche, that leaves the protagonist in a fit of depression and drug addition that lasts for thirty years. It is not, however, the image of either sister's tragic death that prevails in the novel, or that of the protagonist's defeatism, but of moral bravery which Vonnegut praises in the Shamanlike prologue as "common decency" and "bargaining in good faith with destiny" (2). Vonnegut declares in the prologue that his sister was the person he had always written for—the secret of any wholeness and harmoniousness in his work (15). Now Vonnegut pays homage to her—making good a debt of love and inspiration by dedicating to her his own "opera" and thereby also "bargaining in good faith with destiny."

Part of the critical success of this novel, as in all Vonnegut's fiction, is the achievement of a story whose message of psychic *and* social trauma and healing are perfectly fused, an *artistic* joining equivalent to the power created by the gender-joining of the novel's fraternal twins.[3] On the one hand, Vonnegut uses his twins, their merging and their alienation, to portray the enormous intimacy he obviously felt for his sister, and his subsequent grief and despair at her loss. He also portrays his anger with his parents in contributing to that alienation, insofar as we can take the grotesquely alienating power of the parents on the welfare of that single being, Wilbur and Eliza, as consistent with the novel's other autobiographical revelations. The twins, we will see, are a typical device for dramatizing a single mind on the verge of schizophrenia—a contemporary version of Roderick and Madeline Usher.[4] At the same time, Vonnegut uses the symbolic fusion of male and female sensibilities to portray the painful alienation of an entire society, made whole again by that concentrated brain power that inspires Wilbur and Eliza to dream up numerous improvements for their world. Wilbur's shell-shocked reaction to Eliza's death is the psychological counterpart to his society's social collapse; overcoming the psychological crisis, he then, as a literal physician healer and later as president, is empowered to help overcome the crisis of fragmented identities and loneliness that threatens society at large.[5]

The tragic alienation experienced by Wilbur and Eliza comes at the hands of the same parents (Vonnegut's) described in *Breakfast of Champions* as "that saddened, worn-out father and that suicide mother who babbled of love, peace, wars, evil, and desperation." It is these two ominous presences that now torment the childhood of Wilbur and Eliza Swain with guilt and fear, cruelty and loneliness. Obsessively materialistic, viewing intelligence as a liability in their champagne world of power and appearances, they are so stupefied and humiliated by the ugliness of their strange neanderthaloid children, fossil-looking human beings "with massive brow-ridges, sloping foreheads, and steam-shovel jaws" (29), they entomb them in a spooky old family mansion on an isolated mountaintop in Vermont. Visiting the twins once a year on their birthdays, proffering affection with "bittersweet dread" (61), the parents are the true grotesques of this piece. By the age of fifteen, Wilbur observes that he and his sister are more than unloved. "I am awed," he says, "yet again by the perfect lulu of a secret that was concealed from Eliza and me so long: that our parents wished we would hurry up and die (60) . . . that they were all but strangled and paralyzed by the wish that their own children would die" (65). In this most admittedly autobiographical of novels, it seems significant that Vonnegut should comment at some length in the prologue upon the conspicuous absence of affection, spontaneity, or nourishing family rituals within his own family (3–4).[6]

For a long time, the twins keep the strange nature of their intimacy a secret to everyone but themselves: the realization that each represents a facet of mind that is incomplete by itself, which makes them appear stupid and insecure when apart (28), but which in consort, explains Wilbur, transforms these two ugly ducklings into one lovely swan, or Swain. Never mind that the twins, at their best, putting their heads together, murmur in ancient Greek, secretly read and write English, French, German, Italian, and Latin, do calculus by the age of seven, and have read the family's thousands of books by the age of ten (42); in an effort to please their parents, they proceed to be the idiots they believe their parents expect them to—drooling, speaking incoherent babble, eating library paste, farting in public as a favorite pastime, believing that "idiots were lovely things to be," and that "our intelligence was simply one more example of our freakishness." Wilbur explains that their parents "hoped for only small advancement; they wished us to become toilet trained." "We were glad to comply" (41). Together, Wilbur says, he and Eliza composed not only a whole human being but a "thoroughly populated Universe" (56), one "of the gentlest geniuses the world has ever known" (72). Wilbur's contribution is practical, analytical, functional, while Eliza's talents are intuitive, expressive, and visionary. "She does the great intuitive leaping for us both," Wilbur explains. "I did all the reading . . . it was Eliza who could put seemingly unrelated ideas together in order to get a new one. It was Eliza who juxtaposed" (51).

Functioning as an intimate unity, thinking and feeling as a single, androgynous whole, Wilbur declares, "Thus did we give birth to a single genius, which died as quickly as we were parted, which was reborn the moment we got together again" (50). It is together, overcoming fragmentation and alienation in this union of intellect and spirit, of analytical and intuitive intelligence, that this "gentle genius" composes an essay for reorganizing Americans into thousands of artificial extended families, in effect, a social extension of their own personal, psychological cure for alienation. It was possible, says Wilbur, that the framers of the Constitution failed to recognize the value of persons without great wealth or powerful friends. "Thinking as halves of a single genius," Wilbur says,

> Eliza and I proposed that the Constitution be amended so as to guarantee that every citizen, no matter how humble or crazy or incompetent or deformed, somehow be given membership in some family as covertly xenophobic and crafty as the one their public servants formed. (54)

At the age of fifteen, thinking to please their parents, the twins boldly announce themselves to be the geniuses they know themselves to be. They vow to make their mansion as famous for intelligence as it has been infamous for idiocy (74).The truth only frightens and repels the parents more than ever, unleashing a new form of cruelty, a form of schizophrenic splitting that surpasses the pain of imprisonment. Wilbur and Eliza are turned over to the family psychiatrist, actually, Wilbur says, a "malicious lunatic" (90), and made to undergo a barrage of intelligence tests in isolation from each other. Wilbur likens their plight to that of condemned prisoners who think of themselves as dead long before they die. "Perhaps that was how our genius felt, knowing that a cruel axeman, so to speak, was about to split it into two nondescript chunks of meat, into Betty and Bobby Brown" (107). A second testing produces just this result. In their eagerness to please, checking their answers together, the twins wind up with more than their heads together: "the two of us . . . wound up under the table—with our legs wrapped around each other's necks in scissors grips, and snorting and snuffing into each other's crotches" (103, 104). The next morning, Wilbur is whisked off to a school for severely disturbed children, and Eliza is exiled to an expensive institution for the feeble-minded.

The forced separation not only destroys the harmony and wholeness of their single healthy mind; it is a separation so complete that Wilbur must be reminded over the years of his sister's existence somewhere in a world very different from his. Wilbur has gone to prep school and then to Harvard, and in his subsequent prosperity never inquires into his sister's whereabouts, for which Eliza's hurt becomes so great she calls her brother "a swine" (116). Equally unkind, Wilbur refers to his sister as a "sort of anteater known as an aardvark" (119). With the help of a shifty-eyed attorney named Norman Mushari, whom we remember from *God Bless You, Mr. Rosewater,* Eliza manages to escape the asylum and to regain her portion of the family's wealth. But illustrative of her emotional and mental crippling, the first thing she does is to buy half-interest in the New

England Patriots professional football team (117). With the rupture of their collective soul, both brother and sister resume their former role as idiots, experiencing now the idiot's delights of adults.

The rest of Wilbur's disaster-filled story might suggest that this is the bleakest, most demoralized of novels, those Vonnegut is accused of writing.[7] We see again, for instance, that the agony of personal suffering that Wilbur must undergo has its larger social counterpart in the ominous external collapse of his society; microcosm and macrocosm are poisoned with lovelessness, loneliness, and death. The separation from and then the death of Eliza leaves Wilbur "swooning with sorrow and loathing and guilt" (121), inducing years of self-destructive forms of withdrawal in which he hallucinates, pretends to talk to his dead sister, drugs himself with pills, and finally considers suicide (237), thinking to join his sister in the afterlife. To retain faith in his utopian dreams, and to fight off "Tourette's Disease," he pops tiny green pills which he says accounted for his unflagging courtesy and optimism (161). Sufferers of Tourette's Disease involuntarily speak obscenities and behave insultingly no matter where they are (155). He fails at a disastrous marriage, and wonders openly if he has really gone insane (192). Concurrently, the nation is bankrupt and people are dying by the millions of the Albanian flu and a mysterious plague called "The Green Death." Joining the two forms of devastation, Wilbur taps his head and says to a soldier who has commented on the massive social chaos around them, "You should see what it looks like in here" (192).

But neither of these stories—Wilbur's or Vonnegut's—is ultimately about moral escapism or a failure to cope, but about courage, love, wholeness, optimism, and creative inspiration; about the salubrious effects of loving sisters and sister-muses; and about the healing, self-reflexive process of art that leads Eliza and Wilbur to explore the "alternative universes" of imagination and heart.

During their final visit together, something shocking and remarkable happens to the twins, which gives the novel its ultimate meaning, which allows them to become a single genius again, and which shows Eliza (along with Alice, her real life counterpart) to be the source of that courage, self-belief, and ability to love that will allow her brother to survive and lead a creative, harmonious life without her. Eliza entices Wilbur into an orgy of coupling and "writhing embraces" that lasts a week and seems at first to leave the two of them emotionally shattered (130–31). The deeper consequence appears, however, when Wilbur twice hears his sister's voice, once when he graduates from medical school and again when he becomes president of the United States. Hovering over him in a helicopter during his graduation party, Eliza appears to Wilbur as an allegorical angel, and rather than dropping a bag of excrement on him, which he feels is his due, she showers him with these lines from a Shakespearean sonnet, praising Wilbur as their better half:

> Even for this let us divided live,
> And our dear love lose name of single one,
> That by this separation I may give
> That due to thee, which thou deserv'st alone. (138–39)

Properly moved, the normally emotionless Wilbur says, "I shouted something daring; and something I genuinely felt for the first time in my life. . . . 'Eliza! I love you!' I said. . . . 'Did you hear me, Eliza . . . I *love* you! I *really* love you!'" (139). Then, she says, "I will say in turn something that I really mean, my brother—my twin. . . . God guide the hand and mind of Dr. Wilbur Rockefeller Swain."

It is the abiding memory of Eliza that guides and inspires Wilbur's work as a pediatrician (140), symbolically appropriate to curing his own childhood afflictions, and his work as president when he puts to work his and Eliza's scheme to bring together people without great wealth or powerful friends into membership in "extended families," whose spiritual core is common decency. Even as relative anarchy, disease, and economic collapse grip the country, with everybody being someone else's relative around the globe, people have become less lonely and more merciful. There is no such thing as "a battle between strangers anymore" (220). An antidote has been found to The Green Death. Wilbur observes that the machines have decided not to fight anymore. In a battle he has observed, people were deserting and surrendering and even embracing (220). We learn that in the midst of their orgy, at the point of greatest intimacy, Wilbur had alternated passionate embraces with his sister with passionate sessions at the typewriter, giving birth to what he calls his "intellectual center of gravity," a manual on childrearing that is surely the counterpart of the life stories composed by Wilbur and Vonnegut, the fruit of that therapy and that invention by which the sickness of childhood has been transformed by art into something harmonious and whole.[8] It is no coincidence that, when Wilbur attempts to reunite his mind with that of his dead sister in order to "recreate the genius they had been in childhood" (230), it is through an electronic device called a "Hooligan" that bears a striking resemblance to a typewriter. The Hooligan has obvious Freudian characteristics. Wilbur would have crawled into it if he could, and someone observes that, straddling the Hooligan, he looked like "the biggest baboon in the world trying to fuck a football" (236). The experience is crudely incestuous, but ironically encourages wholeness and growth.

Save for Billy Pilgrim, each of Vonnegut's earlier heroes has shown potential as a healer of self and then a healer of others. But Wilbur demonstrates the greatest potential yet to recreate himself through art. At age fifty, he says, "I found the hospitality of my mind to fantasy pleasantly increased" (145). The bridge, the faith that has eluded previous heroes, but which now produces Wilbur's equilibrium, is the discovery of art and life alike as open-ended, existential structures. Wilbur learns to creatively manipulate such structures by combining harmonious minds (237)—thus answering the challenge of the Universe which Wilbur hears saying to him, "I await your instructions. You can be anything you want to be. I will be anything you want me to be" (96). Wilbur's narrative itself was experienced first as a "daydream," then transformed into the story of this novel (18). *Slapstick* bears out Patricia Waugh's observation that the paranoia that permeates the metafictional writing of the sixties and seventies gradually transforms to more positive forms of fantasy—fabulatory extravaganzas, magic realism.[9] The potentially creative paranoia of Paul Proteus, his stifled gift of invention, gives way to renewal and celebration. The two forms of fantasizing—Paul's and Wilbur's—are contrasted through the desirable social vision of extended families, and the dynamite bouquet represented by Wilbur's delusional visit with a Chinese man the size of his thumb.[10] The latter is induced by the trauma of Wilbur's separation from his sister and news of her death, by withdrawal from reality through ever-increasing dosages of tri-benzo-Deportamil. "Cooked to the ears" (145), Wilbur imagines the tiny Chinese man has brought him greetings from his sister. Indicating that this is a dangerous hallucinatory retreat from fear and guilt, Wilbur notes that "going to China" became a euphemism for committing suicide (145). Wilbur is troubled that the Chinese emissary refuses to answer his questions, insisting Wilbur is too dumb to understand (149). He is made to feel intellectually and spiritually inferior to his "teeny-weeny" visitor as Malachi Constant and Howard Campbell were to the god figures they conjured. Notably, then, we are told that the microscopic Chinese are the cause of "The Green Death," fatal to normal-sized human beings when inhaled or ingested. The allusion links the moral death Wilbur invites by popping the tiny green pills—doping himself to reality—and the larger social disease of apathy and will-lessness that brings Wilbur's society to ruin. His Chinese fantasy occurs in "the first rush of grief"(153), news of his sister's death, but the drag of gravity he experiences is felt throughout the world.

Wilbur's Chinese fantasy is suicidal because it encourages Wilbur to relinquish control of his thoughts and actions to those in higher authority. Like his mother's idiotic image of Heaven as a lemonade paradise, this fantasy subverts Wilbur's quest for wholeness and autonomy. What distinguishes the vision of extended families from the Chinese fantasy is that the former offers no panaceas—no Garden of Eden or womblike hiding place from complex human problems. Its goals require no bloody revolutions, no sacrificial messiahs, no deterministic structures such as Fu Manchu's communist world represents, and no god figures on whom to thrust moral responsibility. Rather its goals are modest, humane, democratic, and almost comically practical. It settles for companionship, fairmindedness, and common decency over perfect love, even if achieved for only a short period of time. Its foremost hope is to increase the individual's sense of personal worth and power in determining his or her own destiny. Families are decided not by background, wealth, or social position, but by new middle names that allow them to claim relatives all over the world (5). As a candidate for president, Wilbur explains the expected results of artificial families in a way that is far from grand or utopian. He tells a prospective voter to consider how much better off he will be when a beggar comes to him for money. You ask him his middle name, and when he tells you " 'Oyster-19' or 'Chickadee-1,' or 'Hollyhock-13,' " you say to him:

> Buster—I happen to be a Uranium-3. You have one hundred and ninety thousand cousins and ten thousand brothers and sisters. You're not exactly alone in this world. I have relatives of my own to look after. So why don't you take a flying fuck at a rolling doughnut? Why don't you take a flying fuck at the mooooooooooooon? (163–64)

In perhaps the most resoundingly affirmative resolution to any Vonnegut novel to date, Wilbur Swain leaves this poem at his death, hoping someone will use it for his epitaph:

> And how did we then face the odds,
> Of swan's rude slapstick, yes, and God's?
> Quite at home and unafraid,
> Thank you,
> In a game our dreams remade. (230)

Judging from the end of *Slapstick,* it appears that Vonnegut has survived what in *Breakfast of Champions* he called the spiritual crossroads of his career—a battle with personal despair—and that with the help of his work as therapy and the inspiration of his sister-muse, he has learned to create for himself and for us that "humane harmony" whose absence, as with Wilbur, may nearly have driven him crazy. Wilbur, like Vonnegut, has learned to resolve personal and social fragmentation by creating fantasies that encourage communal bonding rather than narcissistic withdrawal. In the closing pages of the novel, Vonnegut embodies his optimistic faith that human beings can be anything they want to be in a final act of gender-joining, Wilbur's mating at a time when he has thrown off his addiction to drugs, which eventually produces a granddaughter named "Melody." "Melody," Vonnegut explains in the prologue, "is what is left of my memory of my sister—of my optimistic imagination, of my creativeness" (19). In that spirit, Melody arrives on the scene amid the desolation of New York City with a Dresden candlestick as a gift, climaxing an incredible journey eastward in search of her legendary grandfather and climaxing as well, I think, Vonnegut's long obsession with Dresden.[10] She is surrounded by lifesaving equipment and vital living presences (240–41). She is pregnant; members of her extended family feed and warm her, and point the way; she possesses a compass, an alarm clock, and a needle and thread for weaving—the first for direction, the second for awareness, the third for weaving the loose ends of fictional yarn we are told Wilbur has left behind into more stories of wholeness and harmony such as this.

9

Jailbird: The Madness of RAMJAC

*Sacco and Vanzetti never lost their dignity—never cracked up.
Walter F. Starbuck finally did.*

Jailbird

*Violence comes from powerlessness . . . it is the explosion of
impotence.*

Rollo May, *Power and Innocence*

As surely as Laurel and Hardy prove inspirational for Wilbur Swain, the deaths
of Sacco and Vanzetti lead Vonnegut's next protagonist back into despair. Save
for Dresden, nowhere in Vonnegut's fiction does a single act of sociopolitical
madness so burden the hero's conscience or prove more unbalancing than the
executions of Sacco and Vanzetti. The "Great Depression" (ix) for Walter Starbuck actually describes a lifetime of personal and public degradation that includes childhood alienation, the trauma of war, and successive public humiliations involving his role in the McCarthy hearings, the political machinations
of Watergate, and his relationship with a monstrous capitalistic conglomerate
called RAMJAC.

On the one hand, Walter's Joblike trials mark him one of Vonnegut's most
tormented protagonists—a man so battered and depressed he confesses, "I
wasn't sure I wanted to live anymore" (111). Tending at times to the defeatism
and moral evasion of Billy Pilgrim, he echoes Billy's fatalistic lament, "So it
goes," announcing repeatedly that "It's all right" (48). Someone observes, "You
say that about everything." Walter sees life in America as "a slaughterhouse"
(173), what a character in *Bluebeard* (1988) calls "The Republic of Suicide,"
"Dementia Praecox" in "The Genocide Century" (66). Billy escapes into self-
imprisoning fantasies of Tralfamadore; Walter twice lands in asylums—jails
really, but both have padded cells designed for maniacs (183).

The mood of Walter's story is so subdued that we might indeed mistake him for another Billy Pilgrim rather than the regenerated Wilbur Swain. The fact is that how Billy and Walter differ in their approach to pain and despair constitutes the essential difference between Vonnegut's heroes before and after the spiritual transfiguration of *Breakfast of Champions*. Billy retreats permanently into a schizophrenic shell that isolates and divides him against himself, whereas Walter bears his suffering nobly, resisting that defeatist voice which counsels him to make his mind "as blank as possible" (8).

Walter overcomes crazy vacillation between optimism and despair by embracing suffering rather than running from it. His willingness to suffer for others ascribes a very different symbolism to his entombment as opposed to Billy's. Billy remains dead to life, but Walter emerges reborn, not a "jailbird," but "a canary bird in the coalmine," an agent of illumination and spiritual healing. In effect, Walter inculcates the moral lesson of Wilbur Swain by bargaining "in good faith" with his surrogate parents, Sacco and Vanzetti, and with three powerful female guides who personify psychic healing and creative optimism, his wife Ruth, Sarah Wyatt, and Mary Kathleen O'Looney.

The infamous executions of Sacco and Vanzetti prove the most tormenting of Walter's life-long confrontations with public cupidity. For the impressionable fifteen-year-old Walter Starbuck, the lives of these social visionaries bare the promise of the Sermon on the Mount—the prediction by Christ that the poor in spirit would receive the Kingdom of Heaven.[1] The Christlike passion for mercy and justice in Sacco's letter to his thirteen-year-old son, written three days before his execution, represents Walter's own youthful idealism and desire for public service (xxxix).

By contrast, the poisonous words of the judge who tries Sacco and Vanzetti—venal, cruel, and bigoted—grotesquely betray Walter's faith in democratic ideals: "Did you see what I did to those anarchistic bastards the other day?" (181). Such injustice shatters Walter's trust in the authority of his elders, while the absence of public outcry undermines his idealism for years to come. He observes with disgust the complicity of the "three wise men" appointed by the government to make the executions appear just and respectable—a retired probate judge, the president of Harvard, and the president of Massachusetts Institute of Technology (180). Years later, Walter reflects, "I am compelled to wonder if wisdom has ever existed or can ever exist. Might wisdom be as impossible in this particular universe as a perpetual motion machine?" (180).

In contrasting the gentle humanity of Sacco and Vanzetti with the murderous temper that kills them, Vonnegut distinguishes sanity from insanity as never before. Society applauds the vicious executioners, but throws the idealistic socialist and union leader, Powers Hapgood, into a lunatic asylum for picketing the execution and protesting unfair labor practices. The portrayal of such perversion continues Vonnegut's indictment of America's crimes of injustice and violence against those who are without political power or great wealth—"crimes for money and power's sakes" (xxxvii), described in *God Bless You, Mr. Rose-water* as the force that turned the American dream "belly up." But as surrogate parents, Sacco and Vanzetti also provide an ingenious link between Walter's personal nightmare and questions of public guilt and responsibility.[2] The pair arrives in America the same year in which Walter's mother and father arrive (173). Walter even notes the similarity of their ages, "Father . . . nineteen . . . mother . . . twenty-one . . . Sacco . . . seventeeen . . . Vanzetti . . . twenty" (173). Sacco's son is thirteen at the time his father is executed. Walter is fifteen. That Walter goes to prison for his minor role in Watergate, a crime that itself is as irrational and totalitarian as the executions of Sacco and Vanzetti, establishes the preservation or betrayal of democratic principles as the responsibility of all individuals.

Whereas Walter's spiritual family, Sacco and Vanzetti, foster his love and respect for his fellow human beings, his real parents breed only despair and shame—alienation so great he prefers to think he is adopted (40). He lies to people that his father studied in Europe and is the curator of a famous art collection rather than a penniless chauffeur and household servant. Walter fictionalizes that he is a Nantucket man descended from whaling captains and, before that, the Vikings. The virtual adoption of Walter by his father's employer, Alexander McCone, further confuses Walter's identity, dividing him against himself and from his actual parents. Walter suggests that McCone's wealth had alienated Walter from his father in a way that he only later understood:

> In my youth . . . I had often ridden in the backseat with Mr. McCone, with a glass partition between myself and my father. The partition had not seemed strange or even suggestive to me at the time. (82)

The "partition" metaphor reveals the power of artificial wealth to divide human beings in numerous ways: from one another, from self, and from the Father of Creation.

The portrait of Vonnegut's own father in the preface to *Jailbird* bears a striking resemblance to the fictional fathers of *Jailbird* and *Slapstick*. The loss of material wealth leaves Vonnegut's father "in full retreat from life," with "only unfriendly things to say" (xii). It was not easy, Vonnegut writes, to be good friends with a man who was not particularly companionable, who was perpetually nine years old, and whose ambitions were reduced to "making mud pies all day long." Vonnegut's remarks about his mother—who "surrendered and vanished" into a spiritual void, then vanished completely (xi)—explain the intriguing nonpresence of Walter's mother in his narrative. Her absence is eerie, the most immediate and deep-rooted source of Walter's loneliness and emotional instability. While wistful about his sad and broken father, Vonnegut is disgusted with a mother so generally inept she could "not cook a breakfast or sew a button" (xiii), so addicted to wealth that its loss meant she simply "declined to go on living, since she could no longer be . . . one of the richest women in town" (xi).

Thus originates the abysmal "air of defeat," the legacy of failure and guilt which Vonnegut says became his—now Walter's—permanent life's companion (xiii).[3] He had flunked out of Cornell as a student of chemistry; he had experienced "planetary economic collapse" (xv); he had returned penniless from Europe in July of 1945 at age twenty-two, to discover his father's architectural firm had gone defunct; his mother had taken her life; and the first atomic bomb was about to be dropped on Japan. Scant allowance here for the development of a stable psychic life.

While Walter does not share Vonnegut's experience as a combat veteran, he has been as ineradicably scarred by memories of war as those who lived the terrors of the trenches and gas chambers. He sees the wreckage of war first-hand in 1945, arranging for the Nuremberg trials as a civilian employee of the Defense Department. His wife-to-be, whom he meets in Nuremberg, had emerged from a concentration camp "an asexual stick," trusting no one and uninterested in life (21). The psychological effect is as wearing as literal warfare on Walter. He pictures himself dead on a beach with a fascist bullet between his eyes (15); he sees himself a corpse in the mud on a battlefield (79); and a friend dreams of Walter with a rifle on a beach somewhere, dead in the water (156, 157). Though not a literal survivor of Dresden, Walter inherits its psychic aftermath. Fire is part of his personal and cosmic nightmare.[4] He dreams of becoming a skid-row drunk and of being doused with gasoline and set afire. In the subbasement of his executive office building, he hears sounds overhead similar to those heard by Billy Pilgrim from his underground meatlocker (12). The fact is, Walter confesses, nothing else in life was nearly so obsessive with him as "war, war, war" (28).

Walter's postwar retreat with Ruth into their "little bungalow in Chevy Chase, Maryland" bears a superficial resemblance to the "Nation of Two" formed by Howard Campbell and Helga Noth in *Mother Night*. Like Campbell, Walter deludes himself that the pursuit of personal salvation exempts him from involvement in the political madness raging around him—not the Nazism unwittingly promulgated by Campbell, but the more immediate insanity of McCarthyism. In his job with the Department of Defense, Walter is pressed by a young Congressman named Richard Nixon to explain his college association with communists and to prove his loyalty to the United States of America. Walter's testimony inadvertently implicates an acquaintance and fellow government employee named Leland Clewes, whose political career is subsequently ruined forever. It is a betrayal so demoralizing that Walter asserts, "my wings were broken forever," and "I realized I would never soar again" (42). Their names, "Starbuck and Clewes," Walter says, became as famously linked as those of "Sacco and Vanzetti" and "Laurel and Hardy" (44).

Walter's next government job literally bears out his prognosis of soured dreams and broken wings. While he himself takes seriously the upbeat title of "President's special advisor on youth affairs" (12), cynical advisors relegate Walter to the White House basement, where his presence is but once acknowledged: as the butt of a joke by the president (32). At a White House meeting with the president, Walter is so nervous he discovers he has lit four cigarettes at once. Quips the president, "we will pause in our business . . . while our special advisor on youth affairs gives us a demonstration of how to put out a campfire" (33). While Walter stays up all night drafting suggestions as to what honorable and healing things the president might say about the Kent State tragedy, the president's men above plan out burglaries and other crimes on the president's behalf.

Ultimately Walter is jailed as a Watergate conspirator, for acquiescing in hiding illegal campaign contributions, and emerges five years later more despondent and self-deprecating than ever. His self-respect is so reduced he calls himself "a piece of garbage" (2). He is dead broke—one hundred and twenty-six thousand dollars in debt to lawyers for "a futile defense" (30);[5] his wife has died of congestive heart failure, and his son no longer speaks to him, blaming his mother's death on Walter. "Woozy with disgrace" (119), "strangling on shame" (118), Walter appears close to schizophrenic. He is "petrified" (10) of the future; he feels neutered and disembodied; he hears "alien" voices speak cynically of love (9); and he sees his fate as that of a man "in the bottom of a well" (30). "I entered a period of catatonia again," he says, "staring straight ahead at nothing, and every so often clapping my old hands three times" (81).

Walter sees his condition reflected in the ominous schizophrenic imagery— fragmentation, disembodiment, isolation, and death by fire or drowning—of a story told by a fellow jailmate. The setting of the fantasy is Vicuna, a planet made uninhabitable by "patriotic bonfires" (56) and indifference to ecology. Chronological anomalies, gravitational thunderstorms, and magnetic whirlpools (symptoms of psychic disturbance) tear Vicunian families apart and scatter them far and wide in space. "Great rifts in reality were appearing everywhere" (56). The delusion that he can leave his body, dissociating himself from material cares or responsibilities, causes a Vicunian judge to escape into outer space. But his flight from reality proves as tragically illusory as Billy Pilgrim's escape to Tralfamadore. He falls in with "a flock of Turkey buzzards . . . carrion eaters" (57), members of the ruling class on earth, and winds up in a minimum security prison for white collar criminals. We are told later that the judge enters the head of Walter Starbuck (59).

Out of jail but part of one full day, Walter loses his sanity when he is subjected to still further public humiliation: on the streets of New York City he is accosted by a pitiful and seemingly deranged shopping bag lady; then he is absurdly, wrongly, arrested for theft of clarinet parts from the American Harp Company, placed in a padded cell in the basement of a police station, and left without food, water, or toilet facilities. He sobs, bounces off walls, defecates in a corner, and screams a fatalistic poem from his grammar school days: "Don't care if I do die / Do die, do die!" (189). It is this final blow to Walter's self-respect that causes him to reflect, "Sacco and Vanzetti never lost their dignity—never cracked up. Walter Starbuck finally did" (182).

The repeated association of Sacco and Vanzetti with Walter's public and personal agony establishes the ironic affirmation of Vonnegut's story. Intense and inexplicable suffering makes Walter temporarily mad, but it also completes a life-long process of spiritual chastening and growth that unites him with the martyred, universal community of sufferers and prophets including Christ, Joan of Arc, Sacco and Vanzetti, Laurel and Hardy, and Mary Kathleen O'Looney. It is the supposedly demented Mary Kathleen O'Looney, bag lady but once political activist and Walter's college sweetheart, who doubly proves Walter's salvation.

From the moment of their reunion it is apparent that the relationship between Walter and Mary Kathleen will be redemptive. She leans her shopping bag against Walter's legs "as though I were a convenient fireplug" (134). Though this ragged scarecrow in basketball shoes is worse off than Walter, *she* offers to look after him (135). Walter notes that but for her, "I might at this very moment be sleeping off a wine binge in the Bowery, while a juvenile monster soaked me in gasoline and torched me off with his Cricket lighter" (143).

Walter is shocked to learn that Mary Kathleen O'Looney is also the legendary Mrs. Jack Graham, the majority stockholder in the business conglomerate known as RAMJAC. As the latter, she rescues Walter from the police and makes him an executive vice-president of the corporation. As the former, she restores Walter's divided soul—proving by example that deep suffering may strengthen the spirit's capacity for love and service. Though fear for her life drives Mary Kathleen to hide in the dismal catacombs beneath Grand Central Station, Walter finds that "only her body was decrepit. Her voice and the soul it implied might well have belonged to what she used to be, an angrily optimistic eighteen-year-old" (154). Walter marvels that in the face of interminable grief—the death of her husband, fear for her life, time in a sanitarium, and electroshock treatments—Mary Kathleen "dared to be sane" (154), by which he means, merciful, hopeful, and socially engaged. Her double identity as Mary Kathleen O'Looney, bag lady, and Mrs. Jack Graham, secret head of RAMJAC, preserves her life, while empowering her to offset RAMJAC's brutal business practices with actions that are merciful and just.

While Mary Kathleen's indomitability revives and invigorates Walter's idealism, the fact is that Walter has never lost touch with the idealistic young man he had been, nor, through all his tests of sanity and moral fortitude, has he betrayed the moral vision of Sacco and Vanzetti and the Sermon on the Mount. Though after the war Walter's future appeared absolutely grim, he both gives and receives love by taking his wife's suffering onto himself. He is the Christological age of thirty-three when he and Ruth marry and he declares, "my unflagging optimism prevailed" (27). Walter may no longer be the utopian socialist and Roosevelt idealist who believed absolutely in the ending of war, equal distribution of wealth, and the establishment of "one big happy and peaceful family on earth" (14), but he keeps his reforming instincts alive by devoting himself to restoring Ruth's mental health. Until such time as he can become "a cautious believer in capitalistic democracy gain" (13), he vows, "My optimism became bricks and mortar and wood and nails" (29).

Walter's Watergate imprisonment results more from his refusal to add to human misery than from a betrayal of public trust. Refusing to name names as during the McCarthy hearings, he observes: "It was sickening to send another poor fool to prison. There was nothing quite like sworn testimony to make life look trivial and mean ever after" (53). Walter's contempt for brutal capitalistic power and money games sets him well apart from the jailed, unrepentant white-collar criminals around him. As he listens to real thieves boast of fortunes made through swindling poor people, Walter asks that he be remembered as "a striking exception" (52).[6]

The fact is that Walter's elected suffering—his Watergate entombment—deepens his compassion and creates a more honest and mature idealism, which is the paradoxical lesson in suffering Leland Clewes shares with him:

> Life is supposed to be a test. . . . If my life had kept going, I would have arrived in heaven never having faced any problem that wasn't as easy as pie to solve. Saint Peter would have had to say to me, "you never lived, my boy. Who can say who you are?" (136)

Walter recognizes that his own untested identity has belonged more to his father's employer, Alexander Hamilton McCone, than to himself. Walter had allowed himself to become "a robot invented and controlled by . . . McCone" (96) in exchange for a Harvard education. "I was a robot," Walter explains, "programmed to behave like a genuine aristocrat" (103).

Appropriately, Walter's clothes, reflecting his old identity, no longer fit when he is released from jail; he announces that "he may have found his clothes in a rich man's ash can" (66). The clothes no longer fit because this former

McCone clone has been transformed by suffering into a bonafide student of oppression and injustice—no mere abstract theorizer of democratic ideals, playing at revolution. Walter's early political vision was sincere but hopelessly utopian, predicated upon "simple needs" and simple antagonisms between the forces of good and evil, "Hell and heaven" (13). Sobered by five years of reality therapy, Walter is mystified by the "newborn" earth-bound self reflected in the prison mirror, but he gives himself over to the metamorphosis: "I performed what was the most obscenely intimate physical act of my life. I gave birth to a broken, querulous little old man by doing this; by putting on my civilian clothes" (65).

It is the fellow jailbird—artist Bob Fender, alias Kilgore Trout—whose multiple symbolic roles assist Walter's transformation from jailbird to canary bird.[7] Fantasist, tailor, supply clerk, and veterinarian, Fender is a lover of "subtlety and delicacy of all things Japanese" (62). His genteel humanity provides a literal "alternate universe" (63) for Walter. Fender mends the hole in the crotch of Walter's pants (restores potency), and his fantasies supply, or "tailor," Walter with a moral vision that discourages schizophrenic withdrawal. Fender's apocalyptic tale of Vicunian schizophrenic destruction presages moral disaster for those who adopt either futility or simplistic utopian solutions as ways of coping. The judge who flees the self-created madness of Vicuna may come to infiltrate Walter's mind—to "stick to his feelings and destiny" (59) until death do them part—but it is Walter's capacity for hope and caring that dominates his new identity. There are no Titans or Tralfamadores on Walter's mental horizon, and the earth-bound role cast for him by Mary Kathleen O'Looney will further shape the Shamanlike identity for which he is headed.[8]

While characters such as Paul Proteus, Howard Campbell, and Eliot Rosewater invent false selves to escape from suffering and responsibility, Mary Kathleen O'Looney masks her identity as head of RAMJAC to operate creatively and humanely in the real world. In short, her schizophrenia is not moribund but crafty and practical—a necessary response to those who would murder her and take control of the RAMJAC corporation. References to her as Christ and as God establish her spiritual nature, but as opposed to such prophets of doom as Bokonon and Winston Niles Rumfoord, Mary Kathleen's holiness is authentic and efficacious. She uses "cosmic powers" (88) to achieve economic justice and to reward human virtue. She thwarts RAMJAC greed by returning profits to the American people; and she redeems the lives of those she admires as honest and kind by assigning them leadership roles in the RAMJAC corporation. It is thus that Walter becomes vice-president of the RAMJAC Down Home Records Division—fulfilling what the chief executive, Arpad Leen, says is RAMJAC's purpose of "putting good people where they can use their talents to the fullest" (207).

The giant corporate machinery of RAMJAC calls to mind such malevolent, spirallike systems of control as EPICAC, the electronic computing machine in *Player Piano,* and Magnum Opus in *Sirens of Titan.* RAMJAC employees are directed to "acquire, acquire, acquire" (229), an end achieved by absorbing or overrunning any business which threatens its corporate goals. RAMJAC owns 19 percent of everything in the country, from match book companies, taxicab fleets, and furniture rentals to major publishing houses, television networks, and banking firms. In the course of Walter's story, RAMJAC gobbles up the *New York Times,* MacDonald's Hamburgers, and the largest catfood company in the world. The second largest conglomerate in the so-called free world was only half its size. RAMJAC's power is so pervasive it even helps topple weaker, smaller foreign governments.

The secret to RAMJAC's success is cold efficiency and complete indifference to human suffering. Its businesses, Walter observes, "were as unaffected by the joys and tragedies of human beings as the rain that fell on the night that . . . Sacco and Vanzetti died in an electric chair" (231). He notices that RAMJAC's business practices were as murderous as the battlefields of World War I—both "places of hideously dangerous work, where a few men could supervise the wasting of millions of lives in the hopes of making money" (175). By associating the predatory nature of RAMJAC—its materialist lusts and absence of feeling—with the deaths of Sacco and Vanzetti and the slaughterhouse of war, Walter suggests the inevitable, symbiotic relationship of all those public and private horrors that burden his conscience: the Great Depression, the Cuyahoga Massacre, the Nazi concentration camps, the McCarthy hearings, Hiroshima, and Watergate. References to symbolic clocks enforce the message that such soulless mechanisms as RAMJAC stimulate and perpetuate the age-old impulse to violence, cruelty, and injustice that underlies mankind's inhumanity to man. Walter's wife characterizes the Nuremberg trials as "the closing chapter to ten thousand years of madness and greed" (25). As she speaks, a four-hundred-year-old clock strikes, as if confirming her indictment. The clock's spirallike edifice consists of robots representing centuries of world violence. The clock had stopped briefly; now it goes again. Billy Pilgrim might have said, "So it goes."[9]

It is from the factory clock tower of Cuyahoga Iron and Steel that RAMJAC executives view dispassionately the slaughter of protesting workers on Christmas morning. Aided by the police, the National Guard, city administrators, company guards, and Pinkerton agents, four sharpshooters "primed for action" kill fourteen people outright, and wound twenty-three others. The massacre drives the Guard's commander mad, and Alexander McCone, the traumatized son of the factory's owner and Walter's Harvard benefactor, develops a machine-like stammer and devotes the rest of his life to atoning by donating to the fine arts.

While RAMJAC's most obvious and immediate victims are those with little money or power, its cruelty and aggression kill or gradually drive mad members of its own elite. The wealthy family of one of Walter's sweethearts named Sarah Wyatt, a clock heiress, kills fifty female employees through the negligent use of radioactive radium. But Sarah's grandfather commits suicide, and both she and her father develop schizophrenic tendencies out of guilt and remorse (100, 107). The daughter of one of the women killed by radium poisoning later rises to the top of the RAMJAC spiral, its conelike rim, to be known as Mary Kathleen O'Looney. But Mary Kathleen attempts to reverse the inhumanity of RAMJAC's insidious spirallike mechanism, caused by brutality at the top and passivity at the bottom. The Vicunian judge who represents moral escapism is described as "encased in cone-shaped armor," which secretes a glue from the "rim of its cone" (55). The verbal associations of McCone, clone, and cone demonstrate Vonnegut's use of word play to subvert conventional patterns of perception and behavior. Notably, Alexander McCone, a static, machinelike being who literally sputters like a motor, is poor with words. His neurotic obsession with power and money structures turns him into "a bumbling booby of totally blocked language" (8). Walter Starbuck's use of language becomes increasingly inventive as he dismantles the conelike prison of his McCone identity, and authors a more holistic and creative self.

Sarah's grandmother says that "what was insane" (96) was the way members of the financially elite such as the Wyatts and McCones saw their wealth as divinely appointed—"the way we all imagined that God was watching, and simply adoring us, guaranteeing us all seats at his right hand" (96). Another story by Robert Fender Trout satirizes the delusion that the spiritually elect are identifiable by their material worth. To get into heaven, the people in Fender's story must prove at the Pearly Gates that back on earth they have exploited fully the economic opportunities God's angels had offered. God's inquisitors are former certified public accountants or investment counselors or business managers. The auditors find that Albert Einstein is miserably unfit for heaven as a result of his disdain of wealth and material goods. He had sinned by failing to exploit the numerous investment opportunities opened to him in the uranium market, before telling the world that $E = MC^2$. Einstein has been, they conclude, "asleep at the switch" (185). A notably stupid and callous God thus threatens to deprive Einstein of his most prized possession throughout eternity—his fiddle—if he continues to challenge God's right to accept or deny people entrance into heaven based upon financial worth on earth.

Walter recognizes such cruelty as less divine than human, residing more in the earthly designs of RAMJAC executives than in the mind of God Almighty. Mary Kathleen O'Looney's position as majority stock holder of RAMJAC may lead Arpad Leen to confuse her with God, but Walter knows that as "a mistress of disguise" who "could be anyone" (192), her spiritual potential is decidedly, if ambiguously, human. An indirect reference to

RAMJAC employees as Tralfamadorians exposes the delusion that human destiny is controlled by absolute forces from above. In a RAMJAC limousine, Walter becomes hypnotized by a pretend steering wheel attached to the glove compartment. The physical attributes of the imaginary wheel are exactly those of the Tralfamadorians described in *Slaughterhouse-Five:* a green object protruding from a shaft attached to suction cups. But Walter is far more prepared to resist Tralfamadorian fatalism or messianic callings than such earlier heroes as Paul Proteus, Malachi Constant, Jonah, Eliot Rosewater, and Billy Pilgrim. Descent into the catacombs (his own underworld) teaches Walter more about the Evil Larkin (evil lurking) in himself—his capacity for moral escapism—and puts him in touch with the "secret purpose of RAMJAC" (122), the complex potential of the human spirit for good or for evil.

RAMJAC is no more an evil empire than a certified paradise; the supposed paranoid bag lady, Mary Kathleen, can inject sanity into RAMJAC's soulless, mechanistic processes by using the raw economic power at her disposal to achieve concrete reforms and by putting good people in positions of power and influence. Though one of her appointees, Leland Clewes, pulls down one hundred thousand dollars a year at RAMJAC, much of the money goes to the Foster Parents Program, a scheme that provides support for individual children in unfortunate circumstances in many parts of the world (231). By appointing Walter Starbuck an executive vice-president of RAMJAC, Mary Kathleen performs a double humanitarian service: she advances the public good by providing RAMJAC with a leader devoted to honesty and kindness, and she gives Walter's long-frustrated drive for human service practical direction. Appropriate to what Kathryn Hume calls *Jailbird*'s "Christian mythic exostructure,"[10] Mary Kathleen's suffering and death make Walter's salvation possible. Though she dies in Walter's arms weary of trying to improve the world, Walter rises from her underground tomb to assume her spiritual identity and to carry on her moral commitments.[11] Though Walter suffers no grandiose illusions or messianic calling, he declares that, "I was in an extraordinary position theologically with respect to millions of employees" (230).

Walter recognizes that RAMJAC's operations are so vast, diverse, and impersonal that the good he can do is limited to minor reforms, yet the fact that RAMJAC's top executive confuses Walter's identity with that of Mary Kathleen informs him that he can be as powerful as "I wanted to be" (211), and he determines, in Kathryn Hume's words, to show "what an individual can do to alleviate the pain inherent in the human condition."[12] Corporate infighting drives Walter "mad" at times; bureaucratic inefficiency diverts much of Mary Kathleen's legacy away from the people; other greedy conglomerates threaten RAMJAC businesses; and Walter himself faces a third jail term for unlawfully hiding Mary Kathleen's will from those who would thwart her plans for economic reform. But in answer to Walter's question, "How well did I do at

RAMJAC?" (227), he can boast of significant sponsorship of the arts, and of singlehandedly extending the moral life of RAMJAC by placing more good people in positions of executive power.

Clearly Walter Starbuck inherits the grace of human awareness of *Breakfast of Champions,* and by reaffirming his youthful idealism, he keeps faith with Wilbur Swain's efforts to improve the lives of others. It is spring and raining when Walter asserts his inviolable belief in the "Family of Man."[13] "My idealism did not die," he says (14); "I still believe that peace and plenty and happiness can be worked out some way." It is the voice of Vonnegut's canary bird, the Shaman, who denounces public apathy: "the total lack of seriousness . . . about what's really going on, what's going to happen next, or how we ever got into such a mess" (238). And it is the compassionate, heroic spirit of Sacco and Vanzetti resurrected in Walter that responds thus to Nixon when the president asks Walter why he was so ungrateful to the American economic system: "Why? The Sermon on the Mount, sir" (241).

Walter learns to deal with schizophrenic suffering directly from the three women he describes as "more virtuous, braver about life, and closer to the secrets of the universe" than he could ever be (9). Kathryn Hume locates the increased affirmation of *Jailbird* in Walter's more productive relationship with these women. She perceives that having exorcised the mother who "so contaminated his inner picture of women," Vonnegut can now accept the female principle in himself and espouse "a more active response to the hurts of the world."[14] The prominence of the creative force as female in *Slapstick* and *Jailbird* may even be an attempt by Vonnegut to atone for what Walter calls "the publication of some of the most scurrilous books about women ever written" (9).

Hume's suggestion that Starbuck's success with women corresponds to Vonnegut's own heightened creativity carries over to Walter as well. Walter achieves his metamorphosis from jailbird to canary bird through Wilbur Swain's awareness that reality is a fictional construct—a "perpetual motion machine" (180) whose meanings are self-created and undergo constant transformation. Both Wilbur's and Walter's autobiographies are cast in the form of dreams, realities re-formed and humanized through the creative imagination: Walter refers to the world of his narrative as "a game our dreams remade" (230), and his story is a "dream of a jailbird" (192), "my dream" (194), in which "anything was possible" (191).

Walter's awareness of the possibilities of existential authorship in life as in art comes across in metafictional references to life as "theatre"(140) and to himself as an actor/creator. Walter plays with the knowledge that he can author humane or destructive parts for himself, or for RAMJAC, by drawing contrasts between spiritual realities perverted by machines and machines of destruction converted to good. He refers to the electric chair as the "invention of a dentist" (xxxviiii) and observes a fighter plane that "destroyed enough energy to heat one hundred homes for a thousand years" (3). But he also testifies that what was once "military" became "beautiful" through poetic recreation (222); and it is the former counsel for Joseph McCarthy, Roy M. Cohn, who ushers Walter from jail. The Cuyahoga Massacre exemplifies human brutality and injustice, but is also "an invention, a mosaic" of tales of historical riots composed by Walter or Vonnegut, to inspire human compassion and awareness (xxi). Walter realizes, in short, the intimation of Paul Proteus that the most "beautiful peonies" may be grown in "pure cat excrement." As an artist of positive suggestions, as well as an artist of suffering, Walter demonstrates new creative potency through the playful, self-conscious manipulation of illusion and reality. The story's index mixes real and imaginary names, a clue to the symbolic value of Walter's title as Doctor of Mixology. Walter acknowledges that most of the speeches in his story "are fuzzy reconstructions" (110), but that he himself "was not at all uncomfortable with the lies" he has told on behalf of self-rehabilitation. "I was pure phlogiston," he says, "an imaginary element of long ago" (95).

The redemptive significance of Walter's ascending creative self is conveyed through the wedding gift Walter gives to Ruth, a wood carving of an old person with hands pressed together in prayer. It is, he stresses, a multidimensional creation ("my invention") whose attitude of hope and love he himself has designed (28). The next incarnations of Vonnegut's hero, Rudy Waltz, Leon Trout, Rabo Karabekian, and Eugene Debs Hartke, move closer yet to that final artistic identity by which they merge with their creator, Kurt Vonnegut.

10

Deadeye Dick: **The Resolution of Vonnegut's Creative Schizophrenia**

Choose life, that you may live, you and your descendants.

Deuteronomy 30:19

On the other hand the great works of art, those that are not afraid of admitting the Unconscious as a collaborator, *are "social" in the most magnificent sense.*

Hans Sachs, *The Creative Unconscious*

From Vonnegut's prefaces alone it seems clear the author experienced the tragic disharmony of family relationships that turn his child protagonists into emotional grotesques. In *Deadeye Dick* (1982), Vonnegut devotes another entire preface to explaining the symbolic correspondence between personal traumatic experience and the ailing unconscious of his protagonist, Rudy Waltz. "The neutered pharmacist who tells the tale is my declining sexuality," Vonnegut explains. "The crime he committed in childhood is all the bad things I have done" (xiii). Rudy's and Vonnegut's cathartic accounts of guilty, blood-stained pasts converge in the Grand Hotel Oloffson in Port au Prince, Haiti, where both tell their stories. Vonnegut explains that the hotel is haunted by a ghost, possibly because of "an uneasy conscience about something it did or saw done when the cottage was an operating room" (xi). The identity of the ghost is problematical. Its evocation suggests not only the guilt and anger of marines who died while protecting American financial interests in Haiti, but all the sinning and sinned upon ghosts in Vonnegut's and Rudy's pasts.[1] The common identity of Rudy and Vonnegut climaxes in the novel's epilogue; both appear as artist-priests with the power to raise ghosts from their graves (227).

In his book of personal essays, *Wampeters, Foma, and Granfalloons,* Vonnegut confesses that "One thing *Breakfast* did for me was to bring right to the surface my anger with my parents for not being happier than they were."[2] But it is more than just anger that surfaces in *Deadeye Dick,* which presents a view of childhood so perverted by parental morbidity, boorish insensitivity, and spiritual vacuity that its immediate victim, Rudy Waltz, emerges from adolescence with "no more feelings than a rubber ball" (144). The most visible source of Rudy Waltz's suffering—the tip of the iceberg—is the fact that he becomes a double murderer at the age of twelve: on Mother's day, 1944, he fires an unaimed round from a rifle in his father's gun collection and accidentally kills a pregnant woman doing housework a mile away.[3] Rudy is jailed, viciously beaten by the police, bathed in ink,[4] caged, displayed to selected visitors who are encouraged to punch him out, and nearly persuaded by Patrolman Squires to kill himself with another gun. Lawsuits from the bereaved husband, Mr. Metzger, ruin the Waltz family financially; and Midland citizens bestow on Rudy the mocking nickname that gives the book its title, Deadeye Dick.

From the second his "peephole" opens in 1932 to the explosion of the neutron bomb that depopulates his hometown, Rudy's is a world of perpetual injustice, violence, and death. He encounters the same grisly discoveries, fears, and insecurities marking the traumatic transition from innocence to experience as do such previous spiritual orphans as Huck Finn, Nick Adams, and Quentin Compson—each of whom also has a notoriously weak, absent, or impotent father who cripples the child's search for personal identity.[5] The theme of absent, impotent, or fragmented parental authority goes back at least as far as *The Odyssey,*[6] and certainly this is what turns Rudy Waltz into a potential schizophrenic. Rudy bears out the view that those who appear vulnerable to schizophrenia as adults are usually people with troubled childhoods, children unusually sensitive, easily hurt, and particularly responsive to the feelings of others. Rudy also fits the profile of patients whose relatives have been hospitalized for schizophrenia.[7] His mother, father, and brother are all certified to be crazy at some point in the story. Still more pertinent to Rudy's case is the fact that such people often gravitate to the arts.

When Rudy says he thinks he would have had a very different sort of soul if his home had not been so "vast" (9), he might well have said so "vastly schizophrenic." Vonnegut describes himself in *Breakfast of Champions* as a physically and emotionally warped human being standing directly beneath a "clock my father designed" (3). The narrator's childhood home in *Deadeye Dick,* the scene of endless trauma, is structured like a "human watchtower" (8); insanity is as sure to come round to him as to his mother and father and their parents. Rudy learns from his mother that his father's mother was "as crazy as a bedbug" (9). Rudy's father, a man whose artistic ambitions are perverted into a passion for beautiful guns and a flamboyant enthusiasm for Adolph Hitler, is depicted as someone who has lost all touch with reality (8). He is a dangerous presence who has turned Rudy's childhood home into an inferno of violence. Rudy observes,

> Many people found our house spooky, and the attic in fact was full of evil when I was born. It housed a collection of more than three hundred antique and modern firearms. Father had bought them during his and Mother's six-month honeymoon in Europe in 1922. Father thought them beautiful, but they might as well have been copperheads and rattlesnakes. They were murder. (11)

By the end of the novel Rudy's mother suffers a literal personality derangement, but Rudy notes that "she was never what you would call demonstrative" (93). He calls her "a cold and aggressively helpless old bat" (163). She is the first person Rudy encounters after he shoots Mrs. Metzger, and he opines that "She wasn't about to hug me, or cover my inky head with kisses" (93). When Rudy's brother, Felix, had gone off to war, she had shaken Felix's hand by way of encouragement and then blown a kiss to him when his train was a half a mile away (92–93). She is so incapable of imagining what Rudy might want that, after he shoots Mrs. Metzger, she does not even get out of the doorway so he can come inside. "I wanted to get into my bed and pull the covers over my head. That was my plan. That is still pretty much my plan" (93).

Consistent with this impulse to hide from pain, the most potentially deadly ingredients in Rudy's family's emotional legacy are persistent morbidity and lack of will. His father, the master of grand gestures and attitudes but finally as collapsible as a paper cup, kept going at the end only because all that money, which could buy almost anything, "kept coming in and coming in" (95). Emma, Rudy's mother, becomes a cynical, hick-town Voltaire near the end of her life. An autopsy would reveal several small tumors in her head that would account for the change in personality (94). It is ironically appropriate that Rudy's father should die "in cold storage" of double pneumonia and that his mother's character should be emblematized by severe frostbite; these conditions occur as a result of Midland City's terrible winter blizzard, a storm so severe that Rudy was "expecting to find bodies as hard and stiff as andirons" (160). This "dead storage" (160)—Rudy's term—is an apt metaphor for the living death of coldness and lovelessness that had claimed his parents long before.

Rudy too is in danger of becoming so much dead storage. During his time in the cage, he concluded that the best thing he could do for himself and others was to want nothing, to be as unenthusiastic and unmotivated as possible so that he would never again hurt anyone. "To put it another way," says Rudy, "I wasn't to touch anything on this planet, man, woman, child, artifact, animal, vegetable, or mineral—since it was very likely to be connected to a push-pull detonator and an explosive charge"(112). Rudy's paranoia, his need to withdraw into some cozy, womblike hiding place, is understandable. Drowning in shame and guilt, believing he has ruined the lives of his family, he decides he is a defective human being, one who should no longer be on this planet. Anybody who would fire a rifle over the rooftops of a city, he concludes, has to have a screw loose: "If I had begun to reply to the people, I think that's what I would have babbled over and over again: 'I have a screw loose somewhere' " (79).

While at first it seems that Rudy's only response to the endless aggression and fear that have tormented him from birth is withdrawal into a schizophrenic shell, the cultivation of a deliberate death-in-life existence, another, healthier impulse has been working in him as well. When his high school English teacher asks him to share his thoughts with her, Rudy maintains his resolve to remain isolated from the outer world: "It seemed safest and wisest to be as cold as ice to her, and to everyone" (110). Nevertheless, Miss Shoup discovers Rudy's "divine spark" in his essay on "The Midland City Person I Most Admire," and encourages him to write. She judges his essay on the mythical kingdom of Katmandu to be "the finest piece of writing by a student that she had ever seen in forty years of teaching.... 'You really must become a writer,' she said, 'And you must get out of this deadly town, too—as soon as you can' " (109).

However, Rudy's father exerts his most destructive influence in thwarting Rudy's deepest, creative instincts. Just as he had repressed his own artistic aspirations,[8] he counsels Rudy to "plug your ears with wax whenever anybody tells you you have a creative gift of any kind" (112). Rudy explains:

> The night I told Father I wanted to be a writer . . . he ordered me to become a pharmacist instead, which I did. "Be a pharmacist. Go with the grain of your heritage! There is no artistic talent in this family, nor will there be. . . . We are business people, and that's all we can ever hope to be." So I became a pharmacist, but I never gave up on being a writer too. (116–17)[9]

Thus does Rudy acquire that agonizingly divided soul, that separation of his several selves that eventually causes Howard Campbell of *Mother Night* to commit suicide. As long as he succumbs to his father's fatal advice, Rudy's yearning, creative self will be neutralized by the "dead storage" self created by his parents. By deciding to play dead, to muffle the cry of conscience with a variety of anesthetizing devices, he will become an emotional vacuum as defeating as the misery he seeks to escape. Within his self-spun cocoon, Rudy lacks sufficient will and moral strength to love or be loved, or to nurture his creativity.

Rudy is well aware that he has within him these separate, warring identities. "It was the Deadeye Dick in me," he says, "who felt he had to nourish all those people back to health" (130). Guilt-stricken, claiming to be a "social leper" (108), Rudy becomes not only one of his family's walking dead but their personal servant as well:

They were zombies. They were in bathrobes and bedroom slippers all day long—unless company was expected. They stared into the distance a lot. Sometimes they would hug each other lightly and sigh. They were the walking dead. (108)

Rudy goes shopping for food right after school, and he starts supper as soon as he gets home. He does the laundry in a broken-down Maytag wringer-washer, serves supper to his parents and occasional guests, cleans the day's dishes afterwards, does his homework until he can't keep his eyes open any longer, and then collapses into bed, often sleeping in his clothing. At six in the morning he gets up, does the ironing and vacuuming, serves breakfast to his parents, puts a hot lunch in the oven for them, makes the beds, and goes to school.

None of this leaves him much time for nurturing the artist within, and his decision "to go with the grain," to become a pharmacist, distances him further than ever from his artistic self. Still living with his parents, he goes straight from pharmacy school to a midnight-to-dawn job at Schramm's Drugstore six days a week. The job is dangerous because Schramm's is the only business establishment open all night, a "sort of lighthouse for lunatics and outlaws" (122). Far more dangerous than the threat of physical assault, however, is the enemy within Rudy that encourages him to pretend to be invisible, to avoid his pain, and to offer "pills for everything" (165) to the schizophrenics and near-schizophrenics who wander into the store. Dispensing drugs is also a part of the family legacy. Otto, the father, had inherited the "Saint Elmo's Remedy" fortune. This quack medicine was made of grain alcohol dyed purple, flavored with cloves and sarsaparilla root, and laced with opium and cocaine. "As the joke goes, it was absolutely harmless unless discontinued" (2).

Rudy is keenly aware that the amphetamines he dispenses are frequently abused, and that abuse creates extreme psychological dependence, often resulting in severe social disability and personality change, and can lead to a psychosis that is often indistinguishable from schizophrenia.[10] He notes that his father's old friend Hitler was one of the first to experience the benefits of amphetamines, and with bigger and bigger doses remained "bright eyed and bushy tailed" (122) right up to the end. Closer to home, Rudy believes amphetamines caused the suicide of Celia Hoover and the "drug-inspired madness" (191) of his brother Felix. Rudy's nemesis is Dr. Jerry Mitchell, who builds a lucrative practice on the principle that nobody should be ill-at-ease when pills are so readily available. Dr. Mitchell encourages Celia, his own wife, and countless others to destroy their minds and spirits with drugs. He used to torture cats and dogs, saying he was performing scientific experiments.

Rudy's contempt for amphetamine abuse does not extend to the more subtly mind-numbing activities he uses to dull his own pain. Still pretending to be invisible, he cannot get waited on in a restaurant because nobody sees him. Refusing to love or be loved even at the age of fifty, thirty-eight years after the shooting, he thinks he may possibly be a homosexual. But he can't be sure because he has "never made love to anyone" (99). As late as the death of his mother, the police conclude that he is not sociable. And, while he criticizes his brother for purchasing a Rolls Royce to soothe an aching conscience, Rudy admits that he derived an indecent degree of pleasure from his Mercedes.

Rudy's early creativity is as dangerous as those opium-laced amphetamines that destroy so many of his acquaintances. We learn that his father's penchant for romantic fairy tales and myths causes Rudy to fantasize his murderous home environment as an enchanted kingdom of the imagination (44). It is thus "second nature" for Rudy to write his high school essay about a place where no one ever tried to hurt anybody else, and where everybody was happy and nobody grew old. Given the subject, "The Midland City Person I Most Admire," Rudy chooses a man with a past as remarkably traumatic as his own. Childless, his wife dead from cancer, his family dairy farm bankrupt, John Fortune "suddenly took off for the Himalayas in search of far higher happiness and wisdom than was available, evidently, in Midland City, Ohio" (32). His goal was the imaginary Garden of Eden called Shangri-La, in the tiny, isolated country of Katmandu described by James Hilton in his novel *Lost Horizon*. Rudy's dramatized version of John Fortune's adventure clarifies the escapism that links Rudy's interest in Shangri-La with that of John Fortune. The actor playing John Fortune asks Rudy to help him interpret Fortune's compulsive quest. He never says why he wants to get to Katmandu, he tells Rudy.

> All these people either try to help him get to Katmandu or keep him from getting to Katmandu, and I keep thinking, "Why the hell should anybody care whether he gets to Katmandu or not? Why not Tierra del Fuego? Why not Dubuque?"

Rudy explains that his hero is looking for Shangri-La but appears mystified when the actor tells him he has written this into the play thirty-four times. The actor has counted, he explains, because he finds these recurrences rather obsessive—"especially if the person who says it says practically nothing else" (131). The actor asks Rudy to tell him again about the great death scene in Katmandu, in Shangri-La. He is bothered by the fact that he knows he is sick and dying while still professing to believe he is in Shangri-La.

> Another thing I say all through the play is that nobody dies in Shangri-La. But here I'm dying, so how can I be in Shangri-La . . . Seventeen times . . . seventeen times I say that nobody dies in Shangri-La.

When Rudy says he will have to think about that, the actor answers, "You mean this is the first time you thought about it?" (133).

This is indeed the first time Rudy confronts the contradictions in his dream of utopia. Until now the source of his compulsive search for refuge from life's storms in an illusory paradise like Shangri-La has befuddled him. He can only say, "I seemed to know less about the play than anybody. If I was asked about this line or that one, I was likely to say something like, 'My goodness—I wonder what I meant by that' " (130). But what Rudy knows at the time his play is produced and what he knows when he begins to tell us his life's story from his residence in Port-au-Prince, Haiti, at the age of fifty, are literally and spiritually worlds apart. The essential narrative principle of this novel, of Rudy's story, is the most important key to its meaning, which is that it is told in retrospect by a narrator who after great struggle with his own soul has learned to deal with his compulsions and to recreate himself through art. When Rudy tells us that "Katmandu was my one fling away from Midland City, my one experience, until now, with inhabiting a place where I was not Deadeye Dick" (106), he means that he has freed himself from the deadly influence of his parents, from his guilt-ridden past, and from the lure of escapist fantasies. In effect, the writing of his life's story allows him to rid himself of the very illusions that inspired him to write *Katmandu* in the first place. Unlike John Fortune and munitions maker, art-lover Fred Barry, who go to their graves drunk as ever on utopian dreams, Rudy is drug free. Described as half eagle, half cow (156, 157), sick with loneliness, Fred Barry dreams of giving south-eastern Ohio its own Taj Mahal in the form of a performing arts center, the same southwestern Ohio destroyed by a neutron bomb and appearing as lifeless as a polar ice cap (174). John Fortune dies of double pneumonia in his search for absolute peace of mind, but nevertheless offers as his final message from the Taj Mahal, "To all my friends and enemies in the buckeye state. Come on over. There's room for everybody in Shangri-La" (120). "They were words," says Rudy, "that so much deserved to be spoken in a theatre" (118). It is from this illusion-free perspective that Rudy declares, "It was Deadeye Dick, tormented by guilt in Midland City, who had found old John Fortune's quite pointless death in Katmandu, as far away from his hometown as possible, somehow magnificent. He himself yearned for distance and death" (130). Rudy observes that once upon a time even educated men and women believed that contentment might be "hidden . . . on the map, like the treasure of Captain Kid" (113). In the interim between the writing of *Katmandu* and his residence in Haiti, Rudy has evidently researched the facts underlying this fool's paradise, and can say, "I agree now that *Katmandu* was a ridiculous play" (118).

Whether in the form of Oedipal fantasies or an imaginary paradise like Shangri-La, Rudy has learned that "Beauty seldom comes cheap" (214). Through with fantasized nirvanas, Rudy declares that "this" is as much Shangri-La as anywhere:

> Here in Haiti, I have begun to verbalize that sentiment, so intolerable to me when I was a
> teenager. . . . In any event . . . I have in conversation given Midland City this code name . . .
> Shangri-La. (114–115)

Maturity teaches Rudy that he himself must create peace and harmony, a lesson bodied forth in his existential vision of life and art as a tabula rasa. Rudy observes that the morning after *Katmandu* opened and closed, he and Felix flew over a landscape as white and blank as their lives. The image simultaneously suggests bombed-out Midland City and the desolation of Rudy's past. It also enforces the view that one can author one's own existence rather than submit to the tyranny of prestructured systems of control, closed scripts in which one serves as a robot character in someone else's drama, that, for instance, of God, parents, government, or the military.

Critical to Rudy's moral and literary evolution, he also learns that unless human beings understand that the smallest acts of aggression are connected to the world's larger, bloodier deeds, we are doomed to complete "the suicidal flight we are on" (151). The treachery of romantic literary illusions, the deaths of human beings used to create the Taj Mahal, the murder of Eloise Metzger, Rudy's father's gun collection, Fred Barry's armaments business, Hitler's annihilation of ten million Jews, the destruction of Midland City by a neutron bomb explosion, even the shooting out of Bernard Ketchum's eye with a beebee gun—all are part of the lunatic aggression that perpetually threatens human life and has brought the planet to the edge of nuclear annihilation. Benjamin De Mott argues that Vonnegut sees these acts of violence as "causeless," that irony, paradox, or incongruous juxtaposition are not on "Vonnegut's map." Like Christopher Lehmann-Haupt, De Mott wonders what all the guilt in the novel is about.[11] Is it that the guilt of anyone is visited upon everything else, asks Lehmann-Haupt?[12] What is the possible connection, asks De Mott, between the child of a gun-loving father who emerges as a double murderer and human beings who take satisfaction in creating neutron bombs? De Mott dismisses Rudy's father as "an opinionated parent."[13] The interconnected horrors of the novel are, in fact, called "random," "accidental," or "innocent." No one takes responsibility for the various acts of violence—except Rudy, and a group of farmers in Midland City. Rudy recognizes the aggression behind the creation of weapons of all kinds and sizes that sooner or later go bang, accidentally or on purpose, like the bomb that depopulates Midland City. Like Walter Starbuck, a scapegoat and Shaman, Rudy possesses the awareness, imagination, and nerve to bear the sins and the shame of his family, his nation, and his world. Rudy knows that, however subtly connected, the madness that murders innocent women, makes armaments, drops bombs, assassinates statesmen, and throws Christians to the lions emanates from mankind's heart of darkness; and he knows that it is the denial of responsibility for such violence—seeing it as "playful," "accidental," or "innocent"—that makes the deadly spiral circular and unending.[14] Ultimately Rudy decides that the bombing of Midland City was not as accidental as imagined. He guesses that the government decided to test the bomb in a city they believed nobody cared about, "where people weren't doing all that much with their lives anyhow (234).[15] The satire is double-edged. The government is insane for rationalizing destruction under the guise of "friendly bombs" (230) and for believing that the people of Midland City are so boring and uncreative that they can be slain without inspiring long-term regrets. But it is also true that the automated, uncreative environment of Midland City produces an emotional void that prepares for the physical destruction of the bomb. Rudy learns that a hundred thousand people have died in Midland City, but that every one of the television sets in the new Holiday Inn, all the telephones, and the ice cube maker behind the bar are still operable. He asks, "Have the people of Midland City lost anything they loved?" (34). Vonnegut writes that well before the neutron bomb hit Midland City, "the city was already dead . . . the planet itself was breaking down. It was going to blow itself up sooner or later" (197).

On its social level, *Deadeye Dick* is Vonnegut's personal antinuclear weapons protest. It is Vonnegut as well as the husband of Eloise Metzger who asserts: "We cannot get rid of mankind's fleetingly wicked wishes. We can get rid of the machines that make them come true. I give you a holy word: DISARM" (87, 97). But Vonnegut does more than propagandize against aggression and the existence of weapons of all kind; the subtlety of imagery and symbolism that connects and explains the allegedly random violence makes this one of Vonnegut's most ingeniously crafted novels. Again it is largely the use of spiral and clock imagery that unifies the novel's myriad acts of aggression. The dominant spiral is the "conical slate roof" of Rudy's childhood home (130), which implicates a world of violence and death, a historical roller-coaster for which all bear responsibility. It reaches back at least as far as ancient Rome, and forward to the devastation of Midland City by the neutron bomb. "Our father's home had a conical slate roof," Rudy explains.

> It had a naked skeleton inside of noble oak beams . . . a little piece of Europe in Southwestern Ohio, a stone-by-stone replica of a structure in an illustration in her [mother's] favorite book of German fairy tales. An art historian explained that the original might have been a medieval granary built on the ruins of a Roman watchtower from the time of Julius Caesar. Caesar was murdered two thousand years ago. Think of that. (11)

Immediately under the conical slate roof is the father's gun room, which houses hundreds of antique and modern firearms Rudy's father thinks beautiful. The guns are as deadly as the larger bomb that destroys Midland City. As Rudy says, "They were murder" (11). He notes that this father's guns, including the fatal Springfield, had been donated to a scrap drive during the war, along with the weather vane. "They might," he says, "have killed a lot of people when they were melted up and made into shells or bombs or hand grenades or whatever" (167).

We are told that the innocent-looking radioactive mantelpiece that kills Rudy's mother comes from a scrap heap in back of an ornamental concrete company outside Cincinnati. The cement that went into the mantelpiece was traced all the way back to Oak Ridge, Tennessee, where pure Uranium 235 was produced for the bomb dropped on Hiroshima. The government had allowed the cement to be sold, says Rudy, despite knowing its danger: "The government was about as careless as a half wit boy up in a cupola with a loaded Springfield rifle—on Mother's Day" (215). The word "scrap" connects the final murderous effects of the guns that belong to Rudy's father with the death of Mrs. Metzger, as well as with Rudy's mother. It is also toward the conical roof of Rudy's home that two youthful immigrants head, Gino and Mario Martino, having come to America the Beautiful to escape injustice, cruelty, and violence. Yet the realities symbolized by the conical roof suggest horrors as great as those the youths have fled. They are robbed at knife point by American hobos, who take their suitcases and all their clothes. "They were lucky," says Rudy, "they didn't have their throats cut for fun" (15). The conical slate roof, the peak of the cone, is rightly identified as "the hellish Fujiyama, the sacred volcano of Japan, glistening white like snow" (153). The image of *snow* also unifies various forms of violence. Rudy's parents freeze in a snow storm, and snow links the holocaust of Dresden with the disaster in Midland City (158, 160).

It is only at first that this drug dispenser cum creative writer fails to resolve his psychic dilemma. Nearly every night some prankster calls Rudy at the drugstore to ask him if he is Deadeye Dick; "I always was, I always will be," Rudy replies (125). While stifled, however, neither Rudy's conscience nor his creativity has come to a halt: "My conscience was active as I worked" (184), he claims, and when a playwriting contest comes to his attention, "The next thing I knew, I was back in the stock room, pecking away on the rattletrap Corona portable typewriter we used for making labels. I was writing a new draft of *Katmandu*. And I won first prize" (76). As a result, after dinner one night Rudy at the age of twenty-seven addresses a declaration of personal independence to his parents.

While the play opens and closes in a single night, Rudy's process of exorcism and liberation is not a failure. He faces and frees himself from tormenting family ghosts, triumphs over the Deadeye Dick in himself, and enables the creative artist to ascend. "To have been a perfectly uninvolved person," he says, "a perfect neuter, I should never have written a play" (176). "I was startled not to be Deadeye Dick anymore." He declares, "I felt like a gas which had been confined in a labeled bottle for years, and which now had been released into the atmosphere" (130). The play allows Rudy to come to terms with his blood-stained, guilt-ridden past. The curtain rises on *Katmandu* just as Rudy's father dies back in Midland City; and Rudy finally acknowledges that, while his father never murdered anybody, he was still a terrible father to have (145). With reference to Lacan, John Bleikaster explains that successful initiation requires eradication of the father, at least subconsciously, as a prerequisite for establishing independent identity.[16] The desire to foreclose the father's name, and to establish a name for one's self, has been one of the mainsprings of Western art and literature ever since the Renaissance. For Faulkner, for instance; literature was a way to singularize himself—to prove and proclaim his difference. No sooner did he begin to publish than he changed his patronymic from Falkner to Faulkner. No doubt Vonnegut's decision to remove the "Jr." from his name was a similar case of literary autogenesis. Rudy's symbolic "eradication" of his father is final "testimony" to his father's criminal negligence. In effect Rudy had begun to resolve the Oedipal complexities of Paul Proteus by identifying his father's very real transgressions, by beginning to forgive him for his natural authority, and by taking that authority onto himself. Earlier in the novel, Rudy had observed, "The law was through with me, except as a witness. Under the law, I was only a witness to my father's crime of criminal negligence. There would be a coroner's inquest. I would have to testify" (90). Testifying to his father's criminal negligence is what Rudy does throughout his story. Lacan explains that by symbolically rejecting the father, the subject reinstates the authority of the phallus.[17]

Actually, Rudy had long been accustomed to venting the artist pent up within himself through a variety of muted creative acts: scat signing, tinkering with imaginative recipes, improvisation, daydreaming. Each is a formative experience that helps Rudy offset the aridity and paralysis of his death-in-life existence, gain emotional stability, and achieve a final artistic fusion with his creator. As with Wilbur Swain and Walter Starbuck, the strategies of metafiction help Rudy to order the chaos of his former life. His creative efforts in the retelling of his life story, in the writing of a play called *Katmandu,* and in a number of ingeniously interrelated minidramas, comment upon and embody the transforming power of art by which Rudy survives his somnambulistic stupor and restores himself to life. But it is what he calls his playlets, "wheels within wheels" or plays within the novel, that carry the essential existential message of Rudy's story and of all Vonnegut's fiction—the demonstration that one can author one's existence in life as in a story rather than submit to the tyranny of prestructured systems of control.

"I have this trick," Rudy explains, "for dealing with all my worst memories. I insist that they are plays. The characters are actors. Their speeches and movements are stylized, arch. I am in the presence of art" (83). Rudy constructs his first playlet to exorcise the memory of his imprisonment in the Midland City jail, which he calls "pure regional theatre . . . the Rudy Waltz show" (82).

> They were frank to call me a show . . . and the six remaining policemen were the producers . . . and their pauses in the basement indicated that we had reached an intermission, that there was more to come. They ignored me for the moment, as though a curtain had descended. (82)

Reminding us that it is Rudy who structures and controls the unfolding scene, he comments that "It wasn't exactly like that, of course, I don't have total recall. It was a lot like that" (87). Art has allowed Rudy to absorb and transform trauma into healing, personal truth, just as Vonnegut has informed us in his preface that he has transformed real life people and events into fantasy-inventions, truths of *his* own.

Rudy's second playlet, which he calls "Duplex: A New Comedy by Rudy Waltz," furthers his existential-literary education, his awareness that reality or truth is no more absolute in life than in a play or novel, recipe or scat song, and that as a writer or artist in life, he can embellish, delete, or revise. Rudy has just let himself into his brother's New York apartment, which reminds him of his childhood home, but in which he and Felix have "already rearranged some of the furniture" (134). With the help of the playful strategies of art, Rudy rearranges the scene in a way that transforms chaos into order, and pain into understanding. What floats up to him on his perch above the living room is "the final dissolution of my brother's second marriage, and some unkind character sketches of Felix and myself and our parents and Genevieve." But "it wasn't eavesdropping," Rudy says. "It was music appreciation" (135).

Rudy explains, "Down below me, and out of my line of sight, an acrimonious, atonal duet for viola and string bass was improvised. They both had such noble voices. She was the viola, and he was the bass" (135). "Or maybe it was a comedy," Rudy adds. The point is that the genre and the content of Rudy's dramatic restructuring of reality will have been significantly determined by Rudy. Felix's wife Genevieve, described as "Anyface," will have her features, according to the stage directions, "painted on like those of a China doll" (136). Nothing in the scene has a finite quality. Rudy's brother is described as an "actor," and we hear that "it was *almost* as though New York City were true" (140). One of the characters will say to Rudy, "But you've been keeping house for your parents for years and years, haven't you? Or isn't *that true?*" (146).

The substance of this playlet involves not just the trauma of the moment— the dissolution of the brother's marriage—but a recapitulation of other major traumas from Rudy's tormented past. Genevieve refers to Rudy's childhood home as "a crazy house," and to Rudy as a "circus freak" (138, 139). She notes that Rudy was born defective, "that the umbilical cord had strangled him or something" (142), which symbolically, of course, is nearly true. She is appalled that he hasn't taken a bath since his arrival. Yet again we remember that Rudy is simultaneously actor, character, and creator, that *he* is authoring this scene, dealing with family ghosts, and transcending his past by creating a healing, saving perspective. It is here that Rudy declares his father's responsibility in the cycle of violence that has institutionalized his mother and devastated the family. "That's what growing up was like for Felix and me," he says. "We had no father when we got through. Mother still thinks he's the greatest man in the world" (146). Rudy agrees with Genevieve when she calls him "an idiot savant," "somebody who's stupid in every possible way but one—like playing the piano." Felix says that he cannot play the piano, but that he wrote a play, and sometimes he says something that is really very funny or wise (142). "Idiot savant," Rudy nods. "No good at life, but very funny sometimes with the commentary" (145). Actually Rudy's aptitude for invention makes him adept at life as well as art. Soon he would be able to say, "And then, step by step, I would experiment with having a home of my own and a life of my own, maybe pairing off with this kind of person or that one, to see how that went" (132).

Rudy's next playlet is important because it shows how he has resolved his essential psychic dilemma—the split between his aspiring creative self and the isolated, moribund side of his character. As with Vonnegut's previous heroes, Rudy's creative impulse has been neutralized by his withdrawal into some cozy, womblike hiding place—indicated by his choice of Shangri-La as the subject for his high school essay and for his play, *Katmandu*. Now Rudy repudiates dangerous escapist fictions, dealing directly with his specterish past as he insists Celia Hoover deal with her drug addiction. Celia had once been humiliated by Rudy's father through an ostentatious show of family wealth. Now "the raddled, snaggletoothed ruins" of what was once the most beautiful girl in town (179) appeal to Rudy's sympathy where he is most vulnerable. "I love you," she says, which at first causes Rudy to freeze. When she asks him to write her a play with "the medicine of [his] . . . magic words" (180), he insists she has come only for amphetamines, "And I wouldn't give you any more of that poison, if you had a prescription signed by God Almighty" (182). When Celia retorts, "Give me a hug or give me some Penwalt Biphetamine" (183), Rudy shows he is learning to love, not drug, by refusing her the temporary, addictive peace of mind she seeks. Celia brands him Deadeye Dick, calls him a killer and a mama's boy, and proceeds to wreck the store. "My feeling was," Rudy says, "that chemicals had wrecked her brains, and that she wasn't Celia Hoover anymore. She was a monster" (184). The thought of altered reality activates Rudy's creative instincts. "If I did write a play for her new face . . . what wonderful things could a writer put into the mouth of a crazy old lady like her anyway?" So he tinkers with the possibilities of a recreated Celia Hoover. "I tinkered too," he says "with the idea of having the voice of God coming from the back of the theatre. Whoever played God would have to have a voice like my brother's" (185).

In his playlet, Rudy emphatically illustrates the existential message that life and art are both fictions whose truth is determined by the courage and imagination of the artist-character, artist-creator. This miniplay abounds with epistemological game playing. Numerous references to interchangeable realities, defined as "joke" and "real," "sane" and "insane," invite the reader to make such distinctions to determine, if possible, what is real or unreal, sane or insane. "A story," Rudy says, "is as artificial as a mechanical bucking bronco in a drinking establishment" (210). One can ride or dismount as one pleases. The playlet focuses on the funeral of Celia Hoover, whose drug addiction has finally led to suicide. "It was like a scene in a cowboy movie," Rudy says, "with the townspeople all huddled together, and with a half-broken, tragic, great big man going to meet destiny all alone" (201). "If this confrontation scene were done as a playlet," Rudy says, and proceeds to exorcise a final family ghost.

The confrontation here is outwardly between Celia's husband Dwayne and Rudy's brother. Dwayne is puzzled to find Felix crying uncontrollably because Felix and Celia had been childhood sweethearts. But the *important* encounter is between Felix and his mother, Emma, providing a final purge of Rudy's tormented memories of the mother he described as "a cold and aggressively helpless old bat," whose inability to love helped create the living death of Rudy's childhood. Whereas Felix claims his crying makes him the sanest man at the funeral, "the sanest person in this whole shitstorm," Emma calls him mad, berates him for being a weakling ("He can't fight, he never could"), calls him a public disgrace, and tells him, "Go ahead and get your brains beat out." Felix replies, "You must be the worst mother a person ever had. . . . You never sewed on a button. . . . You never hugged or kissed me. . . . You never did anything a mother's supposed to do." Emma says, "Who could blame me?" and publicly wishes him dead (204, 205).

When Rudy tells an actor in the production of *Katmandu* to go ahead and say anything he wanted to say, the actor replies:

> Maybe you don't realize this . . . but actors don't make up what they say on the stage. They look like they've made it up, if they're any good, but actually a person called a "playwright" has first written down every word. (132)

But as Rudy has learned and his playlets attest, life is pure theatre, in which the player must forge his own identity. The Reverend Harrell is right when he says, "the most important arts center a city could have were human beings, not buildings . . . there in the back (pointing to Rudy) sits an arts center named

Rudy Waltz" (199). Through his apprenticeship as dramatic artist, Rudy has learned, he says, "to be comforted by music of my own making." The Deadeye Dick in him will always exist to a degree, but Rudy Waltz, the Waltzer, the singer, the writer, the creator, has come into ascendance, closer yet to the consummate artist-hero Rabo Karabekian, whose painting Rudy's brother has purchased (188).

Rudy's emotional and artistic restoration climaxes in one of the novel's most comical but philosophically important scenes—Rudy trapped in an airport toilet, battling diarrhea. Rudy reports,

> In I flew, and up to the men's room, noting in flight that somebody was running a floor-waxing machine. I relieved myself, and became as calm and respectable as any other citizen again, or even more so. For a few moments there, I was happier than happy, healthier than healthy, and I saw these words scrawled on the tiles over a wash basin:
> "To be is to do"—Socrates
> "To do is to be"—Jean-Paul Sartre
> "Do be do be do"—Frank Sinatra. (224)

Unconsciously, at least, Rudy associates the murdered Mrs. Metzger (vacuuming at the moment of her death) with the improvised graffiti. With ingenious concision, the scene suggests Rudy's catharsis: his release of guilt, his repudiation of escapist illusions (he has got the Katmandu out of his system), his awareness of existential responsibility, and his recognition that he is free to author a new essence.

In a double sense, Rudy becomes his own creator. "Katmandu was my one fling away from Midland City, my own experience, until *now,* with inhabiting a place where I was not Deadeye Dick" (106). Rudy's "now" is Port-au-Prince, Haiti, "a nation born out of the only successful slave revolt in all of human history" (105). Vonnegut greets the reader there at the start of the novel, and their mutual liberation rightfully brings Rudy and Vonnegut face to face in a mirror at the novel's conclusion. If Lacan is right that the individual's childhood mirror image is his first experience of fragmentation in the world, this reflection of wholeness and artistic fusion assumes ever larger symbolic value. Rudy's recognition of his Vonnegut-self occurs at the grave sites of his parents and of those who have died tragically young (198). Accepting the demise of his own innocence, putting his parents finally to rest, Rudy experiences a solid sense of self—an identity that is autonomous, whole, and harmonized.

Climactically, the identities of Rudy and Vonnegut connect in the image of an artist-priest with the power to raise ghosts from the grave. In the novel's epilogue, which occurs at the mass grave of those killed by the neutron bombing of Midland City, the gifted metaphysician Hippolyte Paul De Mille offers to raise the ghost of anyone Rudy thinks should haunt Midland City for the next few hundred years. Rudy tells him to go ahead; then he declares, "And I, Rudy Waltz, the William Shakespeare of Midland City, the only serious dramatist ever to live and work there, will now make my own gift to the future, which is a legend" (239). This is the story that Vonnegut, through Rudy, has told. Rudy and Vonnegut know that fictions can kill as well as liberate, deaden the spirit or raise it up and teach it to sing. Both will eschew fantasies that suggest instant panaceas for existential pain, and create honest myths to live by, like *Deadeye Dick*. Each writer, one writer really, has confronted the painful chaos within and without to create new and humane perspectives. As Rudy learns to affirm life, Vonnegut provides his most life-affirming novel.

Galápagos: **Oedipus at Galápagos**

The fateful question for the human species seems to me to be whether and to what extent their cultural development will succeed in mastering the disturbance of their communal life by the human instinct of aggression and self-destruction.
Sigmund Freud, *Civilization and Its Discontents*

His big brain must have been sick in some serious way—if giving a damn what happened next was a sign of mental health.
Galápagos

I argued earlier that the author used the novel *Breakfast of Champions* to purge himself of his more embittered and cynical self, that eternal harbinger of doom Kilgore Trout. What I had not sufficiently noticed in *Breakfast of Champions* was that Vonnegut, at the end of his story, had quietly merged two presences he had associated with death and void throughout his fiction—Trout and that of his own father. The author first draws a line between a father described as being of little help to him when Vonnegut was growing up, a mother "crazy as a bedbug" whose bizarre phobias and chaotic mind led to suicide, and his own demoralized condition (181). Equating his father with machinery and mechanistic structures, Vonnegut notes that when he was ill it felt like that syphilitic standing underneath the "overhanging clock that his father designed . . . eaten alive by corkscrews" and unable to fit together the world of self and the world of society (30). Then, from that void which he says is his schizophrenic hiding place from despair and cynicism, comes the wasted face and saddened voice of Trout, which Vonnegut says, quietly but dramatically, is also that of his father (181).

Yet Vonnegut's self-projections through Trout have been so complex that no one could have anticipated the ultimately sinister role that Vonnegut had in mind for him ten years later in the novel, *Galápagos* (1985). The linking of

Vonnegut's father with the life-hating Trout portrayed here corroborates the overview of Vonnegut's work as an autobiographical psychodrama—a career-long process of cleansing and renewal. We observed that as early as Vonnegut's first novel, *Player Piano* (1952), the protagonist's rebellion against organizational machinery appears as a subconscious desire to destroy his father, the phenomenon explained by Freud as the unleashing of the death instinct when the natural organic balance between the forces of Thanatos and Eros was disturbed by "inorganic substance."[1] In the novels following *Breakfast of Champions,* especially *Slapstick* (1976) and *Deadeye Dick* (1982), the destructive father-son relationship becomes still more ominous—the moribund father infecting the protagonist with his own disillusionment and cynicism and inducing years of self-destructive behavior in which the son drugs himself, withdraws into some cozy, womblike hiding place, and thinks of suicide. In *Deadeye Dick,* the narrator's childhood home, where the father's persistent lovelessness, morbidity, and lack of will turn Rudy Waltz into an emotional grotesque, is structured like a "Roman watchtower" (8). The father's artistic ambitions are perverted into a passion for beautiful guns and a flamboyant enthusiasm for Adolph Hitler, Eros into Thanatos, so he thwarts Rudy's deepest creative instinct by counseling him to "plug your ears with wax whenever anybody tells you that you have a creative gift of any kind." Now the artistically failed and morose father of Leon Trout infects Leon with his own bitterness, seeking, as Freud said of Thanatos, "to lead that which is living to death."[2]

A casual reading of *Galápagos* might suggest that the essential autobiographical drama of Vonnegut's work had been resolved in *Deadeye Dick*—that with the raising and facing of haunting parental ghosts, with the exorcism of Trout on the one hand, and his father on the other, he had freed himself from the cynical strain in his work that had constituted the psychic malaise of his main characters. Through most of the narrative, it is Vonnegut as social critic, not psychoanalyst, who holds our attention, functioning as the projective imagination of the Life Force, a directing instrument of the evolutionary process that would help us avoid the kind of sooner-or-later fatal technological horror that occurs in this story.

As its title suggests, the setting of *Galápagos* is that of Darwin's *Origin of Species*. With the benefit of nearly a million years of hindsight, the narrator's ghost, which has survived from the year 1986 to the year One Million A.D., tells of "the suicidal mistakes" nations used to make during his lifetime (140). The end of life in its present form begins with the introduction of an irreversible disease in which creatures invisible to the naked eye try to eat up all the eggs in human ovaries (162), suggesting that nature's directions in the year 1986 have been anything but felicitous. Military scientists finish the job by bringing on an apocalyptic nightmare that changes forever the course of human destiny. It is here, fleeing for their lives on a ship called the *Bahía de Darwin*—the "new

Noah's Ark" (215)—wandering aimlessly about the archipelago and finally marooned on the island of Santa Rosalia, that the future progenitors of the human race come together. In one of the most sardonic moments in Vonnegut's fiction, sixty-one-year-old Mary Hepburn assures the future of the species by impregnating six native Kanka-bono women with sperm taken from the captain (265), a racist who at the age of sixty-six is determined not to reproduce. The Kanka-bonos are described as "apolitical" because they are happy to have any-body for dinner (116). The captain's lack of interest in sex implies a death wish—the hatred of life filled with materialistic and mechanistic satsifactions that substitute for love, and the subsequent unleashing of the instinct to destruc-tion and death.[3] If he could, Leon says, the captain, in the name of science and progress, would find ways to "clog the spring" on Santa Rosalia (271). The supposed blessings of technological progress have indeed dammed up the springs of human emotion; it is a diabolical marriage, man and machine, which has diminished the life force as well as the work force, and "let no man put asunder," says Leon, "what the telephone company hath joined" (88). Machin-ery, symbolized by the twin computers Gorbuki and Mandarax, has created an age of "petrified" (57) "pathological personalities" with no more ability to feel or care about the future than "highly accurate clocks" (60). And not giving a damn, says Leon, was a sure sign of insanity (80). The happiest people on earth, he says, were these robotic personalities, people like Gorbuki and Mandarax, who "merely caused pain to those around them, and almost never to them-selves"(56).

All aboard the *Bahía de Darwin* bear the scars of pathologically unloving parents; all have perverted the instinct to love and creativity into masochistic activities. All, in fact, are potential schizophrenics—"people who respond pas-sionately to all sorts of things which aren't really going on" (149). Leon notes that the semiexposed penis of maniacal Andrew MacIntosh was "no more a secret than the pendulum on a grandfather's clock" (77). MacIntosh has spent his libidinal energy in the frenzied pursuit of property. A hard-on for money and power leaves him uninterested in reproduction. Even his name—MacIntosh—suggests the conversion of the organic (apples) to the mechanistic (computers).

The novel's network of clock and spiral imagery connects the mechanical obsessions of MacIntosh with the blind aggression of others whose life instinct has turned deathly. Leon observes that the entire "clockwork of the universe" was in danger of destroying itself (271), which, in effect, it does. The perverse aggression that fuels MacIntosh's quest for power leads one military madman to individual acts of psychopathic violence and another to mass destruction. Private Geraldo Delgado, "a paranoid schizophrenic" (149), guns down sup-posed enemies in the El Dorado Hotel, and Leon confesses,

> He looked all right and he acted all right when he talked to the recruiting officer, just as I did
> when I enlisted in the United States Marines. . . . When I was through with Marine camp, and
> I was sent to Vietnam and issued live ammunition . . . I did worse things than Delgado. (150)

The absence of love leads a pilot named Guillermo Reyes into intimacy
with his radar dish, likened to the Virgin Mary (211). He consummates his love
affair by firing his rocket at the Guayquil International Airport, which precipi-
tates World War III. Letting the rocket go was "as elating as sexual intercourse"
(213), leaving him "happy . . . awed," and "drained" (188).

The death wish of the *Bahía*'s captain, of the "amazing radar lover" (188)
Guillermo Reyes, and of Andrew MacIntosh, implies a larger pathology, the
sickness of an entire dehumanized age bent upon self-destruction. Freud sur-
mised that such an impasse, i.e., the whole of mankind neurotic with lovelessness and self-hatred, would render the sane and insane indistinguishable.[4] Leon
declares,

> No single human being could claim credit for that rocket, which was going to work so
> perfectly. It was the collective achievement of all who had ever put their big brains to work
> on the problem of how to capture and compress the diffuse violence of which nature was
> capable, and drop it in relatively small packages on their enemies. (189–90)

The rocket is the product of universal technologies: it is conceived by a Japanese
brain, constructed by Americans, armed with Israeli explosives, and delivered
by the Peruvian Air Force. Like the protagonist the age is divided against itself.
Mandarax quotes, "It was the best of times, it was the worst of times . . . it was
an epoch of belief . . . of hope . . . of Light . . . ," and it was an age of
"incredulity . . . Darkness . . . despair . . ." (180, 181). The Viet Nam War,
Leon says, was symptomatically schizophrenic—a war waged by "pathological
personalities" who "might do almost anything on impulse, feeling nothing
much. The logical explanation for the actions, invented at leisure, always came
afterwards" (103).

Has the law of natural selection—freakish and blind—and the carnage
known as survival of the fittest vindicated Darwin's perception of brute survival
rather than divine guidance at work in the evolution of species, creating that
fateful moment when the history of the species takes an inevitable turn for the
worse? Not to judge from the narrator's description of the "perfect happiness"
(186) that has come to humankind on Santa Rosalia one million years hence, a
blissful Eden of blue lagoons, coconut palms, and broad white beaches where
people lie around in a state of innocence and relaxation they have never known
before (186).[5] In bringing humanity into harmony with the rest of nature, the
law of natural selection has made some changes, to be sure. Those hands that
had caused such mischief in carrying out the hair-brained schemes of our supposedly duplicitous big brains have become flippers, perfect for survival in the

watery environment of *Galápagos*. There are still plenty of hallucinators, we are told, but people like that can't get hold of weapons now and they're easy to swim away from (149). Slavery has disappeared. Asks the narrator, "How could you ever hold somebody in bondage with nothing but your flippers and your mouth?" (144)

If, as the narrator concludes, our "preposterously huge and active brains" were indeed mankind's biggest dilemma in 1986, the "once nearly fatal defects in the evolution of the human race" (8), nature has evidently solved that problem too by producing smaller heads, skulls that are streamlined and bullet shaped. Calling them the "only real villain in my story" (270), the narrator says that these infernal human computers, incapable of idleness or restraint, fill him with rage. He wonders how evolution could have permitted "something so distracting and irrelevant and disruptive" as those big brains of a million years ago. If they could be relied upon for truth, he might see their value, but they "lied all the time" (174). They lie, they send contradictory signals, they stimulate insane forms of cruelty, greed, and selfishness, they invent machines that make humans obsolete, and the worst big-brained idea of all, they diffuse the violence of nature into bombs to drop on their enemies. Enough reason, decides the narrator, to rejoice in the dramatic decrease in brain power in the year One Million A.D. People "aren't diverted from the main business of life by the hobgoblin of opinion anymore," he declares. They are no longer conscious of death, nobody cries anymore, love has been simplified to whether people are in heat or not, and the problem of identity—of dishonesty or pretense—is gone because "people are who they are and that is that" (99).

Is the narrator's retreat into the soulless oblivion of prehistoric life forms, engendering a loss of love, feeling, identity, and morality, a meaningful deliverance from the evils of our big-brained lives? Or is regression into a dehumanized state of being, where undifferentiated beings confuse wellbeing with a contentment of mindlessness, a dubious trade-off for relief from the painful complexity of human identity? In a review of *Galápagos,* Dr. Clyde Ralph typifies the uncritical response of most readers to Vonnegut's "dynamite bouquets." Applauding what he mistakes as Vonnegut's condemnation of our oversized brains, he says, "Kurt's solution to the whole problem is devolution . . . reducing the size of our brains, thus putting ourselves back in balance with the other denizens of this planet."[6] As usual, Vonnegut sets us up with counterbalancing texts— unresolvable tensions and intentionally ambiguous experiences that force us into a closer-than-usual examination of the materialistic assumptions underlying a twentieth-century view of progress—forcing us, ironically, to use our "big brains." So doing, we see that the law of natural selection may be responsible for better teeth, but the average life span has decreased to thirty years. Nobody starves and problems connected with aging are unimaginable. But it is killer whales and sharks that keep the population manageable. No one is smart enough to make destructive weapons anymore, but neither can anyone play the piano or interest themselves in sculpture. The painful complexity of human identity, emotional volatility, and the anguish of choice have ceased to be. In fact, no one thinks at all anymore, and everyone is the same.

Vonnegut's credulous narrator—and no doubt a number of readers—has been seduced by what is described in *Cat's Cradle* as "a wonderful idea" that proves to be "hideous in retrospect." These superficially benign bargains come in a variety of packages, but none is more dangerous, Vonnegut demonstrates, than the mind-numbing, fatalistic belief that threatens the will of the narrator of *Galápagos*—the belief that the evolutionary process is inevitably structured and directed by the forces of natural selection which he is helpless to influence, and that in the brute struggle for survival nothing has been so distracting and irrelevant as those great big brains of ours. The narrator speaks several times of the inexorable ticking of the "clockwork of the universe" (191) and sees people as "parts" in the grand mechanistic design of the cosmos (289, 290). References to clocks, to literal computers, proliferate in this novel, but it is apathy bred by the belief that people are machines or machine parts in irreversible mechanistic systems of control that concerns Vonnegut here as always. "What Andrew MacIntosh now said to Jesús Ortiz was . . . that his big brain must have been sick in some serious way—if giving a damn what happened next was a sign of mental health" (80). The laws of natural selection comprise the deadliest clock of all. Wondering what the world looks like to a person of high military rank, the narrator enters the head (one of his ghostly prerogatives) of the deranged captain of the *Bahía de Darwin,* who looks up at the stars and reflects that "his planet was an insignificant speck of dust in the cosmos, and that he was a germ on the speck, and that nothing could matter less than what became of him" (197). The narrator declares, "His [the captain's] feeling that life was a meaningless nightmare with nobody watching or caring what was going on, was actually quite familiar to me" (127). Thus it is that the characters of *Galápagos,* crippled by fatalism and apathy, are steered into an apocalyptic nightmare by military madmen.

Rather than advocating mindlessness, then, Vonnegut has created a psychoanalytic subplot in the form of his dangerously passive, emotionless, death-haunted narrator to comment upon the potentially fatal consequences of a population whose will to survive has become crippled by a paralyzing fatalism. As a ghost, decapitated by a sheet of steel while working as a welder inside the *Bahía de Darwin,*[7] the narrator literally isn't there, and, as an invisible presence, his antipathetic condition, which makes him long for a brain that no longer hurts or feels, may go as unnoticed by the casual reader as by the story's other characters. Vonnegut devilishly calls background information about the narrator "a few not very interesting details tacked on at the end of the story" (292).

Supposedly unimportant details, actually dispersed throughout Leon's narrative, show Vonnegut's headless, paranoid narrator to have experienced a past as brutalized as that of the author's other war-scarred, father-persecuted heroes. He is a traumatized veteran of Viet Nam, with unshakable memories of participating in a military massacre in which he personally shot an old woman (293)—an episode "which made me envy stones" (127)—of artillery barrages, exploding mines, and hand grenades, burning villages, people sneaking up on him to kill him, which at war's end had left him guilt-ridden, sexless, and finally hospitalized for nervous exhaustion (293). Subsequent bouts with syphilis, drugs, alcohol, followed by crying jags and psychiatric treatment, created escapist fantasies of putting down his weapons and becoming fisherman, a desire for eternal sleep not unlike the narrator's dystopian vision of life on earth in One Million A.D., which may in fact be only the hallucinated vision of a very sick ex-soldier, writing, as he says, with "air on air" (290).

But something closer to home than war has created the narrator's willlessness—parents who he says "made each other miserable by getting married" (66), typical of those who commonly "made psychological cripples of their own children," turning them into zombies (78). The narrator remembers a "mother who walked out on Father and me" (likely metaphor for suicide)[8] (71, 122) and a father he says he never liked, a repellent failure as a father and husband and an unread author of notoriously cheap science fiction stories, from whom the narrator ran away at the age of sixteen to search for the mother, whom, as it turns out, the father had driven from home. Calling him an "insult to life itself" (256), the narrator says, "Trout had made me his co-conspirator in driving my mother away forever" (25). Yes, of course, *Trout,* father, or, in a double sense, creator, of our narrator, whose pessimism in *Breakfast of Champions* drove his son Leo from home, and who now, Thanatos incarnate, encourages Leon Trout to self-destruction.

The protagonists' Oedipal war continues. Even from the grave, the father seeks revenge for his displacement by the rebellious son (Rudy Waltz has symbolically killed his father in *Deadeye Dick*); and Leon fantasizes another womblike paradise in his tormented search for "perfect happiness" (108). He projects his obsessive longing for the contentment and safety of his own prebirth in the form of planetary regression into prehistoric life forms. One fantasy is as deadly as the other, a schizophrenic, hallucinatory retreat from humanness that retards awareness, conscience, choice, and creativity and that ironically exacerbates aggression. In the watery environment of Galápagos a million years hence, the soulless mechanisms of natural selection render human identity more mechanical and undifferentiated than ever. As for contentment and safety, most of the *Bahía*'s survivors drown (281) or are eaten by sharks and killer whales (286). The novel's omnipresent "tidal wave" (49, 179, 191, 221) foreshadows the moral oblivion awaiting Leon, too, if he chooses devolution as the solution to the pain of human complexity, dreaming of mindless contentment in reconstituted Edens and protective wombs. Leon remarks:

> Back when childhoods were so protracted, it is unsurprising that so many people got into the lifelong habit of believing, even after their parents were gone, that somebody was always watching over them—God or a saint or guardian angel or the stars or whatever. (122)

That Leon believes the details of his own prolonged childhood "uninteresting" shows the continuing repression of Oedipal trauma. After the death of his mother, he hears his father's inarticulate grief coming from the bedroom (173). Later he says that he talked the same way, but that "I would have no recollection of what I might have said" (173). What could it have been, he wonders, except for "the spilling of useless, uncalled for signals spilling from our preposterously huge and active brains"(173)? These Oedipal signals are as blindly mechanistic as the courtship dance of the blue-footed boobies in the Galápagos—described as "huge molecules" (111) who, Leon says, "have to dance like that."[9] Psychic determinism entraps Leon in a life as static and sterile as that aboard the *Bahía de Darwin,* or as that of the "electromagnetic bubble" created by Andrew MacIntosh for his blind daughter, Selena (73). This is the answer to Leon's question, "What do these slaves of fear and hunger have to do with me?" (253). Unconscious and unchecked, these perverse longings convert to pathological aggression. Says Leon:

> I myself had some highly personal experiences with dreams-come-true of that sort in Vietnam—which is to say, with mortars and hand grenades and artillery. Nature could never have been that predictably destructive in such small spaces without the help of humankind. (190)

Leon's unconscious aggression is as dangerous as that Peruvian rocket that "puts the tip of its nose . . . into that Ecuadorian radar dish" (190).

Like Rudy Waltz, Leon must break out of the Oedipal spiral by renouncing regressive and aggressive structures. He must reject illusions of perfect happiness, censor his father's pessimism but stop blaming him for the loss of his mother, and use his imaginative gifts to benefit humanity as a whole. From Freud's point of view, he must achieve independence from extraneous authorities—his father, specifically—and develop his own conscience in the form of a superego.[10] This is precisely the process by which Mary Hepburn achieves selfhood and converts death to life. Leon notes that she didn't become independent of her parents until she received her master's degree at the age of twenty-two (122). Only then did she accept responsibility for her identity, passing through suicidal impulses to "create," if not Beethoven's Ninth, at least new life for humanity (albeit deeply flawed) from the verge of absolute sterility and annihilation.[11]

The same force that saves Mary Hepburn liberates the creative imagination of Wilbur Swain, Walter Starbuck, Rudy Waltz, and now Leon Trout. Mary sees the mental life of human beings as inherently schizophrenic—consisting of a mechanical big brain, often duplicitous and irresponsible, and a soul, described in *Breakfast of Champions* as a sacred living force at the core of every living being. Roy Hepburn says that "the soul is the part of you that knows when your brain isn't working" (44), but Mary realizes that these twin psychical realities are interdependent and equally vital to survival. She tells her students that there was possibly a lot of good to those preposterously active and contradictory big brains—"people's playing will all sorts of ideas in their heads" (265). She sees reality—the Galápagos Islands, the universe, the evolutionary process—as "imaginary," "pretense," a "game," an "invention" of human will and imagination; she sees "significance" as that which the mind's subjectivity assigns. Human beings write these fictions, not the blind mechanisms of nature. Such stories can "end up any which way"(98). Thus Mary generates life out of an experimenter's "curiosity" as to whether it *can* be done—the same playful "big-brained" impulse that creates the guided missiles. But it is Mary's awareness, coupled with conscience, that allows her to control libidinal energy to evolve new life rather than launch orgasmic missiles.

Leon observes that in the early stage of the captain's disease, "it was still possible for his soul to recognize that his brain had become dangerous, and to help him maintain a semblance of mental health through sheer will-power" (87). Ultimately, evident by his life story, Leon achieves such balance, the integration of his thinking self with the self that feels, cares, and creates. As a welder, he says, "my finest work was inside" (197). It is the evolved will and conscience of this holistic self that successfully resists his father's pessimism. Standing in the mouth of the "Blue Tunnel of Death," a sort of limbo between life and death, Kilgore implores his son to, as it were, give up the ghost, calling his commitment to life, his curiosity, foolish. "Keep moving Leon," he says, "No time to be coy. . . . You come to Papa right now" (252). The suction from the Blue Tunnel—his father's fatalism—exerts a powerful pull, and Leon wonders, "Have I at last exhausted my curiosity as to what life is all about? If so, I need only step inside what I liken to a vacuum cleaner" (252). When Leon asks his father for more time to complete his work—his research into the human mind and heart, and into dehumanizing mechanistic structures—Trout tells him he is nothing better than a machine himself, that the more he learns about people, the more disgusted he will become (253–54). Led by captains like that of the *Bahía de Darwin,* lunatics with no charts or compasses (255), the nations of the world, weapons set to go off at a moment's notice, are doomed (254).

In this deadly, soul-threatening "courtship dance" with his father, the narrator notes, "So I took one step in his direction, but not a second one. I was like a female blue-footed booby at the start of a courtship dance. As in a courtship dance, that uncertain first step was the first tick of a clock, which would become irresistible" (252). Rather than resolve tormenting Oedipal aggression by withdrawing into narcissistic fantasies or accepting his father's fatalism, Leon will dance to his own tune, joining ranks with Rudy Waltz, a waltzer and a writer, who has learned to mend his disintegrated self and to recreate himself through art. Rejecting the noxious Trout, Leon achieves the wholeness and the will to declare, "Mother was right. Even in the darkest of times, there was still hope for humankind" (259).

The protagonist's portrayal of his mother as a positive force coincides with Vonnegut's association of the female with creativity in all the novels after *Breakfast of Champions*. "My father was Nature's experiment with cynicism," says Leon, "and my mother was Nature's experiment with optimism" (82). The mother's optimism informs Leon that mechanistic structures—ticks of the clock such as his father's pessimism, lovelessness, and apathy, the stockpiling of weapons of destruction, evolution itself—all are imaginative constructs open to revision. Noting that "the Galápagos Islands could be hell in one moment and heaven in the next" (16), Leon realizes that it is we who are responsible for our creations, that it is we, as a character says in *God Bless You, Mr. Rosewater,* who "are right now determining whether the space voyage for the next billion years or so is going to be Heaven or Hell" (18).

Rather than following his father into the "Blue Tunnel," the ultimate spiral, the fatal eternal womb, Leon chooses to haunt the earth for a million years to pay in full what he calls "his debt to society . . . doing what he has to do" whether anybody notices or not (257, 259). What he has to do, of course, is serve as Vonnegut's "canary-bird" in the coal mine—encouraging us to eschew the dynamite bouquet of mindlessness, to change our minds about experiments with destruction, and to experiment instead with kindness, intelligence, and restraint. For the characters of *Galápagos,* it is too late, says Leon, to "crawl from the ruins of *their* creation" (140). As for their chances of making a comeback, says Leon, "they would have to do it with their beaks this time" (185). For us, by learning "to give a damn," and with that sometimes frustrating big-brained capacity for choice, there is still time to steer the floundering *Bahía de Darwin* in a more humane and intelligent direction.

Bluebeard:
Redemption and the Unwavering Light

"You have no use for truth?" said Beatrice.
"You know what truth is?" said Karabekian. "It's some crazy
thing my neighbor believes. If I want to make friends with him, I
ask him what he believes. He tells me, and I say, 'Yeah, yeah—
ain't it the truth?' "

Breakfast of Champions

The will is one of the principal organs of belief; not because it
forms belief, but because things are true or false according to the
side from which they are viewed. The will which likes one side
better than the other, dissuades the mind from considering the
qualities of those which it does not care to see; and thus the mind,
walking abreast of the will, stops to observe the aspect which
pleases the will, and judges of the thing by what it sees there.

Pascal, *Pensées*

In *Breakfast of Champions* (1973), the character Kurt Vonnegut says that he has conquered pessimism and is getting himself reborn. "Chaos," he announces, "was about to give birth to a new me" (218). A painting by the minimalist artist Rabo Karabekian contained the secret of Vonnegut's renewal—a vertical, unwavering band of light, which Vonnegut identifies as the symbol of something sacred at the core of every living being, an imaginative faculty capable of resisting subversion by dehumanizing machinery within and without (221). The revelation produces a rush of orgasmic emotion seldom experienced by a Vonnegut protagonist. It causes Vonnegut to view modern art not as a conspiracy to make poor people feel stupid (209), but as dynamic process, which shows "everything about life which truly matters, with nothing left out" (221). An ecstatic Vonnegut declares: "At the core of each person who reads this book is a band of unwavering light. . . . God bless Rabo Karabekian" (225).

No wonder that Vonnegut should devote an entire novel to the character derisively described in *Breakfast of Champions* as "a man . . . paid fifty thousand dollars for sticking a piece of yellow tape to a green piece of canvas" (214), but who emerges symbolically as the main regenerative force in the author's spiritual evolution, and the end product of his artistic metamorphosis. And what a resurrection, the transformation of the moribund Billy Pilgrim into the consummate artist, Rabo Karabekian. This most radically alienated of men, with his hideous psychic wounds—the traumatized child, the war-scarred soldier, the failed husband and father—has come through the fires of Dresden to be symbolically reborn in *Breakfast of Champions*, then, as Rudy Waltz says, to be healed by music of his own making in the novels of Vonnegut's "second career"—*Slapstick, Jailbird, Deadeye Dick,* and *Galápagos.*

While the "new me" affirmed in *Bluebeard* is a natural progression in the spiritual evolution of Kurt Vonnegut and his renascent artist-hero, Rabo Karabekian represents a quantum leap in psychic healing. Conceived in the grand epiphanaic light of Rabo's painting in *Breakfast of Champions*, Wilbur Swain, Walter Starbuck, Rudy Waltz, and Leon Trout survive their defeatist selves to work out an "aesthetics of renewal"[1]—the existential possibilities of authoring one's identity in life as in art. But the retrospective visions of these emergent artists—of ghosts laid to rest and emotional recovery—is more tentative than triumphant. The malignant voice of Father Trout lingers on in *Galápagos*, encumbering the protagonist's spirit with unpurged images of death and destruction. It remains for Rabo Karabekian to complete the hero's transformation—an achievement of wholeness and artistic identity Rabo calls his "renaissance" (278) and Vonnegut calls the birth of the "new me."

Rabo's recovery is so complete that when a friend observes that there is something in Rabo's work he identifies as "Chaos," Rabo responds that not even the Chaos should be there, that he'll come back to paint it out (241). But the affirmation in his narrative, his "hoax" autobiography, is neither sentimental nor simple. Nothing in Rabo's calamitous past—childhood unhappiness, the horrors of war, profound depression—differs from that of Vonnegut's former schizoid heroes. Rabo's parents are as unfeeling and materialistic as the parents of Eliza and Wilbur Swain, Rudy Waltz, and Leon Trout. "I can't recall our ever having touched before," Rabo reports (73). They too hold the arts in contempt and discourage Rabo's artistic yearnings (19).

Having barely survived the attempt by the Turkish Empire to exterminate its Armenian citizens, Rabo's parents develop terminal pessimism. Rabo looks into the eyes of his father and sees what every Vonnegut hero has seen, a zombie (65). "There wasn't anybody home anymore" (64). Worse, his mother, says Rabo, "up and died on me" (147).

Rabo, like Leon Trout, holds his father responsible for his mother's schizophrenic collapse and death (14), accusing the father of cheating himself and his mother by becoming "the unhappiest and loneliest of men," bent upon self-immolation (31). But Rabo is at peace with himself about this father, who dies alone in the Bijou Theater wearing his cowboy boots. While he has forgiven his father hundreds of times, *this* time he's going to accept. There are, he says, no bodies in his barn (48).

Neither have the wounds of soldiering or the failure of two marriages proved permanently disabling. Rabo has lost an eye while commanding a platoon of army engineers in Luxembourg near the end of the war, after which he was imprisoned in a camp near Dresden. Pertinent to the imagery of schizophrenia, Rabo thinks of escaping the war experience by drowning in the Arno (225). He refers to the threat of family dissolution as "a marriage on the rocks" (219). When Dorothy calls his art childishly unimportant and literally destroys his paintings, Rabo links their destructive marriage with the traumas of war by labeling Dorothy's mutilations a "massacre" (268). But offsetting any harm he may have done in battle, he has saved the lives of several fellow soldiers (49). Even grim memories of the concentration camp, about which he says he will marvel for a lifetime (208), have been tempered and redeemed by art, as we learn from his painting—the mysterious "watchamacallit" at the close of his narrative.

Rabo's most troublesome memory, he says, is his failure as a husband of "the good and brave Dorothy, and the consequent alienation of my own flesh and blood, Henri and Terry, from me, their Dad" (243). The fact is that the "good and brave Dorothy" had hated his work, insisting he take a degree in business education, and doing everything possible to erode his artistic confidence. In spite, she tells him he couldn't draw something real if he had to (266). Rabo's second wife, Edith, doesn't hate his work, but ignores it, turning him into a social animal and smothering him with kindness. Though his sons no longer talk to him, Rabo's remonstrances to family members are gentle and amicable—those of a man at peace with his transgressions and satisfied that his priorities have been right.

The centrality in Rabo's narrative of the demonic figure, Dan Gregory, reminds us that the Vonnegut hero has battled more than antagonistic wives and parents in his quest for artistic authenticity. In the manner of such previous lunatic projections of the protagonist's fatalistic self as Niles Rumfoord, Bokonon, Frank Wirtanen, and Kilgore Trout, Gregory is that allegorized spook of cynicism and self-doubt who tempts past heroes to moral suicide—to seek escapist solutions to complexity and moral responsibility. Manifested as a devilishly clever commercial artist, Gregory has shortened his last name from Gregorian to Gregory—suggesting his capacity for deception and work that is without warmth or soul. Rabo's parents have supposedly delivered their son into the hands of the rich and famous illustrator of novels, magazine stories, and advertisements with the hope that Gregory will introduce Rabo to all his rich friends (54). But the prospective betrayal is Rabo's alone. Gregory is no more real than those hallucinated Tralfamadorians who offer Billy Pilgrim peace of mind at the expense of selfhood and personal integrity.

This Lucifer of a "papa" (166) is known as the "champion" commercial artist of his time (77), a master of illusions—a perfect copying machine, in fact, with "absolute" control of its paintbrush. "Nobody," Rabo explains, "could counterfeit better than Dan Gregory" (88). Even under Gregory's spell, Rabo is repelled by this "lord and master's" sterile and mechanical creations. Though technically perfect, there is nothing human about them, nothing of that vision of human sacredness and imaginative wonder which in his own work would one day provide so startling an epiphany in the novel *Breakfast of Champions* (190). Gregory's work is not just passionless, but dangerously reductionist—stagnant and morally simplistic. "Nobody," says Rabo, "could put more of the excitement of a single moment into the eyes of stuffed animals" (84). Pablo Picasso is Gregory's idea of Satan, and he calls paintings in the Museum of Modern Art, where Rabo is forbidden to visit, the "vomit of lunatics and degenerates and charlatans" (167). Gregory, of course, is the "lunatic" for portraying life in the form of human stereotypes and moral absolutes. His paintings, Rabo says, were truthful about material things, but they lied about the human spirit and the nature of reality—"that one moment was no more important than any other, and that all moments quickly run away" (84).

Rabo knows that the tendency of people to imitate art makes the "lies," the allegedly objective representations of artists like Gregory, as lethal as bombs or bullets—as dangerous as those toy machine guns with plastic bayonets that look so real (147). Rabo uses a fifteenth-century painting to illustrate the power of creative fantasy: "Compressed into a small space and in bizarre combinations were the most powerful forces of the universe . . . a renaissance effort to make an atom bomb" (217). Rabo fills his narrative with examples of lives perverted by the sentimental, patriotic, or romantic mystifications of life by art. Dan Gregory's assistant Fred Jones, for instance, is ingenious at counterfeiting the accents of movie gangsters and cowboys, roles he imitates in real life. Marilee Kemp worries that Nora's heroic declaration at the end of Ibsen's *A Doll's House* that she will make her own way in the world sends a sentimental message to impressionable female readers, since Nora has no skills or education or money, and no prospect of a job (149). Rabo worries that young people will believe, from movie versions of World War II, that wars are fought by old men instead of babies, with blank cartridges and catsup for blood (257).[2]

Gregory loves most to paint historical scenes of violence and bloodshed, military "heroes" like Mussolini (63), and episodes from romantic adventure stories, such as Robinson Crusoe and Robin Hood, of good triumphing over evil. Adept at ideological camouflage, Gregory actually inspires insane political and racist passions in democratic and fascist nations alike. By no coincidence does a real estate and insurance millionaire in Lubbock, Texas, own the most complete collection of Dan Gregory paintings in the world. Thus Rabo decides about the "delusions of moral grandeur" of painters, storytellers, poets, playwrights, historians, and essayists who play at God, or, at least, justices of the Supreme Court of Good and Evil, that perhaps the most admirable thing about the Abstract Expressionist painters was that they refused to serve on such a court (141).

For the impressionable Devil's apprentice, neither the romantic illusions Gregory peddles nor his moral and artistic authority are easy to resist. Rabo's early self-concept comes from reading romantic histories and novels, and from self-help books about how to get ahead in America (183). He dreams of himself as a crusading knight who will fetch the Holy Grail for Gregory's mistress, Marilee (182), rescuing her from the death dealer who sends her alone to a clinic to dispose of the fetus she carries. As surely as the sister-muse figures of Marilee and Circe Berman serve as agents of life for Rabo, Dan Gregory is an Antichrist in artist's clothing. His projects for Rabo are "diabolical" (106); he appears to Rabo "motionless and silent and shapeless in a voluminous black caftan," crouched before a fireplace as if engaged in satanic ritual (96); his studio, his "one indubitable masterpiece," is filled with image-distorting mirrors (97), antiques from a romantic past, pictures of false paradises (93), and numerous glowing fires. At one point, the master of deceptions appears to Rabo only as a head and hands, declaring: 'I was born in a stable like Jesus Christ, and I cried like this': From his throat came a harrowing counterfeit of the cries of an unwanted baby" (99)—Yeats's bestial, substitute Christ, no doubt.[3]

Gregory's studio teems with hellish omens. Rabo recalls a mantelpiece with eight human skulls arranged in order of size, with a child's at one end and a great-grandfather's at the other—"a marimba for cannibals" (96). The knocker on Gregory's door resembles a Gorgon's head, infected with verdigris (96), an appropriate symbol for one whose work is loveless and stagnant and turns to stone the humanity of all who look upon it. In Gregory's entrance hall is "a spiral staircase," Vonnegut's favorite trope for mechanistic systems of control. No wonder Rabo should reflect, "So reluctant was I to come any further into this dumbfoundingly complex and mirrored environment" (98).

Considering the malevolence of the man in black to whom Rabo entrusts his artistic soul, it is unsurprising that falling asleep in Gregory's sumptuous chamber of a "gilded cage" at the top of Gregory's spiral staircase, he dreams of danger signals at a railway crossing (99). Looking back upon this as the spiritual crossroads of his career, Rabo reflects that he was damnably close to becoming what Gregory was, and "regrettably did in many ways" (134). He admits that he still remains "capable" of the same sort of "commercial kitsch" Gregory used to do (148)—a facility for drawing or painting a likeness of anything "my eye could see" (264).

Rabo knows he could easily have become another soulless Gregory imitation, the Devil's "errand boy," "cunning as a sewer rat" (15), putting his perfect mechanical dexterity to work in pursuit of a dishonest commercial success. "Sewer rat" is a portentous drowning image—the protagonist's fate if he relinquishes his will to Gregory. The image no doubt reflects Vonnegut's dissatisfaction with his own early concessions to commercial success. Rabo's early paintings are clearly an embarrassment, a negation of art, "black holes from which no intelligence or skill can ever escape" (126). The paintings appropriately fall apart due to an unfortunate choice of materials and chemical reactions between the paint he uses and certain pollutants in the atmosphere. The work disintegrates, leaving only a blank canvas and what looks like moldy Rice Krispies on the floor. He reflects that he had given up his boyhood dream of being a serious artist, convinced by Gregory that he would never be anything but "a reasonably good camera" (44). But while in thrall to Gregory, Rabo had begun to serve a second apprenticeship to the great modern masters in the Museum of Modern Art—the Impressionists, Cubists, Dadaists, Surrealists, and Abstract Expressionists.[4]

Their intensely psychological canvases speak to Rabo's deepest spiritual needs; they provide a sympathetic analogue to his personal struggles with fragmentation and despair; they confirm his sense that the important realities are those inside himself; and they encourage him to explore his own subconscious for a deeper understanding of the chaos within, showing him ways to transform schizophrenic fragmentation into works of art that are paradoxically beautiful and whole. These paintings are not petrified like Gregory's but "liquid"—open, emotional, complex, and protean, "old stuff in music," Rabo explains, "pure essence of human wonder" (294).

That Rabo had become an artist with "options"—a disciple of spirit versus a devotee of the machine—is that familiar schizophrenic dilemma in which the forces of Thanatos and Eros battle for the protagonist's divided soul. The potential perversion of Rabo's yearning, authentic self by a complacent, "counterfeit" self is enacted here by psychic projections of Terry Kitchens, a fellow artist, and Fred Jones, a military man. Terry and Fred closely resemble each other and Rabo acknowledges that work attributed to Kitchen was really his own (175). The orgasmic moment that comes for Fred Jones when he is killing comes for Kitchens when he is creating. Jones grows ecstatic upon gripping the joystick of his airplane, firing his machine gun, and watching the enemy plane explode into fire and smoke (160). "What beauty," Rabo mocks, "So unexpected and pure! So easy to achieve!"

Kitchens, on the other hand, experiences his greatest emotional satisfaction when gripping a spray gun, watching paint explode on canvas. Same sort of happiness, Rabo says (161). Rabo completes the image of Eros perverted by aggression and death, concluding, "I now compare his [Jones] elation over arcs and spirals and splotches in the atmosphere with what Jackson Pollock used to feel as he watched what dribbled paint chose to do when it struck a canvas on his studio floor" (160, 161). Rabo, of course, chooses art that is soulful, protean, mysterious, and expressive of the inner eye and the labyrinths of the human mind, over art that is coldly mechanical and static. The latter, he decides, "was too fucking easy" (267). "Life, by definition," he says, "is never still. . . . Even a picture of a bowl of pears on a checkered tablecloth is liquid, if laid on canvas by the hand of a master" (84).[5]

Fittingly, a work by Gregory's spiritual opposite, Picasso, highlights Rabo's education in creative transcendence—the knowledge that "Belief is nearly the whole of the universe" (152)—that so-called "real life" is as much a product of mind, an artifact, an illusion, as a painting or a work of fiction. Rabo refers to the new reality Picasso has created by deconstructing a Gregory illustration from an Italian magazine. The original, an advertisement for American cigarettes showing three cowboys smoking around a campfire at night, Picasso has reassembled into a multifaceted collage of a cat (236). Rabo finds it impossible not to translate ideas in his head into actual experience: "This secret fantasy . . . infected and continues to infect my way of seeing scenes in real life. If I watch two people on a street corner . . . I see . . . vertical bands of light inside them" (212). To actualize an exotic relationship with Marilee, Rabo behaves "as though" the fantasy were already real (152). Rabo, himself, becomes a human collage after the war, "patched up" in a hospital near Dresden.

Rabo realizes that Gregory is his own imaginative construction, or schizophrenic invention, and can be dismantled as easily as Gregory's romantic cowboys.[6] "Everything about Dan Gregory," he says, "except for his paintings, had fewer connections with reality and common sense than the most radical modern art!" (168). "Think what a bizarre creation his studio was," Rabo says, "an hallucination created at tremendous expense and effort!" (168). The mirrors in Gregory's studio, from every conceivable period and shape, hanging in crazy angles, are the mind's surreal windows, casting an infinite number of self images onto reality. Says Rabo, they multiplied "the bewildered observer to infinity" (97). As Gregory is "invisible," so Rabo says, I "myself was everywhere." Life with Gregory only "seemed as real as Hell" (163). It is up to Rabo to conceive better illusions—an iconography that turns war to peace, hatred to love, bigotry to compassion, rather than that which "eggs men on to be even more destructive and cruel."[7] For it *is* we, he asserts, who choose (240).

Thus, as Vonnegut had done in *Breakfast of Champions*, Rabo asserts his artistic independence from a sterile and mechanical creator. Rabo is on his way to becoming an "art expert" not just by possessing the largest private collection of Abstract Expressionist paintings in the world, but in translating the spiritual and philosophical message of these surreal wonders into vital and imaginative living. "As for my own work," Rabo says, "the big fields of color before which I could stand intoxicated for hour after hour . . . were meant to be beginnings. I expected them to become more and more complicated as I slowly but surely closed in on what had so long eluded me: soul, soul, soul" (247).

It is not art alone that reforms Rabo's artistic soul or completes his return to psychic health. His emergence from chaos is aided by two powerful, life-directed, female figures who renew his will to live and open his emotional nature, as the Museum of Modern Art has opened his artistic vision. Whereas war and childhood alienation had left him a "blank brained, deep breathing hermit" (35),[8] these surrogate mothers, lovers, and sister-muses lead him away from self-doubt and hermetic isolation, rejuvenate creative energies, and teach him sympathy and self-acceptance. Vonnegut evokes in Circe Berman his favorite image of humanitarian aid. She goes to fund-raisers for volunteer fire departments. Both she and Marilee Kemp extend the protagonist's "female rescue squad" (299) begun by Eliza Swain and Melody in *Slapstick,* agents of Eros who not only make the hero a whole man, but teach his soul to sing. It is to these women that Rabo devotes his magnum opus, the masterwork he calls "Now It's Women's Turn," and whose humanity explains his narrative's title, *Bluebeard.* By contrast to the obscenely destructive male of the seventeenth-century fairy tale by Charles Perrault, Rabo notes that it is the female of the species who plants the seeds of something beautiful and edible.[9] "The only missile they can ever think of throwing at anybody," Rabo says, "is a ball or a bridal bouquet" (225).

Circe Berman joins Rabo as his house guest after the death of his second wife has left him alone in a nineteen-room house on the waterfront of East Hampton, Long Island. A candidate for schizophrenia, Rabo is so listless, undernourished, and neglectful of personal hygiene that Circe teases him that she is afraid of catching leprosy from him (127). The loss of an eye in the war has left Rabo with a horrible scar he calls "his most secret disfigurement" (118),[10] but the term more aptly describes his unhealthy solitude and obsession with a haunted past. Circe operates on Rabo's ailing psyche as if he were a machine (22) trapped in a time warp. She herself lives outside linear time. At the moment she admonishes Rabo and his "gun-shot" war buddy Slazinger, "you and your ex-pal here never got past the Great Depression and World War Two" (125), her watch, which has never run anyway, crashes to the floor as if to break the hold of Rabo's death sleep. Willful by design, Circe in her first words to Rabo, "How did your parents die?" (13), shocks him into dealing constructively with the present, which now, like Circe, "nips at his heels like a rabid fox terrier" (54). Circe forces Rabo to become "unstuck" in time by insisting he take up painting again and that he write his life story. Reversing the chronic regression of Billy Pilgrim, Rabo announces, "Back to the present" (159). The writing produces a symbiotic experience in psychic healing and self-creativity—literary exorcism in the form of autobiography, which pries Rabo from petrifying memories—and emotional renewal in the form of a diary which assimilates the past and revitalizes the present. Suggesting Rabo's sense of life as always becoming—open, protean, and mysterious—he exclaims, "I had no idea that this was going to be a diary as well as an autobiography" (199). Rabo's memoirs take him into that world of space-time where past and present realities flow together in the manner of those prized Abstract Expressionist paintings.

Circe, then, true to her mythological namesake, is a sorceress who turns men into the animal closest to their nature. Rabo's second wife Edith made him a pet raccoon (260), an animal so docile in spirit he ceases to grow. Circe makes him feisty again, stimulating the artist within. Not only does she bring this "Lazarus . . . back to life again" (299); she makes him a celebrant of Eros. Says Rabo,

> This one house by the seaside, so empty and dead only a few months ago, is now giving birth to a book about how to revolt successfully, a book about how poor girls feel about rich boys, and the memoirs of a painter whose pictures all came unstuck from canvas. And we are expecting a baby, too! (201)

Marilee Kemp also serves as a harbinger of new life for Rabo. He wonders if he might be "a replacement for the Armenian baby which had been taken from her womb" (71). Whereas Circe is more Rabo's spiritual bride, Marilee, patron and mistress, makes him a lover of art and an artful lover. She provides him with the best of art materials from Gregory's mansion and leads him directly to the Museum of Modern Art, but also to the bedroom and the ecstasies of sensual love.

This affirmation of Eros is critical to Rabo's final psychic healing. The hero's most visible psychological wound has been a schizophrenic dissociation of mind and body—a separation of "my soul and my meat," in Rabo's words (258)—the inability to enjoy normal male-female relationships, and disdain for sexual experience. At first Rabo is only mechanically curious about what sort of "devices" he and Marilee might be (180). But Marilee's lovemaking is so simultaneously tender and erotic—Rabo has splendid successive orgasms he calls "retroactive" and "prospective" (172)—that he is carried again into that fluid space-time which fuses past and present, flesh and spirit.[11] Clocks stop while they make love, and Rabo declares that "Life itself could be sacramental" (170).

Just as Rabo and Vonnegut form one identity, so art and love form a single potent force for meaning and renewal in a mechanical world. Thus Rabo remarks, "Our love-making anticipated Abstract Expressionism in a way, since it was about absolutely nothing but itself" (17). Once again, these saving revelations are neither sentimental nor simple. Rabo requires rude jolts from the women in his life to remind him that he and they are human beings, not machines. Only when scolded by his cook for treating her as invisible, and by Marilee for having forgotten to "worry" about her, does he promise to change (241).

Marilee and Circe do more than "anticipate" modern art; they personalize its spiritual dynamism, offering Rabo further lessons in the subjective epistemology by which he learns to reconstruct his life and art. Marilee seems to appear almost mystically from the pluralist world of Picasso's *Les Demoiselles d'Avignon*. Her infinite diversity allows her to pose for nine different female illustrations. That she undergoes five major character transformations—coalminer's daughter, Ziegfeld Follies show-girl, Countess Portomaggiori with a palace in Florence, the biggest Sony distributor in Europe, and Europe's greatest collector of Armenian postwar modern art—suggests the eternal dynamism of Picasso's painting, and disputes the monologic of Gregory's own static representations.

The multiple personalities of Circe Berman, alias Polly Madison, author of best-selling novels for young adults, so disturb Rabo Karabekian that, on the eve of her departure, he says his feelings were so contradictory he was both glad and sorry to see her leave (261). Agitator and nurturer, sorceress and redeemer, lunatic and humanitarian, Circe generates the necessary spiritual angst to make Rabo an "untamed raccoon" again (278), a creative rather than vegetative being. Complexity allows her to serve paradoxical symbolic roles—a sorceress whose supernatural power raises Rabo from the dead, and an all-too-real human being whose schizophrenia reminds Rabo of his narrow escape from that disease.

Circe, like Rabo, writes "to keep grief away" (298). A husband who sees himself as a machine and a father who commits suicide leave her so "petrified by insanity" (191) she becomes nearly catatonic at the sight of Paul Slazinger in a straitjacket (193). Circe's and Slazinger's craziness throws Rabo's own sanity into sharper relief. "What was our bond?" asks Rabo. "Loneliness and wounds from World War Two which were quite grave" (169). Numerous references link Slazinger to Rabo and to former scapegoat psychic projections in Vonnegut's fiction. "It is well known that he was a veteran," Rabo says. "It is well known that I am a veteran" (191). Both come from a family of cobblers. "It takes a molecule to know a molecule," Slazinger tells Rabo (197). Paul has delusions of grandeur—"I was put on Earth . . . with two missions" (197)—he hallucinates visions of paradise, and he rejects literature as a vehicle for human improvement. But it is Paul, not Rabo, whose dreadful war injuries and troublesome pessimism land him in the psychiatric ward of the Riverhead V. A. hospital, and Circe who takes drugs. When Rabo asks of his two schizophrenic friends, "And which patient needed me most now in the dead of night" (195), we see that Rabo has overcome personal fragmentation and despair to become a healer of others.

Rabo Karabekian is the furthest indeed of all Vonnegut's protagonists from belonging in a prison or asylum. The question of Paul Proteus's sanity posed fifty years earlier in *Player Piano* has been answered with an unequivocal assertion of restored mental health. The vigor of Rabo's narrative alone, the energy of Eros, tells us so. But it is the amazing painting in Rabo's potato barn that climaxes and confirms his achievement: a harmony of self and society, body and soul, man and artist, that makes him not only sane but happy—Vonnegut's most emotionally fulfilled hero. At age seventy-one, high time! Soul clap its hands and sing. Rabo subtitles his autobiography, "Confessions of an American Late Bloomer or Always the Last to Learn" (194).

If Circe Berman is "subdued, humble, awed, and virginal" (279) at the prospect of viewing the forbidden contents of Rabo's potato barn, the sight of "the perfectly tremendous whatchamacallit," the gem of his collection, transports her to a state of postcoital languor (298). Like Gregory's studio, Rabo's potato barn is a psychic projection, "an improbable dwelling . . . invisible from the main house" (6), and a metaphor for organic imagination. Circe's sexual response to the painting climaxes her relationship with Rabo as spiritual lovers, and intensifies the coupling of art and love as a redemptive force. Circe cannot imagine how Rabo or anyone could make such a "big, beautiful painting about something so important" (297). What the painting is "about"—"an exorcism of an unhappy past, a symbolic repairing of all the damage I have done to myself and others during my brief career as a painter" (275)—mirrors, climaxes, and augments the meanings of Rabo's narrative and of Vonnegut's work as a whole.

Suggesting Vonnegut's novels from *Player Piano to Breakfast of Champions,* the protagonist's psychodrama is played out over five hundred twelve square feet of canvas, eight surrealistic panels stretched side by side.[12] The painting strikingly resembles *Slaughterhouse-Five*. Its canvas has been "purged," and it is found "entombed in a locked chamber by an inspector looking for fire hazards deep underground" (272). In panoramic view, the painting presents the century's petrifying face, a Guernica-like record of apocalyptic suffering and death, nations of lunatics at war, whose madness has produced the protagonist's own dreadful pessimism and near-schizophrenia. Dresden—Vonnegut's unfading nightmare—is there. Its factories, prisons, and asylums pour forth thousands of scarecrow figures that surround Rabo in a sea of suffering humanity, not just soldiers "from everywhere" (207) and survivors of concentration camps, but fleeing civilians, German soldiers waiting to surrender, slave laborers, criminals, and lunatics—ten survivors to each square foot of painting (283). Half these victims, Rabo explains, are women, who aren't, he stresses, "what might be called movie stars" (285). Illustrating the spirallike, mechanistic, and universal impulse to cruelty that produces such suffering and despair, the painting's victims spill out onto the "rim" of a great valley (208); a posturing Japanese soldier stands by a medieval watchtower, preferring to die than give up his sword (286); and a Polynesian corporal in the New Zealand Field Artillery, descended form a warring tribe of cannibals, is captured in Torbruk, Libya, sitting on a discarded German ammunition box, reading an anti-Semitic newspaper published in Latvia (295).[12]

But the dominant force in this painting is Eros, not Thanatos. Rabo's rescue squad—Circe and Marilee—are not only present, but the painting's supporting pillars. When Circe searches the canvas for images of healthy women, Rabo notes, "You'll find healthy ones at either end—in the corners at the bottom." Suggesting organic life, Rabo says, "The healthy women are in the cellar with the beets and potatoes and turnips" (285). Most importantly, Rabo himself is there, confronting the Gorgon's face head on. In answer to Circe's question, "Are you there?" (284), Rabo replies:

> I pointed out myself at the bottom and right above the floor. . . . I was the largest figure—the one as big as a cigarette. I was also the only one of the thousands with his back to the corners, so to speak. The crack between the fourth and fifth panels ran up my spine and parted my hair, and might be taken for the soul of Rabo Karabekian. (284)

If the horrors of Dresden split the soul of Rabo Karabekian right up the middle, à la Paul Proteus, art puts the ailing hero together again. This painting is Rabo's "duty dance with death," as *Slaughterhouse-Five* was for Kurt Vonnegut. Through exorcism and the reconstructive processes of art, the hero's fate is not the schizophrenia feared by Paul Proteus—petrification or "descent into the maelstrom"—but wholeness and new life. In the manner of those dynamic Cubist constructions of his champion, Pablo Picasso, Rabo's fragmented selves are reconstituted and harmonized by the unifying power of art—in Yeats's words "transformed utterly . . . a terrible beauty is born" ("Easter 1916"). Rabo notes that the painting, even literally, expresses organic balance. It is "animal, vegetable, and mineral with colors and binders taken from creatures and plants and the growth beneath us" (279). Rabo remarks (appropriately) in a double entendre, "I changed the subject from war to peace" (239), and Circe subtitles the painting "The Peaceable Kingdom" (238).

Rabo's painting is compellingly autobiographical, but, paradoxically, its ontological integrity requires that it have a life of its own—that it be only the reality of itself (239).[13] Illustrating his belief that reality never holds still, Rabo tells Circe that the meanings of his painting are beyond his ability to control— shaped by artistic environment and by the viewer's subjectivity. "I lay on the first stroke of color," he says, "after that, the canvas has to do at least half the work" (171). Rabo observes that the barn itself is part of the painting. The point is precisely that which Patricia Waugh makes in defining a metafictional text: "The author discovers that the language of the text produces him or her as much as he or she produces the language of the text."[14] The painting's shifting surfaces and visual ambiguities entice the audience to textual participation, as creators rather that interpreters of meaning. Once upon a time Rabo explained to people the meanings of the fictions in the painting, but gave up in exhaustion. Now he insists viewers author their own texts: "Make up your own stories as you look at the whatchamacallit" (283). As Waugh explains, every interpretation becomes a "reconstruction or re-reading."[15] The reader reassembles the text, or Rabo's painting, as Picasso reassembled Gregory's advertisement. Rabo removes himself from the position of privileged creator by referring to himself as awed or surprised by his own creation.[16]

To demonstrate that an artistic objectification of Rabo the creator is impossible, Rabo shows Circe that his face is obscured by a thick fog "which wasn't there" (284) (the mind's impressionistic haze); he shows how the painting's figures dissolve into textual space, how the painting's organization into frames denies a totality or unified overview; and how the frames' vistas shift with every change of perspective. In effect, the artistic values Rabo identifies in his painting—those of Abstract Expressionism, Cubism, and Surrealism—mimic the pluralistic world of Rabo's narrative. "What could not be put into words" (276) is.[17] Rabo's memories drift in time and space. The reader must determine the structure of events from nonsequential fragments of information. Not only are characters fragmented and dispersed in the manner of Rabo's canvas; they are multiplied and presented from different angles simultaneously. The effect is ceaseless movement—the eternal dynamism by which Rabo achieves his own metamorphosis.

The parodic nature of these schizophrenic inventions suggests that *Bluebeard* comments upon more than the spiritual progress of Rabo Karabekian and a reborn Kurt Vonnegut. The identification of Rabo's story as a "hoax" autobiography, about the "why and how a painting came to be" (276), sets in motion an ingeniously interwoven complex of interdependent semiotic systems—linguistic games, parodies, jokes, fantasies, dreams—which cut across one another in a kaleidoscopic display of arbitrary invention. While nonmimetic systems have always been central to Vonnegut's aesthetics, *Bluebeard* is a metafictional masterpiece. Its proliferating "hoaxes" nullify traditional distinctions between reality and illusion, and foreground art and life as playful imaginative constructions—inseparable existential ventures in self-creativity. The novel abounds with examples of realities whose fluctuating meanings are determined by the perception of the viewer, shifts in language convention, or changes in historical or cultural context. Someone is fooled by a painter who *looks* to him like a musician, a lawyer, or a professional athlete (25). Fred Jones is mistaken for a World War I ace and an aviation pioneer (207). Fred looks and acts like Terry

Kitchens, but Fred was "a genuinely dumb, sweet lunk, whereas my own buddy
. . . was a graduate of Yale Law School" (247). Rabo's first wife thinks she is
getting "a mature, fatherly, retired military gentleman" for a husband as opposed to (Rabo's version of himself) "an impossibly self-centered and undisci-
plined jerk of nineteen or so" (258). Marilee's husband is the Italian minister
of culture, but also a British agent. Illustrating Saussure's proposition that signs
function not through their intrinsic value but through their relative position,
Rabo "transmogrified" his first wife "from her being Mrs. Richard Fairbanks,
Jr. into being Mrs. Rabo Karabekian instead" (6). "Not bad" becomes another
term for "disappointing" (154). Rabo muses that his name could easily have
been "Robert King" (204). Realities also metamorphose as the result of historical or cultural perspective. What "used to be a whaling port" is "just another
tourist trap nowadays" (261). Americans perceive Marilee to be "a dim-witted
floozy," whereas Italians find her an "incomparably beautiful and gifted actress"
(228). The Dominican monk Girolamo Savonarola reconstitutes reality from
pagan to Christian by scraping the walls of a Medici palazzo in Florence (217).
The criminal Vartan Mamigonian, originally Marktieh Kouzoumdjian, subsequently Marc Conlomb, becomes known as a hero of the French Resistance and
the resplendent chairman of the most extensive travel organization in the world.
Even an oceanliner converts to a troopship (124), and the foyer of Rabo's home
("a big joke") converts from Victorian to modern with the change of decor. By
noting the unreliability of signs as verifiers of objective reality, Rabo is encouraged to reevaluate the status of "truth" and "fiction" and to appreciate their
interchangeability—that reality can be made over by imagination.

The "galleries" in Rabo's narrative are "imaginary"; the ones in his head
are "real" (29, 30). The stepfather of Rabo's children "is the only real father
they'd ever had" (292). "We could have been plumbers," Rabo says of himself
and his artist colleagues (293). Gregory's model for the master criminal Fu
Manchu is a "simperingly" polite Chinese laundryman named Sam Wu (90).
Marilee determines that Italy was "her real love" and its people her "real companions" (223). An artist named Beskudnikov takes counterfeit money as real
and rejects real money as fake (102). In a scene reminiscent of Italo Calvino's
Mr. Palomar, Rabo searches the faces of women at a train station, looking for
Marilee, and despairs that his earnest looks will only confirm for each woman
that the darker races are indeed "leeringly lecherous" (78). Finally, Rabo fills
his narrative with people form real life—Al Jolson, W. C. Fields, Jackie Kennedy, the Abstract Expressionist painters—whose identities merge with fictional
creations. These actual people are forever acting out fictional roles, as the fictive
characters give an appearance of reality.

The novel's most elaborate "hoax" is what Julia Kristeva call "the poly-
phonic text"—a plurality of discourses which fragment and disperse the speaker
through intertextual space.[18] Vonnegut disseminates *his* speaking voice over

intertextual space that includes his real life experience, his fictional life as Rabo Karabekian, and his life as twice refracted and compressed in Rabo's autobiographical painting. The problematical interplay among the various texts produces constant interchange and circulation of meaning, intercourse as open and mysterious as the lovemaking of Rabo and Marilee Kemp, and as organic as the interpenetrating frames of Rabo's painting.[19] Again metalovemaking and meta-art come together as one—announcing themselves as twin loving ventures in self-creativity by which the fractured, Picasso-like Vonneguts are made harmonious and whole.

Vonnegut's metafictional strategy in offering us alternative versions of Kurt Vonnegut exposes, in a sense, his own fictionality and therefore the possibilities of existential authorship within and without the text. Yet in *Bluebeard* the metafictional game takes an unexpected twist. Whereas in earlier novels Vonnegut establishes his fictive existence by entering the story directly, he makes no such personal appearance in *Bluebeard*. This time he appears more interested in stressing his reality, or wholeness, than his existence as a literary fragment, standing in opposition to his artist hero. Instead of splitting the identity of Rabo the created and Vonnegut the creator, as in *Breakfast of Champions,* Vonnegut becomes Rabo Karabekian, the most complete and human of all Vonnegut's creations.

As he assesses his career at the end of his narrative, Rabo's confidence falters momentarily. He wonders if the popular appeal of his work will continue to cost him serious critical understanding (283)—or whether a critic will ever come along who sees more in his work than a "Disneyland attraction" (283), art which expresses the most serious concerns of his age, rather than ephemeral entertainment. Yet Vonnegut's protagonist is at peace with himself at last. He ends his story praising the unity of body and soul that created "a painting such as the world had never seen before" (239): "Oh, happy meat. Oh, happy soul. Oh, happy Rabo Karabekian" (300).

But what of Rabo's announcement that he has written "the end" (1) to the story of his life? One might wonder if Kurt Vonnegut were saying his artistic "goodbyes." Au Contraire. Rabo has shown us, after all, that meaning is always being newly created, that every ending is a new beginning, which makes him a true member of what Circe Berman calls the "Genesis Gang" (241). Certainly, like Rabo Karabekian, Vonnegut has every reason to feel "at home . . . a place I never thought I'd be" (236), to rest from his long psychic journey, and to feel "twangingly proud and satisfied" (295). Yet while Rabo's artistic priorities have been met, Eugene Debs Hartke submits to a reckoning even broader and deeper, vowing to leave no sins hidden, not only those of art, but of his basic humanity.

13

Hartke's Hearing:
Vonnegut's Heroes on Trial

Must a written book be brought forth in which everything is contained from which the ashes should be judged?

Vonnegut, *Mass Promulgated*

While there is a lower class I am in it. . . . While there is a soul in prison I am not free.

Eugene V. Debs

At first glance, the protagonist of *Hocus Pocus* seems not to benefit from the psychic "repair" of Rabo Karabekian, a man at peace with his transgressions. The world's fundamental lunacy so burdens the mind of Eugene Debs Hartke, he agrees that human beings are "about 1,000 times dumber and meaner than they think they are" (*Hocus Pocus* 55), then consoles himself with the thought, "At least the world will end . . . very soon" (13). In the land of the free and the home of the brave, the forces of stupidity, cruelty, and injustice appear so irresistible—on the order of tidal waves or earthquakes[1]—that the split personas of *Hocus Pocus,* Vonnegut the novelist and Hartke the teacher-narrator, offer this dose of sobering iconoclasm: "I see no harm in telling young people to prepare for failure rather than success, since failure is the main thing that is going to happen to them" (60).

Such expressions of despair prompt a majority of reviewers to conclude, as always, that Vonnegut is a novelist of "pessimistic" or "defeatist" novels, that, in fact, futility—charting the planet's helpless drift toward apocalypse—is the primary subject of *Hocus Pocus.* According to Pauline Mayer, Vonnegut seduces us again with an "irresistible message of pessimism and doom"—a "fable of hopelessness" about injustice, greed, war, the destruction of our planet, and our "inability to do much about these and other calamities" (6D). For Jay Cantor, the depressed memoirs of Eugene Debs Hartke offer Vonnegut an opportunity to "model his despair." For the reader, they provide "a long education in the unchanging senselessness of life, unlikely to be transformed except for the worse" (15C). "Descent into disillusionment" (9C), Dan Cryer agrees. "Society's obituary" (2H), echoes Lisa Anderson. Even if Vonnegut *used* to be the "canary-in-the-coalmine," Anderson concedes, offering "not-too-late-to-wake-up parables of the perils of war, technology, pollution, and other 20th-century horrors," the author's present view of a crumbling American civilization is a "nightmare from which there is no hope of awakening" (lH) .

So it goes. Such unfortunate readings (this is Vonnegut's thirteenth novel) continue the familiar argument that those "crazy lunkers" (190) from outer space, Vonnegut's infamous Tralfamadorians, are at it again, reflecting the author's own sense of life's futility. Eugene Debs Hartke does appear infected with that same cynical world weariness that threatens to petrify earlier protagonists. Early childhood trauma, deforming experiences in Vietnam, and public humiliations that include family insanity, being fired late in life as a college physics teacher, and imprisonment for treason suggest to Eugene that human beings are so dumb and aggressive that the planet's destruction as imagined by the science fiction writer, Kilgore Trout, is inevitable. According to the story Eugene reads in *Black Garterbelt* called "The Elders of Tralfamadore" (188), the Tralfamadorians will render the earth "as sterile as the moon" (192), first by making the planet a hell of hatred and aggression through a rewriting of the Genesis myth and second by populating the universe with microscopic spacemen—self-reproducing germs which Earthlings will appropriate as new chemical weapons. The Elders instruct the writer of the Genesis story to encourage humans to "fill the Earth and subdue it: and have domination over the birds of the air and over everything that moves on the Earth" (189). Believing that the Creator Himself thus wants them to "wreck the joint" (190), Earthlings proceed to make the deadliest weapons and poisons in the universe, annihilating strangers as if doing "Him" a big favor (192).

After the war, rife with guilt and self-doubt, Eugene is understandably anxious to assign the calamities of his life to the Tralfamadorians, or to the two "prime movers" in the universe, "Time and Luck" (30), suggesting that Tralfamadorian fatalism does indeed, as Goldsmith and others say, help Vonnegut and his psychically scarred protagonists cope with their wartime nightmare. To wit, the Tralfamadorians are right that the horrors of life are something it does no good to worry about. Appropriately, Jay Cantor notes that while Eugene repeatedly counts the cost of being a Vietnam veteran, he "sounds more like a sad, wised-up WWII dogface than a Vietnam desperado" (15C). "If I were a fighter plane," says Eugene, "instead of a human being, there would be little pictures of people painted all over me" (284).

At the age of thirty-five, Eugene has seen so much death and destruction that, as with Malachi Constant and Billy Pilgrim before him, he drugs himself to reality—making himself "dissolute with alcohol and marijuana and women" (59)—

and dreams dangerous escapist fantasies such as Tralfamadore. Says Eugene: "What a relief it was to have somebody else confirm what I had come to suspect toward the end of the . . . war . . . particularly after I saw the head of a human being pillowed in the spilled guts of a water buffalo . . . that Humanity is going somewhere really nice was a myth for children under 6 years, like the Tooth Fairy and the Easter Bunny and Santa Claus" (194).

But rather than providing a saner or more mature perspective, the pain-killing philosophy of Tralfamadore reinforces Eugene's cynicism, threatening him with the same fate that claims Billy Pilgrim at the end of *Slaughterhouse-Five* (1969)—a form of moral paralysis that precludes responsibility or action. "I did not realize at the time," Eugene explains, "how much that story (Tralfamadorian) affected me. . . . Reading it was simply a way of putting off for just a little while my looking for another job and another place to live at the age of 51, with 2 lunatics in tow" (194).[2] It is this same emotional malaise—a tendency to paralysis and withdrawal—that separates Paul Proteus from his sanity, that lands Eliot Rosewater in an asylum, and that leads Howard Campbell to suicide.[3] But if Pilgrim's flight from the responsibility of "wakeful humanity" leads directly to what John Tilton calls a "spiritual oubliette" (101), it is precisely Eugene Debs Hartke's willingness to face the painful complexities of human identity and the anguish of choice that separates him from these earlier fragmented heroes.

Like Christopher Lehmann-Haupt—Vonnegut's most hostile and uncomprehending critic—those who see Vonnegut as a fatalist and view pessimism as the subject of *Hocus Pocus* do so without understanding the role of pessimism in the psychological plot central to this novel and to Vonnegut's career as a whole. Lehmann-Haupt is precisely right that Eugene "loathes" himself for all the killing and lying he did in Vietnam, observing that "If there's anything you don't like about Eugene, he has probably beaten you to it" (16).[4] But failing to keep his own counsel, i.e., to think "as carefully about the pessimism as Mr. Vonnegut seems to want you to do," Lehmann-Haupt concludes that Eugene's acrid self-criticism means an increase in Vonnegut's own "darkness and despair" and warns the reader against succumbing to the author's unreal "nuclear apoplexy."

Failing to understand the divided nature of Vonnegut's latest hero, as he previously misunderstood Rudy Waltz, Lehmann-Haupt hears Eugene's nihilistic voice, the Eugene who feels powerless and despised, but ignores the efforts of a healthier, aspiring self to overcome apathy and to evolve from jailbird to Vonnegut's canary bird, the humane voice exemplified in *Hocus Pocus* and *Fates Worse Than Death* by the Sermon on the Mount. No Vonnegut protagonist since Howard Campbell, in fact, has chosen to explore his shadowy inner world so directly, or to nurture awareness and moral responsibility more avidly than Eugene Debs Hartke, whose potential as a healer of self, then a healer of others, distinguishes Vonnegut's protagonists after the spiritual transfiguration of *Breakfast of Champions.*

It is the essential narrative structure of *Hocus Pocus* —a retrospective vision in which Eugene puts his own troubled soul on trial—that keys this novel's creative affirmation much as it did so ingeniously in *Deadeye Dick*. While Eugene awaits a literal trial for treason for supposedly masterminding a mass prison break at the New York State Maximum Security Adult Correction Institute, his lawyer seizes upon Eugene's remark that he is addicted to older women and housekeeping as credible grounds for a plea of insanity (109). Since in his own mind a history of killing and dying and of invented justifications he calls "lethal hocus pocus" (148) leaves his sanity much in doubt, Eugene determines to conduct a kind of pre-trial, an inquiry both moral and psychological, in which he weighs the sane things he has done, the hopeful, caring, merciful side of his nature, against his insane deeds, the cruel and aggressive acts of an unfeeling, cynical, or indifferent self. As if, he says, there really was a "judgment day" and "a big book" in which all things were written (150),[5] he will compile a kind of moral account book which he hopes will prove his sanity—"that I could be compassionate" (290)—despite what he calls his "worst sins," the lives he has taken, the lies he has told, set against his life-enhancing deeds. When his lawyer sees Eugene's tortured marginal notes about this or that damaged human being, this or that corpse, the lawyer observes: "The messier the better . . . because any fair minded jury looking at them will have to believe that you are in a deeply disturbed mental state, and probably have been for quite some time" (150).

When, imprisoned and awaiting trial, Eugene declares, "I haven't been convicted of anything yet" (18, 19), he effectively invites the reader-turned-psychologist to become his co-analyst and judge, probing his culpability and his sanity. As with Vonnegut's former heroes on trial—Paul Proteus, Howard Campbell, Eliot Rosewater, Kilgore Trout, Walter Starbuck—the interpretive challenge is complicated by the ambiguity of Eugene's psychological condition and by the fact that, as Eugene's lawyer demonstrates, notions of sanity are either hopelessly ambiguous or convenient labels that suppress independent thought and protect the status quo. Eugene's lawyer knows that Eugene's accusers will judge him insane because "They believe that all you Vietnam veterans are crazy, because that's their reputation" (150). When Eugene protests that it all really did happen, that his lists have not been "hallucinated" by the flying saucer people or the CIA, his lawyer sighs, "all the same—all the same." Vonnegut discourages, and Eugene learns to resist, easy categorizations. "All subjects," Eugene insists, "do not reside in neat little compartments" (143). In fact, he says, people are never stronger than when they think up their own arguments for believing what they believe. In the pluralistic manner of those dynamic surreal paintings Rabo Karabekian so admires, Eugene recognizes that reality is a projection of mind, whose meanings defy absolute interpretation. Foreshadowing the difficulty Eugene will have in differentiating the contending "enigmatic" proofs of his sanity or insanity, Vonnegut's verbal destabilizations as always force the reader into a debate as to what sanity is or is not, along with the protagonist "thinking up" interpretations that reflect the quality of the humanity of the perceiver.

At age sixty-one, in the year 2001, from Eugene's prison-home in the Tarkington bell tower library, Eugene's self-inquiry indicates that by war's end he was indeed a "seriously wounded man both physically and psychologically" (116)—a potential "burned out case" (103) prone to "psychosomatic hives" (290, 299) and dangerously tempted by "good old oblivion" (119). The computer Griot finds him so unsalvageable it projects him as hopelessly depressed, dying of cirrhosis of the liver on skid row (105).

While it is the entire last half of the twentieth century (115, 116) that has potentially unbalanced Eugene—the spiraling brutality of childhood, West Point, Vietnam, and humiliating experiences at Tarkington College and Athena prison— he locates the most immediate source of the "something wrong with me" (149) in what he calls his "family image problem" (34), a father "as full of excrement as a Christmas turkey" (14) and a "blithering nincompoop" (15) of a mother so vacuous she agrees with "every decision" his father ever made.[6] He finds his parents' lack of integrity so deeply troubling (34) he fantasizes that his father was actually a war hero and that both parents were killed heroically on safari in Tanganyika (35). Ultimately, he suggests that an appropriate epitaph would be, "OK, I admit it. It really was a whorehouse" (206).

In the mold of Felix Hoenikker, whose coldness turns his children into "babies full of rabies" *(Cat's Cradle* 47), Eugene's father is a research scientist who whores for Dupont, a manufacturer of high explosives (32). Eugene reflects that during the war, which was about "nothing but the ammunition business" (14), he may have done his father's bidding when calling in a white-phosphorous barrage or a napalm air strike on a returning Jesus Christ (14). His father's success at finding new synthetic plastics to make lighter weapons earns him the company's vice-presidency in charge of Research and Development, which in turn earns one of Tarkington's trustees a fortune when Dupont is sold to I. G. Farben of Germany, the same company that manufactured cyanide gas used to kill civilians of all ages, including babies in arms, during the Holocaust (37). The greed and human indifference that Dupont and Eugene's father represent transform Dupont's employees into robots unaware of the "miracles" they package and label (39). And, says Eugene, "never mind what he did to the environment with his nonbiodegradable plastics. Look what he did to me!" (15)[7]

Specifically, Eugene refers to the embarrassment he feels when his father forces him to cheat on a high school science project about crystallography for the County Fair. Eugene has so little to do with the exhibit his father constructs that when he inquires what his father is doing he is told to be quiet. "Don't bother me," his father scolds (42). The unfair competition makes Eugene so literally sick he throws up. Thinking back to when they were caught, Eugene discerns ominous spiral-like connections between his father's aggression and absence of conscience—the desire to win at any costs—and that of the Vietnam war: "Generals George Armstrong Custer . . . Robert E. Lee . . . and William Westmoreland . . . all come to mind" (44). Disclaiming guilt, his father declared that they were not about to go home with their "tails between their legs" (45).

About the "spider web" of guilt and futility his father has fashioned, which Eugene likens to a microscopic universe (119),[8] he concludes, "at least it wasn't a hydrogen bomb" (118). Yet he emerges from the war zone of childhood with psychological wounds so severe that only "a whole new planet or death" (48) would cure them. The planet, perhaps, is Tralfamadore; the "death" is the death of the spirit for those who succumb to Tralfamadorian fatalism as a defense against pain. After all, Eugene says, "If my father was a horse's fundament and my mother was a horse's fundament, what can I be but another horse's fundament" (142). References to having been "zapped" during the "darkest days" of childhood (40), to both childhood and Vietnam as "battlefields" (35), and to Eugene's reliance upon drugs to survive both ordeals effectively merge Eugene's childhood nightmare with that of his war experience. He concludes that "at the age of 35, Eugene Debs Hartke was again as dissolute with respect to alcohol and marijuana and loose women as he had been during his last 2 years in high school. And he had lost all respect for himself and the leadership of this country, just as, 17 years earlier, he had lost all respect for himself and his father at the Cleveland, Ohio Science Fair" (59).

The oblivion of drugs—turning his "brain to cobwebs" (41) with marijuana, alcohol, and their philosophical counterpart, Tralfamadorian fatalism ("failure is the norm," he decides [41])—entraps Eugene further in the web of lovelessness and aggression he seeks to escape. His crisis of trauma and withdrawal is, of course, precisely that which besets Vonnegut's previous heroes, the anesthetic of fatalism now threatening to claim Eugene—to infect him with "existential gangrene"—as it claims Billy Pilgrim. Billy's withdrawal into a world of phantom fulfillment tempts Eugene through "habits" of masking or distorting reality, which he "develops very young" (36) and which leave him as dangerously "unprepared" (41) for complex experience as the brain-damaged victims of Athena or Tarkington.

It is here that Eugene's father does his damage, creating that separation of Eugene's several selves that Howard Campbell calls schizophrenic (136), a split between the protagonist's aspiring, creative self, and the isolated, moribund side of his character. As Eugene ignores or lies about unpleasant experience, he buries or hides his youthful idealisms, that part of himself that wants to tell the truth, so that his hopeful voice, the voice of conscience, the spirit of the man he is named after, Eugene Debs, is neutralized by his father's voice, the voice of Tralfamadorian futility.[9]

Just as Rudy Waltz's father in *Deadeye Dick* counsels Rudy to "plug your ears whenever anybody tells you you have a creative gift of any kind" (112), Eugene's father discourages Eugene's deepest creative instincts. Eugene's happiest, even ecstatic moments come as a musical innovator with his high school band—"cutting loose" on the piano with "never-the-same-way-twice" music (15), which resembles Rudy Waltz's love of scat singing, or tinkering with imaginative recipes. But, like Rudy, Eugene's parents turn him into their family servant, who does most of the family marketing after school, and most of the housework and cooking, leaving him little time to nurture the artist within. Eugene's father also subverts Eugene's literary ambitions by deflecting him from the school of journalism at the University of Michigan to the school for homicidal maniacs at West Point (14). His father believes that the prestige of a son at West Point may atone for Eugene's mediocre high school career, letting his school years go by without scoring a touchdown, or doing anything but making "jungle music" (37). So just as Rudy's father turns Rudy into a druggist, and the father of Rabo Karabekian delivers his son into the hands of the artist of mechanical creations, Dan Gregory, Eugene's father makes an unholy alliance with West Point recruiter, Colonel Sam Wakefield (Eugene sees them laughing and shaking hands [51]), who desperately wants Eugene's body to mold, "no matter what it was." Sam Wakefield represents the cynicism that tempts past heroes to moral suicide, a false tutor in the manner of Bokonon and Kilgore Trout. Eugene had hoped to take courses in English, History, and Political Science and to serve the public by working on the school paper (33). Instead, because his father considers West Point "a great prize," something to boast about to simple-minded neighbors (15), Eugene's creative energies are diverted into the deathly business of making war, Eros converted to Thanatos.[10] Notably, Vonnegut explains that his own father told him he could go to college only *if* he studied chemistry. "How flattered I would have been if only he said instead that I, too, should become an architect" *(Fates* 54). Vonnegut resists his father's attempts to enlist him in Culver Military Academy, "a little West Point and Annapolis combined" *(Fates* 52), in hopes it would make him "neat." The academy strikingly resembles Tarkington College in *Hocus Pocus*.

By graduation, Eugene's identity is so effectively perverted from musicmaker to death-maker—his father's role at Dupont—he wonders, "Can this be me?" (60). Rather than a free thinker or innovative musician (he hoped to play at peace rallies and love-ins), Eugene is turned into a "homicidal imbecile" in thirteen weeks (15). Cadets at West Point did not make music (33), or if they did, they were under orders to play "as written," and never as they felt about the music. More ominously, West Point regimentation creates such an emotional void that the Cadets, like the unfeeling sociopathic computer game, Griot, feel nothing at all. There was no student publication at West Point, Eugene says, "so never mind how the cadets felt about anything" (34). Thus Eugene concludes about the forbidding presence of Sam Wakefield that the spectacularly dressed man with the paratrooper's wings and boots was what he would become for the next fourteen years (48, 49), a professional soldier programmed to kill "Jesus Christ himself . . . if ordered to do so by a superior officer" (14).[11]

What Eugene appears to become, by his own definition, is "insane," so numb or indifferent to reality that fact and illusion become indistinguishable. West Point so extends the job Eugene's father has begun of numbing Eugene's conscience and perverting his artistic identity that at one point the doped-up soldier feels no difference between the playing of bells and the lobbing of shells—both of which seem to him "very much like music, interesting noises . . . and nothing more" (81). Used to dulling his wits with drugs and cynicism, he finds scenes of mutilation and death "no more horrible than ultrarealistic shows about Vietnam" on television (124), a desensitized condition that allows him to commit unspeakable acts of violence and cruelty. Referring to the corpses he has seen and in many cases created (173), he remembers strangling someone with piano wire (261), throwing a suspected enemy agent out of a helicopter (203), and killing a woman, her mother, and her baby by throwing a grenade into the mouth of a tunnel (236).

But Eugene's freakish parents, with the help of West Point, have spawned not only a temporarily insane, psychopathic killer, but an expert liar whose "elaborate" (36) destructive fantasies carry over to his role as Public Relations officer in Vietnam. As a "genius of lethal hocus pocus," the effect of which he likens to mood-modifying drugs (36), Eugene claims that justification for all the killing and dying becomes "as natural as breathing" (36). The representation of deceit as normal suggests the perversion of Eugene's life-instinct by the instinct to aggression and death. Vonnegut continues here his concern first highlighted in *Mother Night* and *Cat's Cradle* with fiction as a form of play that can be constructive or destructive. All wordplay or fiction, he comments, is really "practical joking" *(Fates* 137). "Hocus Pocus" represents the power of imagination to construct sane fictions that abet the forces of life—of courage, compassion, and engagement (308)—or insane ones that encourage cruelty and violence. Vonnegut refers in *Fates* to the "hocus pocus laundromat" (72), which may turn good to evil or evil to good, calling this a case of "post-modern multiple crossover." Ultimately Eugene's perception is that both forms of aggression, killing and lying about killing, were equally insane, typical of people who rendered themselves "imbecilic or maniacal" (36). Such was the fate of the students at Tarkington and the prisoners at Athena. The crippled human potential of the students with "learning disabilities" passed on to them by materialistic parents and by the romantic success myths—stories of "supposed triumphs" (41)—which dominate Tarkington's library, equates with the dazed and hopeless condition of the convicts. The melodramatic success stories, the puerile and absurdly outdated impression of reality displayed on prison television reruns like "I Love Lucy" and "Howdy Doody" (218) create a mental prison for both populations, effectively isolating them from complexities within and from each other. Underscoring their common plight, Eugene observes that the two communities, so close geographically, yet so socially and economically divided, both name their main street "Clinton Street" (243). He notes too that teaching at the prison was "not all that different from what I had done at Tarkington" (243). The point is that the ease with which the College eventually converts to a prison merely literalizes the intrinsically oppressive nature of both institutions.[12]

Like that of such previously father-persecuted, war-scarred protagonists as Howard Campbell, Eliot Rosewater, and Billy Pilgrim, Eugene's sense of estrangement after the war is so great he wonders, "What is this place, and who are these people, and what am I doing here?" (242). Memories of "orgies" of death and suffering he labels "Unforgettable" (297) fill Eugene with such guilt and moral uncertainty that, again like Billy, like Eliot, he seeks relief from blame in anonymity. "I wanted nothing more than to be left strictly alone with my thoughts" (237), he says. Or he attempts to make everything "all right" (120)[13] through the imagined sanctuary of affairs with off-balanced, middle-aged women. No wonder that like the hallucinating Billy Pilgrim and Eliot Rosewater, who share a room in a mental hospital because of what they had seen in war *(Slaughterhouse-Five* 101), Eugene should be tempted by the same painkilling philosophy of life—the "morphine paradise" *(Slaughterhouse-Five* 99) of Tralfamadore. Eugene likens the feeling that he is the plaything of enormous forces of control to that of his student who gets trapped in a Bloomingdale elevator. The student's sense of isolation and helplessness is magnified by the fact that, as with returning Vietnam veterans, no one cares, no one apologizes, and no one takes responsibility (158, 159).[14] These are the spiral-like systems of control Vonnegut calls a "dynamite bouquet" (290), seemingly wonderful at first, but hideous in retrospect. Demonstrating that these insidious spirals lead to violence and cruelty rather than to the paradise they promise, Eugene notices, for instance, that swirling "spirals of dust" (218) were present when his friend Hiroshi Masumoto was atom-bombed, that it is the belfry of a spiral-like tower that the college president, "Tex" Johnson, turns into a "sniper's nest" (77), and that Athena and Auschwitz are similarly "ringed" with barbed wire and watchtowers (226). Even the TB germs inside Eugene's body exist in spiral-like shells. To show his contempt for liberal ideas, jingoist talk-show host Jason Wilder covers them in "spit" and throws them back with "a crazy spin," which makes them "uncatchable" (266). Eugene links his wife's madness to the maniacal aggression of Sam Wakefield, the rabid Westpoint lieutenant who "blows his brains out," by observing that it is "a clock that made them sick" (164).[15] Eugene has earlier referred to his wife's insanity as "a spider web" (118).

Like Griot, the computer that doesn't care about anything, especially "hurting people's feelings" (103), these hellish mechanisms appear either superficially alluring or too powerful to escape (103). Hence, they lock the unwary individual into cycles of action indifferent to individual will or aspiration, engendering robot-like aggression or the passivity that allows aggression to happen, at both the top and the bottom of the spiral. The convicts particularly hate Griot because when they punch in their race and age and what their parents did, how long they'd gone to school and what drugs they'd used, Griot sends them straight to jail (104). Feelings of futility create in turn the sociopathic madness of the age—the Trustees' complete indifference to the suffering at Athena, the absence of "remorse" of Alton Darwin (78), the lunatic laughter of Jack Patton, who has "the same untightened screw" (77), for whom all disasters are funny (57), and even Eugene's apathy at Tarkington until he is made to empathize with the suffering of the prisoners across the lake. Thus it is that for years to come, believing that the loveless, inhumane spirals of his life are beyond his ability to resist, Eugene becomes a potential moral sleepwalker, threatened by the same petrification of will and conscience that dooms the prisoners at Athena and the students of Tarkington College. Eugene marries unknowingly into a family with a history of madness, saddling himself with a crazy wife and mother-in-law (84), then lives with dread that his two children, who hate him for reproducing, will go as crazy as their mother and grandmother. It is a short distance, Eugene says, to "where I am now" (142)—to getting fired by Tarkington, to teaching the unteachable at Athena, and to eventual imprisonment for treason (50). He might have fared better, he reflects, if his "exit" had not been "blocked by Sam Wakefield." It is another of Wakefield's recruits, the morally dead Jack Patton, who preaches pessimism and introduces Eugene to his crazy sister and bride-to-be.

Of course Eugene's psychological odyssey brings him also to the realization that his "exit"—to journalism, to music-making, to a more courageous and independent identity ("saying and wearing what I goshdarned pleased" [50])—was torpedoed by the father who, upon reflection, Eugene says tried to blame him entirely for their troubled past (36, 37). It is Eugene's present ability to see both his own involvement and his father's responsibility for creating the horrors he has seen and committed—in effect, their common humanity, or inhumanity—that liberates him from paralysis and guilt and that allows the pent-up artist to emerge.

In his search for the compassionate self that would prove him sane, he had hoped that the names of the women he has loved would prevail over the list of people he has killed; at the same time, he worries that by war's end he had become the unfeeling machine ("an electrical appliance . . . a vacuum cleaner" [147]) that his wife and mother-in-law see upon his return—manifesting that absence of feeling that Griot represents and that both Eugene and Griot share with the sociopathic mass murderer Alton Darwin (149). What Eugene discovers, however, is that the contending proofs on his imagined epitaph are "enigmatic" (38), that is, "virtually identical" (195). Not only do they suggest a precarious balance between the forces of kindness and cruelty, aggression and restraint, but each list is itself ambiguous—the impulses of the soldier/lover inextricably mixed, military kills mitigated by acts of mercy, irresponsible seductions counterbalanced by genuine compassion. This is the "argument" (64) within himself that he experiences when the music he makes as a carillonneur at Tarkington echoes off the prison walls and Scipio's empty factories, returning to him as if a second carillonneur were "mocking" him from across the lake. It is also the divided author-persona of *Breakfast of Champions* that Leonard Mustazza so aptly describes in *Forever Pursuing Genesis:* "Kurt Vonnegut, who is alternately a meat machine . . . and the free-willed maker and lord of his own creations" (125). While the prospect of an equivocal nature invites futility, Eugene's inquiry brings him instead to that grace of awareness Vonnegut calls "sacred" in *Breakfast of Champions* (221), an understanding that fragmentation is the universal human condition. Though he playfully observes that, "If there is a Divine Providence, there is also a wicked one" (120), he recognizes that such antagonisms are never absolute, but a complex potential of the human spirit for good or for evil, and that by understanding and controlling their heart of darkness, human beings, not Griot, not the mechanical Tralfamadorians, may shape their lives for the better.

From the ironically regenerated perspective of his bell tower prison, Eugene visualizes the contrary "possibilities" (105) of love or aggression within himself through such psychic projections as Jack Patton and Paul Slazinger, each of whom has grown coldly cynical and apathetic, and through the aware and morally courageous figures of Eugene Debs and Helen Dole. The psychopathic tendencies of Patton, Eugene's "equal" (57), and of Slazinger, who was "echoing" him (115), reflect the Eugene who killed with his bare hands and laughed about it afterwards. On the other hand, Helen Dole, the feisty little black women who teaches physics at Tarkington, and the pacifist/healer Eugene Debs equally represent Eugene's humanitarian instincts. When the Tarkington Trustees try to turn Helen into an uncritical teaching machine, she defies not only the Trustees, but Griot, who finds her so independent and assertive that it can describe her destiny only as "unpredictable" (264). Multilingual and versed in science, history, literature, music, and art, Helen challenges racist stereotypes as well as Tarkington's totalitarian structures, accusing the Trustees of being as exploitative as modern-day plantation owners (264).

As Eugene sorts out the tangled debris of his troubled past, he is surprised to learn that he was never as dispossessed of the Helen Dole or the Eugene Debs in himself as he had thought. He finds marked evidence that though even after the war he succumbed to ingrained habits of lying and evasion to assuage shameful or embarrassing experience, his youthful idealistic and creative self had never ceased to function, the self who identifies with Eugene Debs' credo of love and humanitarian service. Eugene notes, for instance, that whereas Alton Darwin had murdered innocent people for money, he "had never stooped to that" (72). And while as a soldier in Vietnam he had seen mutilations, he "hastens" to say that under his command that would never have been tolerated (52). Eugene's roll call of good and bad deeds reveals not only a painfully active conscience, but a disposition to kindness and moral courage that often prevails over his worst self. If he has been a "gung-ho" warrior (164), his final soldierly act was not militant but merciful—the rescue of American personnel from the rooftop of the U.S. Embassy in Saigon.[16]

Eugene's eventual colleague at Tarkington, Muriel Peek, reminds him of how "kind and patient" he has been with his worse than useless relatives (21), remaining so loyal to his unbalanced wife and mother-in-law that Andrea Wakefield calls him a "saint" (164). When Eugene's estranged out-of-wedlock son Rob Roy assures Eugene that he intends to make no demands on his father's emotions, Eugene welcomes that relationship, insisting, "Try me" (286), determining to behave "as though I were a really good father." "I like life to be simple," he says, "but if you went away that would be much too simple for me, and for you, too, I hope" (288).

In caring for his troubled family, even as he himself battles tuberculosis, Eugene succeeds, as is said of Wilbur Swain, in "bargaining in good faith with destiny" *(Slapstick* 2). But it is as a teacher that he keeps faith with his grandfather's belief that the greatest use a person can make of his or her lifetime is to "improve the quality of life for all in his or her community" (176). First at Tarkington College, an oasis of white in a community dominated by 10,000 black inmates at Athena prison, Eugene is persecuted by the college's dim-witted, mean-spirited Trustees for daring to tell the truth even about "things nice people shouldn't want to see"—the horrors at Athena or Vietnam, for instance, to which the Trustees remain smugly oblivious. When Eugene tells one of the Trustees about the agonies of prison life and about the mental illnesses and feelings of futility of the prisoners, Jason Wilder "closed his eyes and covered his ears" (225). The Trustees believe that the government's first responsibility is to protect them from the lower classes (226), while Eugene's sympathies are those inscribed on the tombstone of his namesake, Eugene Victor Debs: "While there is a lower class I am in it. While there is a criminal element I am of it. While there is a soul in prison I am not free" (9).[17]

Accordingly, when Eugene's efforts to free his students from ignorance and self-serving fantasies are dubbed unpatriotic, and he is fired for being not just un-American but anti-American, he continues at his new teaching post at Athena to make the lives of the inmates "more bearable" (228), however uphill the struggle. Though the inmates are kept literally and figuratively "drugged" to reality (coked to the gills on Thorazine, or rendered docile and unaware by television reruns [243]), he raises their literacy level by 20 percent.[18] When the convicts stage a massive prison break, overrunning the college, and the campus becomes a prison for the recaptured prisoners, Eugene does his best as temporary warden to humanize conditions. "Let it be recorded," he says, that when warden of this prison "I moved the convicted felons out of tents . . . into the surroundings of buildings. They no longer had to excrete in buckets, or in the middle of the night, have their homes blown down" (295). Eugene personally houses and feeds three infirm old men serving life sentences.

Even when Eugene returns after the insurrection to a soldierly role as military commander of the Scipio District, he continues using his authority to combat rather than foster aggression. He turns soldiers into firemen,[19] personally supervises the exhumation of bodies, notifies next-of-kin, and sees that the dead are given decent burials (276, 277). However chaotic his life or disruptive the bizarre changes of career, Eugene continues to find proof positive of his compassionate self. Not only does he oppose the sociopathic indifference to suffering shown by people like Alton Darwin and the Trustees at Tarkington, he reminds us of Kathryn Hume's assertion that in Vonnegut's troubled cosmos the humanity of individuals can still make a difference (*Vonnegut and the Myths and Symbols* 442). We see that rather than pointing to the "pessimism" for which Eugene is fired at Tarkington, or the "treason" for which he is imprisoned for sympathizing with Athenian prisoners, both charges imply the ignorance and duplicity of his accusers. "I wouldn't be under indictment now," he says, "if I hadn't paid a compassionate visit to the hostages" (148). Not only does Eugene directly repudiate his reputation for pessimism at Tarkington ("that was twice within an hour that I was accused of cynicism that was Slazinger's, not mine" [115]), he says that all he ever wanted to do as a teacher was to encourage his students to think for themselves and perhaps to raise questions about the moral contradictions of Vietnam, capitalism, and organized religion, for which he is judged "unpatriotic." The real betrayal here is the suppression of honest inquiry by an economic system so corrupt that it calls a concern for others "un-American" if it threatens the status quo. "What could be more un-American," Paul Slazinger says sarcastically, "than sounding like the Sermon on the Mount" (97).

But Eugene's greatest evidence of sanity, he hopes, will be his salubrious relationships with women. Just as the words on his namesake's tombstone reflect decency and caring, Eugene projects as his own epitaph the names of the women he has loved. He ponders that if at times he has used women irresponsibly, women too "full of doubts" (120) to make emotional demands (Marilyn Monroe would have been perfect, he muses [120]), he believes that rather than exploitative or superficial, these relationships have been soulful and intellectual ("not another infernal device") as well as ardent or libidinal (17).[20] Hence, when artist-in-residence Pamela Hall asks Eugene why he has come to visit her, he replies that he wanted to make sure she was OK (121, 122). And when Marilyn Shaw, also a Vietnam veteran, who "had a rougher war than I did" (164), lapses into despair after the war, it is Eugene who rescues her drunk and asleep on a pool table (105) and who apparently nurses her back to health.

Appropriate to Kathryn Hume's observation that the increased affirmation of Vonnegut's protagonists after *Breakfast of Champions* correlates with their more sympathetic relationships with women, Eugene's connection with this community of female fellow sufferers is, as is said of Zuzu Johnson, not only "deep" but "thoroughly reciprocated" (102). Just as Eugene's final thought is of their well-being (38), *their* courage and love prove cathartic and liberating to Eugene, opening him emotionally and helping him form a more holistic and creative self. Hence Eugene finds himself "spilling his guts" (123) to Pamela about the Vietnam war and purg-

ing himself of unspeakable scenes of cruelty and stupidity and waste by confessing
his nightmares to Harriet Gummer (124).

So the chief irony of Eugene's suspect sanity is not that he feels so little, but
that he feels so much once he discovers the "equation" (298) that brings all spirals
into being: the age-old impulse to cruelty and aggression that perpetually threatens
human life. It is not the Eugene who killed with his bare hands and laughed about
it who writes these memoirs, but the long repressed artist for whom this act of
creative exorcism and renewal has been so humanizing and illuminating that he can
say that was "the old me . . . I think . . . the soldier I used to be" (180, 253). Whereas
he once found it easy to mask or distort the truth, he determines no longer to "play
hide-and-seek" (ll9),[21] which "wasn't my natural disposition" (78). However painful, he will openly acknowledge his crimes. He speaks thus of the corpses "I created" (173), of the slaughters "I myself had planned and led" (246, 247), and when
assigning responsibility for the strafing of a village in which innocent women and
children were killed, he makes clear that the chief transgressor was himself, not his
father, not Sam Wakefield, not West Point, and certainly not the Tralfamadorians.
"You know who was the Ruling Class that time?" he asks. "Eugene Debs Hartke
was the Ruling Class" (236).[22]

The new Eugene conveys his contempt for the totalitarian designs of others
by ridiculing the notion that Tralfamadorian-like forces control his fate. Determining to combat the TB germs that have invaded his body (metaphorically speaking,
Tralfamadorian agents), he declares, "If any of these germs are thinking of themselves as space cadets, they can forget it. They aren't going anywhere but down the
toilet" (194–95). Eugene's reference to the box containing Trout's story of
Tralfamadore as "a sort of casket" (187) presages both the dangers of
Tralfamadorian fatalism and Eugene's rejection of such a philosophy along with
the rest of his dead past, "the remains of the soldier I used to be" (187). But like
Vonnegut's other emergent artist-heroes, Wilbur Swain, Walter Starbuck, Leon
Trout, and Rabo Karabekian (like Rabo, Eugene is also a diarist), Eugene learns not
only that such inhuman mechanisms as Griot, Dupont, or West Point can be resisted, but that they can be reconstituted through the fabulating power—the "hocus
pocus"—of creative imagination. Just as he had once used the "ammunition" of
language (148), his "lethal" hocus pocus, to foster violence and death, he will now
put his "genius" for elaborate fantasies to work for constructive rather than destructive purposes. He will stylize his memoirs—perform "tricks" (130) of imagination—in ways that defy static or arbitrary language convention.

Eugene's venture in self-creativity abounds with references to fact and illusion as interchangeable or indistinguishable realities, so that, like Warden
Matsumoto, the reader finds himself "among structures and creatures both real and
fantastic" (227). Eugene's war memories are like "old movies" (1249), his childhood is "all a dream" (38). Dead American soldiers are "manufactured" beings,

"curious artifacts" (39), and Vietnam is *all* "hallucination" (85), so much "show-biz" (253). For Eugene, playing the bells at Tarkington, which might have been mistaken for an emerald-studded Oz or City of God or Camelot (250), has "absolutely no basis in reality"(64), and for the convicts at Athena there is no distinction at all between television and what might be going on in the real world (252).

Following the example of Rabo Karabekian, Eugene demonstrates further that reality is largely the product of imagination and will, as fluid and dynamic as dreams, providing countless examples of experiences whose fluctuating meanings vary with the perception or invention of the viewer, or are determined by historical or cultural context. Scipio becomes "Pompeii" (140); escaped convicts, "Freedom Fighters" (204); the Christian cross, the Nazi "swastika" (128); and "champagne cases" in Scipio, "cartridge cases" in Vietnam (198). An Italian racing bike might have been a "Unicorn" (1960), "stogies" could be called "mogies" or "higgies" instead (21), "Petrograd" is renamed "Leningrad," then "Petrograd" again (281), and the Mohiga Valley Free Institute becomes Tarkington College.[23] What people call themselves, says Eugene, is not "reality" (204). Thus Arthur Clarke the "fun loving billionaire" (166) is not Arthur Clarke "the science fiction writer," and Herbert Van Arsdale, a President of Tarkington, bears no relation at all to Whitney Van Arsdale, the "dishonest mechanic" (183). Eugene doubts that "Donner" was really the last name of the "John Donner," the "pathological liar" who appears on Donahue: "He could have made that up . . . " (214).

Eugene is encouraged to reevaluate the status of "truth" and "fiction" and to appreciate their interchangeability—that for better or worse reality can be made over by imagination. Eugene's socialist grandfather refers to the foolishness of those who believe that every word is "true" in a book put together by "a bunch of preachers 300 years after the birth of Christ." "I hope," he instructs Eugene, "you won't be that dumb about words . . . when you grow up" (98). In that vein, Vonnegut in *Fates* dramatizes the proposition that language precedes but does not objectify reality by commenting, "In the beginning was the word" (73), illustrating the kinetic power of language to alter consciousness by writing "a new language" (73), transmuting the "sadistic and masochistic" message of the Catholic Mass for the Dead to an appeal for kindness and mercy (71). Eugene observes that whereas Scipio's citizens "daydreamed" of shooting escaped convicts (249–50), Damon Stern envisions that the "tidy checkerboard . . . streets and old stucco two-story shotgun building" of Auschwitz "might have made a nice enough junior college for low-in-come or underachieving people in the area" (280). Alton Darwin "hallucinates" a racially pure, all-black Utopia of the future (258), but Sam Wakefield is transmogrified from a rabid military man to a Christ-like being, with "eyes full of love and pity," who speaks against the war (156). We see that Tarkington's carillon bells are recast from mangled Union and Confederate rifle barrels, cannonballs, and bayonets (63) and that the mobile field kitchen invented by one of Tarkington's founders, Aaron Tarkington, was adopted both by the German Army during World War I and by the Barnum and Bailey Circus (22).

It is finally Eugene's ingenious narrative, or magic act, that signifies his personal transformation from jailbird to canary bird: a brilliant fabrication that illustrates his awesome, redirected powers of invention. Demonstrating the possibilities of existential authorship in life as in art (that it is he rather than Sam Wakefield, Griot, or Tralfamadore who is "the helmsman of my destiny" [162]), Eugene and the "editor" who helps arrange his text continuously identify Eugene's memoirs as "pure fiction" (9), a "game" (50, 296) or "trick" (130) or "joke" (22) whose truths are personal, elusive, and multifaceted. Eugene's editor knows that while Eugene had hoped to amass absolute proofs of "humility" *or* "insanity," what he "is doing is writing a book" (7), an imaginative reconstruction rather than an objective representation of so-called actual events or objects in the real world. "Bear with me," Eugene explains, "this is history" (21). But it is history whose truths are problematized by imperfect memory, recapitulated impressions from second- or third-hand sources and from Eugene's and his editor's own selective storytelling. Past events are pieced together from old newspapers, letters, diaries, and the "*Musketeer*," the Tarkington College Alumni magazine, dating back to 1910 (62), as well as from the *Encyclopedia Britannica* (215) and *Bartlett's Familiar Quotations* (146). At best, Eugene and his editor can only "speculate" (7), can know only "what is likely" (7), or what "supposedly" happened (270–71)—what happened, for instance, "according" to the "story," the "legend," of Adam and Eve (189) passed on to Eugene from Jack Patton and passed on in turn from "the nameless author" of "The Protocols of the Elders of Tralfamadore" (190).

The creative idiosyncracies of Eugene, his editor, and of course Kurt Vonnegut remove the reader still further from representational reality. With references such as, "Before I tell about that" (207), "there is more I want to tell" (271), "that will seem to complete my story" (271), and "I will carry on as though I hadn't heard the news" (271), Eugene establishes himself as a subjective storyteller who will delete or embellish as he chooses. The editor explains that he himself has attempted to improve the "disreputable appearance" (7) of Eugene's text (what else has he tampered with?) by setting in type what did not reproduce well on the printed page (8),[24] but though we have only his editor's word on this, or his editor's editor, it is Eugene's artistic contrivances that compel our attention. The editor explains that the book was written on everything from brown wrapping paper to the backs of business cards (7), that for reasons unexplained (8) Eugene capitalized words which should have been in lowercase, that he let numbers stand for themselves rather than put them in words, e.g., "2 instead of two" (8), and that he drew lines across the page to separate passages within chapters.[25]

If Eugene's grammatical or literary deviations puzzle his editor, the reader sees that such linguistic liberties correspond precisely with Helen Dole's defiance of the repressive moral strictures at Tarkington. Since he had been used as a government propaganda machine to create the horrors of Vietnam, he will now use the "ammunition" of language to expose rather than produce such deceptions—realities uniquely his own. "The expression *I* will use for the end of the Vietnam War," he says, "will be when the excrement hit the air-conditioner" (272).

Pondering the speed with which such linguistics and spiritual hocus pocus may be performed, Eugene marvels that whereas "Only 2 hours before, I had been so at peace in my bell tower. . . . Now I was inside a maximum-security prison with a masked and gloved japanese National who insisted that the United States was his Vietnam!" (220). Yet how different are the bars that imprison the body of Eugene Debs from that mental cage that holds Billy Pilgrim prisoner on Tralfamadore—a fatal dream that assures Billy's descent into madness, but whose repudiation signals Eugene's freedom from self-imprisoning spirals, or "self-serving fantasies," and allows the creative artist to ascend. Eugene is threatened by the same maddening contrasts between sanity and insanity and the same feeling of futility that doom Billy. Eugene's friend, Hiroshi Matsumoto, who is, like Edgar Derby, inordinately innocent and kind, nevertheless commits the "trick" (130) of suicide out of guilt and remorse for horrors for which he appears blameless. Yet Derby's absurd death produces only despair in Billy, while the death of Matsumoto deepens Eugene's awareness and sympathy.

The answer to Eugene's question, "But why would I ever care so much?" (294) reveals a lot about Eugene's quest for the meanings of sanity for both himself and his world. Eugene identifies with Hiroshi in his childhood anguish over the dropping of the bomb on Hiroshima. Eugene is struck by the fact that someone relatively blameless, who "never shirked his duty, never stole anything, and never killed or bombed anyone" (295) should yet hold himself responsible for a legacy of "burning and boiling" (219) before he was even born. The spiritual bond between Eugene and Hiroshi rests on their shared recognition that the smallest or most personal acts of aggression are connected to the world's larger, bloodier deeds. The impulse that boils lobsters alive, or that allows Eugene to kill with his bare hands, emanates from the same heart of darkness that creates the "Rape of Nanking" (297), that drops bombs on Hiroshima (118), that commits the "vainglorious lunacy of Vietnam" (219), and that has turned the entire planet "into an Auschwitz" (226). Hence the trustees of Tarkington "had a lot in common with B-52 bombardiers" (226), and the escaped convicts of Athena "were like a neutron bomb" (28). Eugene and Hiroshi know too that the will to destruction is neither a peculiarly nationalistic nor historical phenomenon. Like Joan of Arc and like the Caib Indians (264), the victims of Hiroshima were "burned alive" (218). Just as Jews and Romans crucified their enemies, Tex Johnson is crucified with spikes through his palms and feet. American forests are in fact being looted by Mexican laborers using Japanese tools under the protection of the Swedes to sell to the Japanese. Eugene and Hiroshi, both reformed warriors, see finally that it is the denial of responsibility for such violence that makes the deadly spiral of aggression circular and unending. But what most disturbs Eugene (he experiences an "attack of psychosomatic hives" [299]) is the fact that self-destruction, the equivalent of Billy Pilgrim's withdrawal into the "morphine paradise" of Tralfamadore (99), should become Hiroshi's only recourse to the world's suffering and pain. The notion so demoralizes Eugene that he is glad he hasn't shown Hiroshi a copy of "The Protocols of the Elders of Tralfamadore," which might have hastened Hiroshi's suicide. Hiroshi might have left a note saying, "The Elders of Tralfamadore win again" (299). "Only I and the author of that story," Eugene concludes, "would have known what he meant by that" (299).

What Tralfamadorian fatalism "means," to Eugene Hartke and to Kurt Vonnegut, is central to our decision about Eugene's sanity, but, more important, to Vonnegut's view of the sanity of his readers and critics. The Tralfamadorians foster the kind of suicidal futility that causes Hiroshi to kill himself, that threatens Eugene with "existential gangrene" after the war, and that encourages the people of the earth to "wreck the joint." Do these "crazy lunkers" who delight in pain (193), who are, "to say the least," indifferent "to all the suffering going on," really speak for Eugene and his author?

As with Eugene's purpose as a teacher, Vonnegut writes more to encourage reflectiveness than to offer specific reforms,[26] so we must decide for ourselves whether Vonnegut uses such fantasies as Titan, Shangri-la, and Tralfamadore, to warn against or affirm such a philosophy. Yet Eugene's own final judgment appears to be a direct rebuke on the author's part of critics who join in calling Tralfamadorian fatalism "a higher order of life" or a philosophy that teaches "un-enlightened earthlings" a tolerance for pain. Contemptuously, Eugene calls "dumb" and "humorless" those "earthlings" who find "acceptable" the "series of side-splitting satires about Tralfamadorians arriving on other planets with the intention of spreading enlightenment" (191). It is hardly coincidental that Eugene's aspiration as a teacher—to expose "self-serving fantasies" (92)—corresponds with that of Vonnegut the novelist and that both Eugene and Vonnegut should be called "pessimists" or "defeatists" by "imbeciles" (36) and charlatans. It appears that both Tarkington's trustees and critics who read Eugene's memoirs as a "model" of despair project their own apathy[27] and cynicism and thus fail Eugene's primary criteria for sanity. It is they, finally, who have been on trial.

As his own new identity attests, Eugene knows that it is belief and its linguistic formulations that determine reality, that what we are therefore sane enough—aware and compassionate enough—to imagine the future to be will influence what it becomes. Indicating *his* belief that destiny will be shaped by human beings, not machines, Eugene observes that "any form of government, not just Capitalism, is whatever the people . . . sane or insane . . . decide to do" (96). "When it came to dreaming up futures for ourselves," say Eugene, "we left Griot in the dust" (178). Whether we view Eugene's text through the cynical, unfeeling eyes of Griot or the Elders of Tralfamadore or, "like life," see it as consisting of better "possibilities" (105) will decide whether we imagine and create for ourselves the sociopathic future of Alton Darwin and Jack Patton or the more humane and responsible world of Helen Dole, Eugene Debs, and Eugene Debs Hartke.

Notes

Introduction

1. *The Modern Temper* (New York: Harcourt, Brace and Company, 1956), p. 81.

2. "The Character of Post-War Fiction in America" in *Our Contemporary Literature,* ed. Richard Kostelanetz (New York: Avon Books, 1964), p. 40.

3. *The Holocaust and the Literary Imagination* (New Haven: Yale University Press, 1975), pp. 90, 91.

4. "The Alone Generation" in *The American Novel since World War II,* ed. Marcus Klein (Greenwich: A Fawcett Premier Book, 1969), p. 115.

5. *Mr. Sammler's Planet* (Greenwich: A Fawcett Crest Book, 1969), pp. 136, 137.

6. Gary Harmon, "The Scene with Kurt Vonnegut, Jr.: A Conversation." This is a transcript taken from conversation that took place at Stephens College, with Jack Lazebnik as the moderator and a group of students joining in the questioning.

7. "The White Negro," in *Advertisements for Myself* (New York: G. P. Putnam's Sons, 1959), pp. 343–48.

8. *Samuel Beckett: A New Approach* (New York: Dodd, Mead, and Company, Inc., 1970). The general term "schizophrenia" encompasses a variety of mental disorders that usually overlap; the aforementioned features, common to Vonnegut's generic schizoid or schizophrenic hero, always appear at some phase of the illness. Associated features prominent in Vonnegut's characters are extreme perplexity about one's identity and the meaning of existence; loss of self (ego boundaries) and self-esteem; loss of individuality and volition; uncertain sexual identity and guilt; inattention to physical appearance; delusions of control by outside forces; nihilistic delusions (or wishes) of personal and world destruction. All conditions described as schizophrenic in this study are confirmed by the following authorities: *Diagnostic and Statistical Manual of Mental Disorders,* 3rd edition. American Psychiatric Association: Library of Congress #79–055868, 1980. The *DSM-III* has become accepted by the psychiatric community for the identification and classification of complex psychiatric disorders. See also James Shields and Eliot Slater, "Heredity and Psychological Abnormality" in *Handbook of Abnormal Psychology: An Experimental Approach,* ed. H. J. Ezsenck (New York: Basic Books, 1961); Ephrain Rosen and Ian Gregory, *Abnormal Psychology,* 2nd edition (Philadelphia: W. B. Saunders Company, 1972); Armand M. Nicholi, *The Harvard Guide to Modern Psychiatry* (Cambridge: Belknap Press of Harvard University Press, 1978); R. M. Goldenson, *Encyclopedia of Human Behavior,* vol. 2 (Garden City: Doubleday and Co., Inc., 1970), pp. 68–180; Frank Fish, *Schizophrenia,* 2nd edition (Bristol: John Wright and Sons, 1976); Sue

Shapiro, *Contemporary Theories of Schizophrenia* (McGraw-Hill Book Co., 1981); Theodore Lidz, *The Origin and Treatment of Schizophrenic Disorders* (New York: Basic Books, 1973).

9. *After the Lost Generation* (New York: The Noonday Press, 1963), p. 91.

10. *Slaughterhouse-Five* (1969; rpt. New York: Dell, 1972), pp. 100–107. All subsequent quotations followed by a page number in parentheses are from this edition.

11. R. D. Laing, *The Divided Self* (New York: Pantheon Books, 1969), p. 38. I have drawn consistently from the psychoanalytical theories of Sigmund Freud, R. D. Laing, Jacques Lacan, and Carl Rogers because, with obvious modifications among themselves and Vonnegut, they offer a remarkably common scenario of the inner world of Vonnegut's hero. In opposition to assertions that responsibility and madness in Vonnegut's fictional world do not mix, the above theorists argue that madness has a meaningful structure and refuse to separate psychoanalytic phenomena from the religious, philosophical, ethical, and social issues important to Vonnegut's or any serious writer's work. Each tries to uncover the psychological structures underlying psychosis by examining the patient's biography and argues that the creation of the psychoanalytical plot is a collaboration between the analyst and the subject. The primal scene is always a construction, never an absolute.

12. *Player Piano* (1952; rpt. New York: Dell, 1975), pp. 61, 266. All subsequent quotations followed by a page number in parentheses are from this edition.

13. *Mother Night* (1961; rpt. New York: Dell, 1974), p. 191. All subsequent quotations followed by a page number in parentheses are from this edition.

14. The reference is in Bernard Shaw's *Back to Methuselah* (Baltimore: Penguin Books, 1961), p. 145. Wavering conviction as to the possibility of human progress causes Vonnegut to remark that "Shaw's optimism in *Back to Methuselah* was science fiction enough for me." In *Wampeters, Foma, and Granfalloons (Opinions)* (New York: Dell, Delta, 1975), p. 260.

15. *Slaughterhouse-Five*, p. 4.

16. In *Bluebeard* (New York: Delacorte, 1987), the protagonist-artist describes his part in "a peculiar membership" with ancient historical roots—people telling stories around a campfire at night or painting pictures on the walls of caves (75, 76, 199). Its purpose is to cheer people up, inspire fellowship, and open up minds that would go on exactly as before "no matter how painful, unrealistic, unjust, ludicrous, or downright dumb . . . life may be."

17. *Wampeters*, p. 238.

18. Ibid., p. 246.

19. "Kurt Vonnegut and the Myths and Symbols of Meaning," *Texas Studies in Literature and Language* 24 (Winter 1982), p. 444.

20. "Blunting" or "flattening" of emotional response varies from the absence of feeling registered by Paul Proteus to the mute and stuporous condition of Eliot Rosewater and Billy Pilgrim (*DSM-III*, 183, 191). In the latter state, the individual provides "motionless resistance" to all instructions or attempts to be moved. Vonnegut's stone, machine, and petrification imagery often represents catatonic rigidity.

21. *God Bless You, Mr. Rosewater* (1965; rpt. New York: Dell, 1981), p. 145. All subsequent quotations followed by a page number in parentheses are from this edition.

22. Social withdrawal and flattened or inappropriate emotional response in Vonnegut's characters are frequently accompanied by inattention to hygiene and grooming. The schizoid withdraws a considerable part of his ego, which leads to physical decay because the restricted false self is feeble and unconcerned with bodily functions.

23. Laing uses the term schizoid, as opposed to schizophrenic, to identify what may actually be a healthy, existential state of mind. The *DSM-III* differentiates between "Schizophreniform Disorder" (185) (less severe and briefer symptoms) and schizophrenia. While most of Vonnegut's protagonists drift into psychosis at some point (severe disruption of the individual's being as a whole), exhibiting marked schizophrenic symptoms, it is better to call them pre-psychotic or schizoidal—

persons especially vulnerable to psychosis but whose isolation and angst may engender a more honest and creative way of living in a world of conformity and aggressive madness. The paradoxical value of separation and loneliness to the artist is discussed in chapters 2 and 3.

24. *The 13th Valley* (New York: Bantam, 1982), p. 496. Vonnegut's heroes are often far more sane than the society that labels them "crazy" for renouncing its own inhumane norms. Mark Vonnegut comments that "Schizophrenia is a sane response to an insane society," *The Eden Express* (New York: Praeger, 1975), p. 111. In *Bluebeard,* Vonnegut writes, "A real doctor might . . . say that millions of people walking the streets every day fell into a gray area, where it was difficult to say with any degree of certainty whether or not their personalities were pathological" (56).

25. *Fabulation and Metafiction* (Urbana: University of Illinois Press, 1979), p. 159. See also Patricia Waugh's *Metafiction: The Theory and Practice of Self-Conscious Fiction* (New York: Methuen, 1984), pp. 8, 9, 34.

26. Catherine Belsey, *Critical Practice* (New York: Methuen, 1980). Vonnegut does not reject meaning *per se,* only the claim to unequivocal domination of one mode of signifying over another. Reflecting Derrida, Belsey observes that as a dynamic, pluralistic universe of its own, the text necessarily signifies something more, something less, or something other than it claims to (104). Accordingly, Bernard Selinger, in *Le Guin and Identity in Contemporary Fiction* (Ann Arbor: UMI Research Press, 1988), observes that "the good psychoanalytic critic reads the work with a sense of its ambiguous and latent meanings, and thus can find new meanings and relations that will increase the importance of the work" (10). Patricia Waugh says that Vonnegut is a master at concocting what Roland Barthes calls the hermeneutic code, problematical surfaces that create the "enigmatic dispositions of the text" (*Metafiction,* p. 83).

27. While understanding of the etiology of schizophrenia is subjective and highly debated, consensus among authorities is that it results from a genetic disposition activated by life experience—what Lacan calls the "lived history" of the patient. See Bice Benvenuto and Roger Kennedy, *The Works of Jacques Lacan: An Introduction* (New York: St. Martin's Press, 1986), p. 265. In his personal account of schizophrenia, *The Eden Express,* Mark Vonnegut counsels his father never to blame society or relatives for schizophrenia—that it is "an internal catastrophe . . . bad genetic luck" (242). Mark's book has been used as a specific case history in *Abnormal Psychology: Experiences, Origins, and Interventions,* ed. Michael Goldstein, Bruce Baker, and Kay Jamison (Boston: Little Brown, 1980). While the author ascribes his own mood disorders and much of the psychotic behavior of his characters to internal chemistry, he says he believes that culture—ideas and artifacts—is also responsible for making healthy people sick, *Palm Sunday: An Autobiographical Collage* (New York: Delacorte, 1981), pp. 241–42. See *Fates Worse Than Death* for Vonnegut's recent thoughts as to causes and cures of mental illness. He concludes that it seems more accurate to classify people like himself as "manic-depressive" than schizophrenic (205), adding that such lack of certainty makes for wonderful intellectual speculation and "absolute hell for patients and their families" (206). Ultimately Vonnegut views mechanistic theories of human behavior as he does all closed systems, as dangerously limiting the individual's sense of freedom of choice and action. He expresses his contempt for such structures by saying that in writing his book about his personal family history, he was "driving my fist into the guts of grandfather clocks" (*Palm Sunday* xv). Schizophrenic episodes experienced by Vonnegut's protagonists are nearly always precipitated by a specific trauma. The *DSM-III* calls these "psychosocial stressors" (185). In the *Paris Review* interview Vonnegut consolidates the calamities of his own life that form the nexus of suffering of his major characters: "depression, war, the possibility of violent death, the inanities of corporate public relations, six children, an irregular income, long-delayed recognition" ("The Art of Fiction LSIV: Kurt Vonnegut," *Paris Review,* no. 69 [Spring], pp. 56–103). The suicide of Vonnegut's mother belongs with this list.

28. Laing, pp. 54, 161. Laing sees this precisely in terms of Vonnegut's portrayal, as a life and death struggle between a true self and a false self system. Armand Nicholi, in *The Harvard Guide*

to Modern Psychology, says that "Schizophrenia like all psychosis is experienced as a life-and-death struggle for emotional survival," p. 202.

29. Ibid., pp. 76, 79, 94. Freud, Laing, Lacan, and Rogers offer similar warnings about the neurotic defense mechanisms by which Vonnegut's heroes shield themselves from intolerable psychic pain and trauma. The tendency to hide behind elaborate facades, masks, or false selves, to withdraw into narcissistic fantasies and daydreams that distort or exclude the outside world, may create a perpetually equivocal nature and render the individual unable to participate in real life. In this light, the challenge to Vonnegut's protagonists becomes what Carl Rogers calls "the stripping away of false facades." See *On Becoming a Person* (Boston: Houghton Mifflin, 1961), pp. 35, 111. The cathartic process of Vonnegut's fiction allows the author and his characters to free themselves from neurotic fears and restrictions and to realize themselves in the present.

30. Laing, p. 82.

31. The checklist of critical essays and books in *Kurt Vonnegut: A Comprehensive Bibliography,* ed. Asa B. Pieratt, Jr., Julie Huffman-Klinkowitz, and Jerome Klinkowitz (Hamden: Archon Books, 1987), pp. 221–72, reflects the many Vonnegut critics who share Hendin's position, viewing Vonnegut as fatalist or nihilist. See, for example, references to Bell, Blair, Bodtke, Bosworth, Bradbury, Bryan, Chabot, Engel, Gardner, Goss, Harris, Hanck, Kennedy, Lowing, Le Clair, McConnell, Messent, Olderman, Pinsker, Ramley, Schulz, Weales, Wolfe, and Wood. Lynn Buck's essay, "Vonnegut's World of Cosmic Futility," *Studies in American Fiction* 3 (Autumn 1975), pp. 182–98, catalogues critics and reviewers who see Vonnegut's work as artistically simple *and* pessimistic. Buck concludes that the only recourse open to Vonnegut's characters "is to laugh and create a world even more insane" (181). In a recent dissertation Marc Leeds concludes that Vonnegut's characters are victims of "an inescapable time-looped fatalism"; all are doomed to "preordained destinies" (26). "What Goes Around, Comes Around: The Naive-Schizophrenic-Resurrected Cycle in the Novels of Kurt Vonnegut" (University of Buffalo, 1987).

32. *The Harvard Guide to Contemporary American Writing,* ed. Daniel Hoffman (Cambridge: Belknap Press, 1979), p. 259.

33. Ibid., pp. 257, 258.

34. Ibid., pp. 259.

35. The following major studies demonstrate a connection between appreciating Vonnegut as an accomplished practitioner of experimental fiction and understanding his vision as basically affirmative. Scholes speaks for the group in asserting that Vonnegut subtly but relentlessly "seeks to make us thoughtful" (160). In *Fabulation and Metafiction* (Urbana: University of Illinois Press. 1979), pp. 156–62, 200–205; see Tony Tanner, *City of Words* (New York: Harper and Row, 1971), pp. 181–201; John W Tilton, *Cosmic Satire in the Contemporary Novel* (Lewisburg: Bucknell University Press, 1977), pp. 69–88; Patricia Waugh, *Metafiction: The Theory and Practice of Self-Conscious Fiction* (New York: Methuen, 1984), pp. 8, 22, 127–29, 133.

36. Of those critics who discuss the psychic dimension in Vonnegut's work, John Tilton, Kathryn Hume, and Leonard Mustazza provide the most compelling and thorough insights into Vonnegut's use of the Freudian and the mythic unconscious. See Tilton's *Cosmic Satire in the Contemporary Novel,* and Hume's "Vonnegut's Self-Projections: Symbolic Characters and Symbolic Fiction," *Journal of Narrative Technique* 12 (Fall 1982), pp. 177–90.

37. Of critics who defend Vonnegut against charges of escapism and triviality, Waugh, Tanner, Hume, Scholes, and Mustazza are particularly incisive about the positive relationship in Vonnegut's work between the actual and the imaginary. Each shows that Vonnegut, like Borges, Fowles, Bartheleme, and Calvino, uses supernatural and superrational structures to express the most profound and serious concerns of the age. These critics show that a measure of Vonnegut's genius has been successfully to fuse the experimental and innovative with the popular and the traditional.

38. *Roots of Renewal in Myth and Madness* (San Francisco: Jossey-Bass Publishers, 1976), pp.

134–38. Perry discusses expressions of apotheosis in the context of heroic archetypes as well as psychic illness. See the *DSM-III* for further discussion, p. 207.

39. The view of Vonnegut's work as thin or facile has been countered in exemplary studies by Jerome Klinkowitz, Peter Reed, Kathryn Hume, Robert Merrill, and Leonard Mustazza, among others. Jerome Klinkowitz has been to Vonnegut studies what Malcolm Cowley was to Faulkner, arguing the complexity of Vonnegut's technique and vision from the time Vonnegut's novels were hardly getting reviewed. Books like *The Vonnegut Statement* (1973) and *Vonnegut in America* (1977) promote Vonnegut as a foremost contemporary American writer. Klinkowitz's *Kurt Vonnegut* (London: Methuen, 1982) is particularly important for portraying Vonnegut's evolution as a major postmodernist. Peter Reed's *Kurt Vonnegut, Jr.* (New York: Warner, 1972) is a careful study that sees Vonnegut's vision as autobiographical and developing. No existing study of Vonnegut defends the author against the charges of defeatism or artlessness more successfully than Leonard Mustazza's *Forever Pursuing Genesis.* Mustazza sees Vonnegut's narrative techniques as complex and original, describing the novels as a whole as a continuous plea for ethical action, for the exercise of reason, and compassion (115). It is my sense that Kathryn Hume has provided the most penetrating overview of Vonnegut's work in her essays, "The Heraclitean Cosmos of Kurt Vonnegut," *Papers on Language and Literature* 18 (Spring 1982), pp. 208–24, and "Kurt Vonnegut and the Myths and Symbols of Meaning," *Texas Studies in Literature and Language* 24 (Winter 1982), pp. 429–47.

40. Laing, pp. 46, 47.

41. Indirectly through character projections and repeatedly in the autobiographical prefaces, Vonnegut comments upon the constricted family relationships that produce his own depression and the bizarre phobias of his protagonists. The parental morbidity—what the *DSM-III* calls "premorbid personality" (86)—and lovelessness visited upon Vonnegut's protagonists often become the first stage of mental deterioration in schizophrenic patients. In serving as his own psychoanalyst, Vonnegut calls himself "an eclectic worker in the field of mental health"—a pragmatic man, a little Jungian, a bit Freudian, a little Rankian, and so on *(Palm Sunday* 243).

42. *Beyond the Pleasure Principle,* trans. James Strachey (New York: Bantam, 1967), pp. 78–110.

43. Laing, p. 49. Mark Vonnegut describes his personal experience with schizophrenia as "the struggle . . . between two opposites, good and evil, positive and negative, yes and no" *(The Eden Express,* 79–80). Vonnegut comments directly upon such a division in himself: "I was fascinated by the good and evil in myself and in everyone" *(Wampeters* 212).

44. *Cat's Cradle* (1963; rpt. New York: Dell, 1975). All subsequent quotations followed by a page number in parentheses are from this edition.

45. Technically, the tendency of organisms to maintain their metabolic processes to enhance individual and race survival.

46. *Wampeters,* p. xxi.

47. *Breakfast of Champions* (1973; rpt. New York: Dell, 1975), p. 210. All subsequent quotations followed by a page number in parentheses are from this edition.

48. *Wampeters,* p. xxi.

49. Ibid.

50. Personal letter, November 30, 1982. Cross-sectional symptoms of depression and schizophrenia may be indistinguishable *(DSM* 187, 210). One disorder may be as dangerous as the other. Patients typically experience a loss of hope, lose the ability to respond emotionally, develop paralysis of will, and become suicidal. Vonnegut claims to have experienced such a deficit of emotional energy on a regular basis since he was six years old *(Wampeters* 252). In *Breakfast of Champions,* the character Vonnegut says he used to think of suicide as "a perfectly reasonable way to avoid delivering a lecture, to avoid a deadline, to not pay a bill, to not go to a cocktail party"

(283). In *Fates Worse Than Death,* Vonnegut acknowledges "committing myself to a bughouse for a short stay . . . three or four books ago" (41).

51. *Wampeters,* p. 283. Vonnegut's quest for psychic integration Robert Scholes sees as nothing less than a universal challenge, *Fabulation and Metafiction,* p. 217. This is Freud's basic argument in *Civilization and Its Discontents.*

52. Bellow, p. 167.

53. *Galápagos* (New York: Delacorte Press/Seymour Lawrence, 1985), p. 140. All subsequent quotations followed by a page number in parentheses are from this edition.

Chapter 1

1. "The Theme of Mechanization in *Player Piano,*" *Clockwork Worlds,* ed. Richard Erlich and Thomas Dunn (Westport: Greenwood Press, 1983), pp. 124–35.

2. Symbolized by the "ghost" at the player piano. *Player Piano* (New York: Dell, 1975), p. 38. EPICAC is a giant computing machine in Carlsbad Caverns that makes godlike socioeconomic decisions. Epicac is an emetic that causes violent stomach spasms.

3. Sigmund Freud, *Civilization and Its Discontents,* trans. James Strachey (New York: W.W. Norton and Company, 1961), pp. 26–30. The concept is Freud's, but the dangers of seeking sexual fulfillment through inorganic means are also argued by Laing, Lacan, and Rogers.

4. Hoffman, p. 25. Raymond Olderman concurs that Vonnegut sounds "more like a social scientist than a novelist," sacrificing "fictive device" for absolute clarity. Olderman feels the best Vonnegut can offer in the way of affirmation is discovering a method of survival. What Olderman sees as the hero's "cosmic cool" I see as the prelude to schizophrenia. *Beyond the Waste Land* (New Haven: Yale University Press, 1972), p. 192.

5. Ibid., pp. 126–32, 134.

6. *Player Piano,* p. 9.

7. *Metafiction: The Theory and Practice of Self-Conscious Fiction* (New York: Methuen, 1984), pp. 8–9. Also discussed by Kathryn Hume and Robert Scholes. The Shah's visit to the home of Wanda and Edgar Hagstrohm shows the lives of "statistically average" citizens to be dull, sterile, and unproductive. The loss of personal freedoms finally drives Edgar so crazy he blowtorches his home, p. 250.

8. Kroner believes that all human problems can be resolved with a few simple, immutable truths. His wife, "Mom," is "a fat repository of truisms, adages, and homilies" (123). The danger of Kroner's delusions becomes clear when he speaks of the spirituality of machines at the same moment he picks off an imaginary bird with his poised shotgun.

9. In *The Interpretation of Dreams,* trans. James Strachey (New York: Avon, 1965), Freud argues that pathological symptoms gain access to the conscious mind indirectly in slips of the tongue and jokes called "derivatives of the unconscious." Lacan accepts Freud's focus upon the unconscious and sexuality, upon ego, id, and superego, but views the source of psychosis as less penetrable, less rigidly structured, than Freud supposed. Following Saussure's premise that language can be only about itself, Lacan views neurotic or psychotic symptoms as influenced by the ambiguities of unconscious language play *(The Works of Jacques Lacan,* pp. 50–51, 108–21, 124–25). See note 21 for Lacan's version of the Oedipal complex.

10. Such "shallowness," called "affect," is always a main symptom of schizophrenia and explains Vonnegut's use of excessively stylized language to convey the effects of psychic dislocation and emotional impoverishment—monosyllabic words, fragmented or elliptical sentences, and dialogue that is mechanical, rigid, and unelaborated. See the *DSM-III,* 184.

11. Laing, pp. 44, 47, 54. Lacan also makes innumerable references to schizophrenics who are decentered, alienated, lacking in being, possessed of an empty center *(The Works of Jacques Lacan,* p. 18).

12. In Laing's view, the schizophrenic is someone whose loss of faith in the stability of existing realities is complete. "I have never known a schizophrenic who could say he was loved, as a man, by God the Father or by the Mother or God or by another man." He or she often "feels in hell, estranged from God" (39).

13. In *The Eden Express,* Mark Vonnegut speaks of his own womb fixation as a primary schizophrenic symptom. "I loved the idea of being in this warm, comfy womb . . . I would draw deep into myself until I could talk, move around, without hurting anyone" (100). Theodore Lidz equates womb regression (when reality gave way before the wish) directly with schizophrenia. Discussed in Sue Shapiro's *Contemporary Theories,* p. 156.

14. *Ecrits: A Selection,* trans. Alan Sheridan (New York: Norton, 1977), pp. 298–99.

15. *Civilization and Its Discontents,* pp. 47–48, 78–79, 81–83. Also discussed in *Totem and Taboo.* Wilhelm Reich says there is no case of schizophrenia which does not reveal unmistakable sexual conflicts, *The Function of the Orgasm* (New York: Simon and Shuster, 1973), p. 60. Lacan, Laing, and Rogers follow Freud in viewing early traumatic or unacceptable childhood memories as the basis of all neurotic symptoms; each sees the exposure of repressed experience as basic to a return to psychic health. Significant to the interrelationship of Oedipal and Dresden related anxieties in Vonnegut's hero, Freud comments upon fire, "phallic tongues of flame," as commonly associated in the unconscious with potency or impotency *(Civilization and Its Discontents,* p. 37). Lacan insists upon greater latitude than Freud in the interpretation of Oedipal feelings. The ambiguities of language by which conflicts reveal themselves produce a never-ending interpretive game—a dialectic of desire whose meanings are always complex and elusive. The mother (the signifier) has for instance her own Oedipal complex. The infant desires the mother and the mother desires the phallus to which she is practically and symbolically bound. See *The Works of Jacques Lacan,* pp. 120–21, 126–33 .

16. See Tilton's *Cosmic Satire in the Contemporary Novel,* and Hume's "Vonnegut's Self-Projections: Symbolic Characters and Symbolic Fiction," *Journal of Narrative Technique* 12 (Fall 1982), pp. 177–90. For valuable discussions of the Oedipal complex as the clearest source of the hero's psychic disturbance, see also Lynn Buck, "Vonnegut's World of Comic Futility," *Studies in American Fiction* 3 (Autumn 1975), pp. 181–98; Jerome Klinkowitz, "Kurt Vonnegut, Jr., and the Crime of His Times," *Critique* 12, No. 3 (1971), pp. 38–53; Charles Berryman, "After the Fall: Kurt Vonnegut," *Critique* 26 (Winter 1985), pp. 96–102; and Josephine Hendin, *Vulnerable People: A View of American Fiction since 1945* (New York: Oxford University Press, 1978), pp. 30–40. Each of these discussions highlights the hero's father as an alien and destructive presence throughout Vonnegut's work. Hendin continues to view Vonnegut as a writer who "makes life easy," who writes to "stop thought," and whose style permits "no development after the laugh" (31). She nevertheless offers excellent insight into the hero's yearning for wholeness and the way parental coldness and indifference create the hero's schizophrenia—betrayal, splitting, and self-division. "Once the irreplaceable mother is lost," she says, "fragmentation is all" (61). Loss of the mother's love runs throughout Vonnegut's work, creating his many images of cold, darkness, and void (36).

17. *Civilization and Its Discontents,* pp. 14–15, 29, 30–31, 47–48, 74–75. Freud views infant sexual love as life's strongest emotional experience, a happiness the individual seeks to repeat over and over. This explains the obsessive search of Vonnegut's hero for mother replacements and what Freud calls "libidinal displacement," dubbed "imprinting" by Konrad Lorenz—the transference of instinctual energy to objects in the external world, property, machines, power structures, social ambition, religion. The individual seeks objects by which to avoid the frustration caused by the unloving mother. See Leonard Mustazza's *Forever Pursuing Genesis* for excellent insight into

the Eden myth as employed throughout Vonnegut's work. Whereas I see Eden-like fantasies as dangerously escapist, Mustazza makes a persuasive case that the quest for such sanctuaries or paradises may frequently symbolize a positive mythic yearning for innocence and transcendance.

18. Laing observes that "if there is anything the schizoid individual is likely to believe in, it is his own destructiveness" (93). See also *DSM-III*, p. 211.

19. *Civilization and Its Discontents*, p. 79. Peter Reed shows that much of the power of *Player Piano* comes from the ambiguity with which machinery and progress are portrayed. We are impressed by American ingenuity, the "ability to invent, continue . . . keep things running." This is a natural byproduct of the hero's ambivalence toward his father, with whom technology and progress are associated. See *Kurt Vonnegut, Jr.*, p. 31.

20. The failure of parental love and direction makes Vonnegut's hero literally crazy with loneliness and uncertain identity. Kathryn Hume notes that all relationships between parents and children in Vonnegut's work are "warped, brutal, anguished, and destructive" ("Kurt Vonnegut and the Myths and Symbols of Meaning," p. 440). The schizophrenic's withdrawal often stems from the loss of touch, affection, or love from the absent or indifferent parents. The incidence of schizophrenia is higher among relatives of schizophrenics than in the general population. Most authorities point out that the chaos, cruelty, and irregularity of a schizophrenic family allow the family member little diversity of behavior.

21. *The Works of Jacques Lacan*, pp. 53–58, 130–33, 207. Whereas Freud views the ego's development as beginning with the infant at the mother's breast, Lacan sets the formation of psychic structure at the "mirror" stage of psychological development, which organizes and constitutes the subject's vision of the world. The subject's ego is formed primarily by the force and gaze of the mother and other human beings who share her surrounding space.

22. *Civilization and Its Discontents*, pp. xiii, 27–29, 66–69. Freud comments that what began in relation to the father is completed in relation to the group—a necessary course of development from the family to humanity as a whole. The evolution of Vonnegut's hero may therefore be described as the struggle of the life of the species. By the time of the post-*Breakfast of Champions* novels, Vonnegut's hero learns to resolve both personal and social fragmentation by creating fantasies that encourage communal bonding rather than narcissistic withdrawal. Such, Freud says, is the artist's special dispensation. Conversely, as Lacan insists, the phenomenon of alienation is an inevitable part of the individual's psychic life and particularly important to the artist. It helps him maintain his subjective sense of his own aliveness and difference—keeping critical distance between himself and existing social institutions and conventions. See *The Works of Jacques Lacan*, pp. 14, 60–61, 128. Patricia Waugh refers to that creative paranoia that corrects some part of the world which is unbearable through the "delusional remoulding of reality," *Metafiction*, p. 86.

23. Ibid., pp. 66–69. Also discussed in *Beyond the Pleasure Principle*. This is Vonnegut's essential subject, the struggle between Eros and Death, the instinct of life and the instinct of destruction, which works itself out within the protagonist and between the protagonist and external machinery. Within the libido lies the psychic energy that manifests itself at opposing ends of a spectrum, developing into positive life energy, Eros, and evolving into the destructive force, Thanatos, as the organism's development proceeds. While Freud's concepts are subjective and highly debated, the important point for this study is that Vonnegut's characterizations repeatedly fit the profile of Freud's theories of the unconscious, of libidinal energy, and of the life and death force. The will to aggression in the Vonnegut hero is passive and inward, expressed through the pathological retreat into private fantasies and the diminution or complete loss of sexual feeling. The hero's fear of life manifests itself in images of castration and devouring or mechanical vaginas. Vonnegut associates Thanatos with an entire generation of life-hating Americans who seek to satisfy spiritual hunger with machines and material goods *(Wampeters*, p. 28). Vonnegut surmises that the perversion of libidinal energy might account for Richard Nixon's association of criminality with sexuality: "I'm bound to conclude that someone told him when he was very young that all

serious crime was sexual, that no one could be a criminal who did not commit adultery or masturbate" *(Wampeters,* p. xxiii).

24. *Civilization and Its Discontents,* pp. 70–73, 76–77, 79, 83–85. Lacan observes that the child's rebellion is a struggle with language as well as the primal father. See *The Works of Jacques Lacan,* pp. 131–33.

25. Peter Reed suggests that Paul needs "a blow severe enough to knock him off the course dictated by the circumstances of his birth and training," *Kurt Vonnegut, Jr.,* pp. 178–79. Laing's discussion of the conflict between the demands of conformity and the demands of potential human growth clarifies the tragic production of one-dimensional human beings at the Meadows (11, 12). Soviet psychiatry is infamous for the forcible detention and even treatment in psychiatric hospitals of entirely healthy people whose only "mental illness" consists of the fact they understand various aspects of the social and political life in the Soviet Union in their own individual manner. The type of maladjustment that eschews so-called objective, socially determined definitions of sanity, questions the status quo, and makes trouble for those in authority, Paul must maintain. Laing argues that the type of brainwashing, acquiring of false selves, that occurs at the Meadows not only betrays individual potentialities of perception and feeling but may result in the abdication of ecstasy. The challenge to Vonnegut's first two schizoid heroes, Paul Proteus and Malachi Constant, is to maintain inner honesty, freedom, and creativity, without negating the outer world altogether.

26. Laing, p. 17. Laing, Rogers, and others note that withdrawal may be marked by obsessive conformity to social standards in order to avoid complex social interaction, criticism, or failure.

27. The language of the Ghost Shirt Society betrays its aims as simplistic, romantic, and adolescent. It longs to "restore the game" and "ride into battle one last time" (273, 274). Its revolutionary activities "promised some excitement for a change" (278). After the revolution, says Finnerty, people will get back to basic values and virtues: "men doing men's work, women doing women's work." Finnerty sees society becoming an "engineer's paradise"—where he can occupy himself with pure invention free of conscience or an awareness of human consequences (313).

28. Vonnegut likens detachment to a comforting drug, *Wampeters,* p. 180. The association of drugging with joking is interesting in light of Lacan's and Freud's view of joking as a psychological defensive mechanism.

29. Rogers, *On Becoming a Person,* p. 35.

30. Hoffman, p. 130.

Chapter 2

1. The tendency to view Vonnegut's space journeys literally rather than psychologically leads critics to undervalue his art. Benjamin DeMott, for instance, sees "Vonnegut forever imagining looney battlefields in the void," then calls Vonnegut's message in *Sirens* "dogmatic" and "simpleminded." See "Vonnegut's Otherworldly Laughter," *Saturday Review* (May 1, 1971), pp. 29–32, 38. Conversely, Patricia Waugh appreciates that the sci-fi apparatus of *Sirens* expresses a deep human ontological insecurity through its central image of a man or woman threatened and on the run. See *Metafiction,* p. 79.

2. Patrick Shaw describes Vonnegut's numerous references to defecation, urination, ejaculation, and expectoration as Vonnegut's "satiric excremental vision" ("The Excremental Festival: Vonnegut's *Slaughterhouse-Five," Scholia Satyrica* 2 (Autumn 1976), p. 4.

3. Lacan says that it is the unknown knowledge of the unconscious that creates "alternate world" fantasies. The psychotic attempts to replace a disagreeable reality with one more in keeping with his wishes. See *Ecrits* (London: Tavistock Publications, 1977), pp. 180–87, ed. Alan Sheridan. For Vonnegut's heroes, such idyllic environments are utopias of escape rather than self-realization. Patricia Waugh observes that the imaginary projections of Vonnegut's heroes, delu-

sional or not, are ventures into self-creativity, but that characters like Malachi Constant must stop using fictional constructs to avoid moral and aesthetic responsibility. See *Metafiction*, p. 85.

4. *Alice's Adventures in Wonderland and Through the Looking-Glass* (New York: Lancer Books, Inc., 1968), p. 282.

5. One may argue that Martin Koradubian is the one certain character in this story. A "genuinely" bearded young man, a version of Malachi (49), he is a writer who repairs solar watches (faulty, fatalistic notions of time) and envisions a "tremendous house cleaning" (50), a potential metaphor for the catharsis of Vonnegut's hero which climaxes in *Breakfast of Champions.*

6. This is another instance in which, as Lacan explains, the subject is "spoken" rather than speaking.

7. Appropriate to the novel's Alice parallels, Peter Reed notes that Vonnegut's fantasy fiction "takes us through the mirror rather than simply showing us the reflections of reality." See *Kurt Vonnegut, Jr.,* p. 61.

8. The supposed agents who kidnap and pilot Malachi to Mars, George Helmholtz and Roberta Wiley, are extensions of Malachi's paranoia. Like Malachi, both are "masters of disguise" (88) who know the consolations of booze and cynicism. "I have to whisper," Helmholtz says, "or somebody will want to lock me up in the crazy house" (96). Malachi observes that an alert person would have noticed "a false note in the behavior of the two" (88).

9. This debasement of spirit by matter again suggests anal aggressivity.

10. We are reminded of the point made by Freud and others that because the tension between the ego and superego is lacking in children brought up without love, "they have no other outlet for their aggressiveness but turning it inwards." See *Civilization and Its Discontents*, p. 77. In *Sirens* the inward aggression results in hallucinated visions of worlds (Mars) where the word "father" was "emotionally meaningless" (146) or where (Mercury) one feels the security of affectionate Mamas and Papas one has never had (214).

11. Theodore Lidz writes that the noxious influence of unloving parents is often not malevolent but rather the product of their own personal tragedies and egocentric orientations. If the parents were not difficult or peculiar, it is unlikely that the child would be schizophrenic. See *The Origin and Treatment of Schizophrenic Disorders,* p. 48.

12. Malachi's schizophrenic episode by the pool resembles the condition described by John Weir Perry in which the ego is swept back into a state dominated by unconscious fears and conflicts. Throughout Vonnegut's work, the protagonist's exposure to and assimilation of repressed emotions is threatened by such psychic breaks. See *Roots of Renewal in Myths and Madness* (San Francisco: Jossey-Bass Publishers, 1976), p. 44. Psychiatrists find that it is often in a drug-induced state that schizophrenics experience a spacial fourth dimension—a beyond, where they are watched and spoken to, or experience religious, grandiose, or nihilistic delusions. See the *DSM-III,* p. 182, and Perry's *Roots of Renewal in Myth and Madness,* pp. 134–38.

13. Further illustrating that Rumfoord's powers are not what they seem, reports implied that he could see the past and the future clearly, "but they neglected to give examples of sights in either direction" (11). Nevertheless, the effect of being chrono-synclastic infundibulated explains the story's scrambled chronology—the typical mental disorientation of the psychotic. It becomes difficult for Malachi to determine not only when a thing happens, but whether it happens at all or is only a hallucination. Vonnegut cites Dr. Cyril Hall's explanation of chrono-synclastic infundibula in Hall's book *A Child's Cyclopedia of Wonders and Things to Do.* Cyril was a Greek prelate and missionary, born Constantine, who lived 829–869 A.D.; hence, Malachi's last name. For Vonnegut's further use of fairy tale paradigms, see Edith Pendleton's dissertation, "Cinderella Imagery in the Fiction of Kurt Vonnegut" (dissertation, University of South Florida, 1993). Pendleton points out that suggesting the twin personalities that society demands of Cinderella, the following characters have double letters in their names: Rumfoord, Hoover, O'Looney, Aamons, and Marilee Kemp.

14. In Lacan's system of ego-formation, the mirror fails to provide Malachi a loving, protective parental image, so he breaks with reality completely in trying to enter the booby-trapped mirror itself in search of surrogate parents.

15. John Weir Perry identifies the most familiar expression of delusional apotheosis as that of being a savior or messiah. See *Roots of Renewal in Myth and Madness,* p. 127.

16. This is vintage Freud on the subject of mankind's infantile need for an all-powerful heavenly Father and a system of religious doctrines and promises to make him feel safe and whole. See *Civilization and Its Discontents,* p. 21. As Space Wanderer, Malachi is "reduced" to a "childish condition" (245) that protects him from adult complications.

17. Boaz is another of Malachi's psychic projections, a mirror image suggestive of Tweedledum and Tweedledee, called enantiomorphs. Boaz and Unk are described as Siamese Twins (136).

18. See Vonnegut's story "Harrison Bergeron" for further development of this theme. Handicapping actually limits human will and imagination and deprives the world of beauty and grace.

19. Vonnegut describes Schliemann Breathing as a technique that enables human beings to survive in a vacuum or poisonous atmosphere. It is assisted by the taking of "Combat Respiratory Rations," popularly known as "goofballs" (148).

20. David Ketterer believes that the movement of Vonnegut's spirals may be either destructive or creative, images of death or potential regeneration. He likens them to Yeats' interpenetrating gyres, one integrated, the other disintegrated. Viewing the spirals as problematical configurations, Ketterer notes that they set up numerous ingenious connections and systems of control. See "Vonnegut's Spiral Siren Call: From Dresden's Lunar Visits to Tralfamadore," *New Worlds for Old* (New York: Anchor Press, 1974), pp. 296–333.

21. This is the kind of motor impairment or robotlike behavior that occurs in the case of catatonic schizophrenia. Such individuals spend hours frozen like statues. See the *DSM-III,* pp. 190, 191.

22. Even before Malachi and Bea are shot into space, Bea challenges Rumfoord's omniscience and the machinery supposedly governing their lives. Her dressing gown has "folds formed . . . in a counter-clockwise spiral." Stepping back from Rumfoord's staircase, she separates herself from "the rising spiral" (42). Told she will be the hapless victim of a roller-coaster ride, she declares that anyone who made such improbable prophesies "was mad" and that such contraptions should be treated as "silly and dirty and dangerous" (63). We see too that Chrono's jet-black hair "grew in a . . . counter-clockwise swirl" (140–41).

23. Vonnegut deals directly in this novel with the paradoxical relationship of the schizoid artist to society. The artist's natural recalcitrance, loneliness, and despair help him or her resist conformist patterns and maintain a humane and creative vision. Hence, we read that on Mars Unk and Bea were constantly sent to the psychiatric ward to have their minds cleansed, but that "this supremely frustrated man was the only Martian to write a philosophy, and . . . this supremely self-frustrating woman was the only Martian to write a poem" (163).

24. The relative affirmation or negation present in the endings of *Sirens* and *Mother Night* is much disputed—appropriate to what Patricia Waugh says is the function of metafiction, "disturbance rather than affirmation," *Metafiction,* p. 82. Vonnegut undermines our sense of a total or comfortable ending and thereby reminds us of the necessary restrictions of any "formulation." According to Kathryn Hume, Vonnegut's "low-keyed and loosely structured" presentations compel us to construct our own defenses against chaos. Vonnegut's answers are the "presumptions of the New Testament," but he prefers we reevaluate our own perceptions rather than accept his. See "The Heraclitean Cosmos of Kurt Vonnegut," *Papers on Language and Literature* 18 (Spring 1982), p. 221.

Chapter 3

1. It would be as impossible to gauge the full impact of the Dresden massacre on Kurt Vonnegut as, in Norman Mailer's words, to "determine the psychic havoc of the concentration camps and the atom bomb upon the unconscious mind of almost everyone alive in these years." *Advertisements for Myself,* p. 338. Though Vonnegut has played down the long-term trauma of his Dresden experience, his work testifies that the shock of seeing nearly two hundred thousand civilians incinerated could only be faced and exorcised gradually. Reviewing his Dresden experience in *Fates Worse Than Death,* Vonnegut relates Dresden to the horrors of the Holocaust—a "nightmare from which . . . there can never be an awakening" (30)—and further discusses the importance of Dresden to himself personally and artistically. J. G. Keogh and Edward Kislaitis suggest that Vonnegut's release of his Dresden tensions is spread out over a lifetime, intensifying from novel to novel and creating "an intriguing polyphony." See *"Slaughterhouse-Five* and the Future of Science Fiction," *Media and Methods* (January 1971): 38–39, 40.

2. By making himself a nonfictional presence in a fictional setting, Vonnegut moves from the tentative use of metafiction in *Player Piano* and *Sirens* to its use as a major strategy of deconstruction. By stepping into his own fictional world, crossing what Patricia Waugh calls the "ontological divide," the author breaks down the distinction between story as life and life as story, asserting the possibilities of invention of self both within and without the text. Various references in *Mother Night* to "play acting," games, pretense (the main schizophrenic game), dreams, fantasies, linguistic games, and parody foreground the mutual fictionality of life and art. See *Metafiction,* pp. 131, 136, 139. See also Scholes' discussion in *Fabulation and Metafiction,* p. 128. Vonnegut, Scholes says, "happily" explores the protean qualities life shares with fictional form.

3. Kathryn Hume discusses the underworld descent of Vonnegut's heroes in its broadest mythological context. As explained by Joseph Campbell, the trials that await the hero represent initiation ceremonies and should bring the initiate a strengthened ego and new identity. Hume observes that Vonnegut's use of the monomythic descent is complexly disturbing. Often the hero emerges reborn into a world which is itself a void or threatened with destruction. See "Vonnegut's Myths and Symbols," p. 437.

4. Freud's view that blocked or deflected libidinal energy discharges aggression aiming to destroy the outside world seems particularly relevant to Nazi Germany. See *Beyond the Pleasure Principle,* pp. 78–106. The pattern of the life-hating dictator who is dying and wants to take the whole world with him is repeated in *Cat's Cradle.*

5. This passage parodies lines from Hemingway's *Across the River and into the Trees* (New York: Charles Scribner's Sons, 1950), p. 257. Brutalized in spirit from many years' association with senseless death, Colonel Cantwell reports a dead GI lying in the road, repeatedly run over by passing vehicles, as if he is nothing more than an obstacle: "That was the first time I ever saw a German dog eating a roasted German kraut. Later on I saw a cat working on him too." Both psychically maimed heroes mask potentially overwhelming horrors through gallows humor or seeming indifference, and both are tragically divided within themselves.

6. This brief portrait of the protagonist's mother exemplifies what the *DSM-III* calls the "premorbid personality." "Mother Night" is a comprehensive image of the coldness, darkness, cynicism, and morbidity associated with the protagonist's mother throughout Vonnegut's fiction.

7. Peter Reed suggests that *Mother Night* puts to a harsh test Bea's claim in *Sirens* that it is better to be used than to be of no use to anybody. See *Kurt Vonnegut. Jr.,* p. 89. Appropriate both to Bea's relationship to Rumfoord and Campbell's to Frank Wirtanen, Vonnegut comments: "It can make quite a difference not just to you but to humanity: the sort of boss you choose, whose dreams you help come true" (*Fates* 118).

8. The schizophrenic typically visualizes himself isolated and trapped by such small enclosures.

9. John Weir Perry describes the most familiar form of apotheosis as that of the individual who understands himself or herself to be leading the good half of the world against the Devil's. See *Roots of Renewal in Myth and Madness,* p. 135.

10. Jerome Klinkowitz asserts that "Schizophrenia indeed seems the proper name for the madness devouring Vonnegut's world," that the disease becomes a metaphor for the "illness of an age." In Laing's precise terms Klinkowitz describes Campbell's schizophrenic strategy as "the desire to maintain the integrity of the self in the face of a too chaotic world." See "Kurt Vonnegut and the Crime of His Times," pp. 42, 43. Tony Tanner notes that nearly all the characters in *Mother Night* exhibit some sort of split between their apparent and concealed selves. See *City of Words,* p. 187.

11. Vonnegut's fictional inquiry into the etiology of schizophrenia in *Mother Night* is typically ambivalent. A policeman observes that the world may improve when scientists find out more about chemicals in the blood, but Campbell reflects that change can come about when "Each person does a little something" (170), and that social conditions can create schizophrenic splitting. He doubts that any child is ever prepared for what is going "to hit him in the teeth, ready or not" (190). The latter words comment ironically upon Campbell's delusion of escaping into the peaceful childhood world of "hide and seek," i.e., "here I come, ready or not."

12. Laing, p. 39. Indicating the dissolution of Campbell's ego, he describes himself as "a meditative invalid" and a "citizen of nowhere" (119).

13. It is a short jump (part of the same spiral) from Campbell's role as an author of melodramatic plays to seeking a pure and reductive life with Helga. It is love of high adventure, a world of heroes and villains, that attracts him to espionage. Campbell ultimately condemns the "capacity for unquestioning faith" generated by the "Nation of Two" (120) and refers to it as Krapptauer's "sort of truth" (133).

14. The womblike hiding place into which Campbell invites Resi, Helga's sister, suggests Alice parallels—a "cozy little burrow . . . a hole in the ground, made secret and snug" (109).

Chapter 4

1. See examples of the standard critical view that Bokonon speaks for Vonnegut in Leslie Fiedler's "The Divine Stupidity of Kurt Vonnegut," *Esquire* (September 1970), p. 203 and James Lundquist, *Kurt Vonnegut* (New York: Frederick Ungar Publishing Co., 1977), p. 1. Fiedler calls Bokonon Vonnegut's "guru," and Lundquist sees Vonnegut embracing "foma," comforting lies and happy illusions. Certainly Bokonon is the most complex and appealing of Vonnegut's spurious prophets. Robert Merrill suggests that "foma" may take on less noxious forms, e.g., Vonnegut's comment in *Wampeters, Foma, and Granfalloons* that "Thou shalt not kill," a good example of foma (personal letter, November 7, 1988). But I see Vonnegut's fictional use of foma as expressed by Dr. Roger Gould in *Transformations: Growth and Change in Adult Life:* "The Truth, as best we know it, must be our goal." Gould explains that every self-deception creates "a crevice in our Psyche" which creates only more pain and deception. The larger the self-deceptions, the larger the section of the world we are excluded from (New York: Simon and Shuster, 1978), p. 165–66.

2. Jerome Klinkowitz observes that Vonnegut's fictional regions express cultural value as well as geographical place. In "Kurt Vonnegut, Jr., and the Crime of His Times," p. 38. What Klinkowitz calls Vonnegut's "Mod Yoknapatawpha County"—a world in which the same characters, places, and situations appear again and again in metamorphosing roles—provides fertile ground for intertextual study. Shifting structures express the essentially metafictional and mythopoetic nature of Vonnegut's cosmos.

3. In citing Felix Hoenikker as Vonnegut's most grotesquely cold and indifferent father figure, Lynn Buck directs us to Newt's traumatic portrait of Dr. Hoenikker: "Cigar smoke made him smell like the mouth of Hell. So close up, my father was the ugliest thing I had ever seen. I dream about it all the time" (21). "Vonnegut's World of Comic Futility," p. 189. What greater comment upon

the father as the embodiment of Thanatos than to make him "father" of the atom bomb. Kathryn Hume notes that the destructive, dismembering mother is constantly associated in *Cat's Cradle* with the frozen earth, referred to as "a very bad mother" ("Vonnegut's Myths and Symbols," p. 433).

4. Vonnegut's reputation as a moderate boozer and chain smoker is legendary. Such asides remind us of the closeness of the author and his protagonists.

5. "Vonnegut's Siren Call," p. 308. Tony Tanner says that this entire novel is an exploration of the ambiguities of man's disposition to play and invent, and the various forms it may take. See *City of Words,* p. 189. About *Mother Night* Tanner says, "The book presents . . . a whole spectrum of fiction-making, from the vilest propaganda to the most idealistic art " (188).

6. Bokonon's concept of "Dynamic Tension" is the form of madness Howard Campbell denounces in Bernard B. O'Hare. Taken from advertisements for the Charles Atlas body-building school, Bokonon's theory is that societies should be built by pitting pure good against pure evil and by keeping the tension between them high at all times *(Mother Night,* p. 74).

7. In this respect, Bokononists are literally insane, victims of apotheosis—nihilistic or grandiose delusions.

8. Richard Giannone says that the oubliette is a metaphor for the "human conscience suffering the consequence of its irresponsibility." "Violence in the Fiction of Kurt Vonnegut," *Thought* (March 1981), p. 64.

Chapter 5

1. Tony Tanner and John Tilton see *God Bless You, Mr. Rosewater* as more successful at critiquing the brutality and greed of a laizzez-faire economic and social system—what Tanner calls "Entropyville, U.S.A."—than at creating engaging psychological tension. See Tanner's *City of Words,* pp. 191–93, and Tilton's *Cosmic Satire in the Contemporary Novel,* pp. 99, 100.

2. The senator's identification of sexuality as criminal activity is a distinct form of anal aggressivity. The neurosis manifests itself in all of Vonnegut's other figures. Its most common symptom is the senator's obsessive-compulsive maintenance of constant cleanliness, the fear being that the contamination of others will bring retribution and destruction.

3. *The Phenomenological Approach to Psychiatry* (London: Routledge and Kegan Paul, 1955). Cited in *The Divided Self.*

4. Fred and Eliot Rosewater are more than blood relatives; they are spiritual twins. Their identities are specifically joined when Fred explains that his greatest satisfaction in life is saving souls through the "miracle of life insurance," and grateful brides tell him, "God Bless You, Mr. Rosewater" (104). As Eliot's psychological counterpart, Fred is a lonely, sexless, suicidal person whose failed utopian community undercuts Eliot's own altruistic ventures. Pisquontuit is a community of shithouses, shacks, alcoholism, ignorance, idiocy, and perversion—illustrating that the wastelandic horrors of a brutal, materialistic social system are experienced by rich and poor alike. This minitale of Pisquontuit's grotesquely alienated haves and have-nots provides a nightmarish portrait of America's capitalistic utopia turned "belly up . . . turned green, bobbled to the scummy surface of cupidity unlimited." The thematic power of these pages climaxes in the image of a fish trap—the "Bowl of Doom"—put out by the godlike character, Harry Pena (128). The Bowl of Doom takes "heartless advantage of the stupidity of fish" trapped by its "purse net," its false materialistic lure. Human beings wander into such nets believing that God has decreed such a universe.

5. Kathryn Hume remarks that Vonnegut felt responsible for the death of his own mother. The author obtained leave from the army to visit his parents on Mother's Day, 1944. The night before his arrival, his mother took a fatal dose of sleeping pills. The mother's distress over her son's participation in a war she abhorred, combined with failing health, caused Vonnegut anguish and

guilt. See "Vonnegut's Myths and Symbols," p. 439. Fred Rosewater's emotional numbness is directly attributable to his father's suicide: "Since he was the son of a suicide, it was hardly surprising that his secret hankerings were embarrassing and small" (107).

6. These manic episodes exemplify the problematical nature of Eliot's sanity. Though he hallucinates and hears voices, though his actions are those of a paranoid schizophrenic, compulsive, disruptive, and socially inappropriate, his sentiments are sanely humanistic. Like the science-fiction writers Eliot praises (18), he and Vonnegut are "crazy enough" to agonize about the future of the planet. Leonard Mustazza particularly stresses the fact that Eliot is genuinely kind and his message worthwhile, "a man crying in the wilderness, crying against the tide of greed and hypocrisy that has swept over America" (98).

7. Diana Moon Glampers exemplifies what Conrad Knickerbocker calls Vonnegut's "frightening sense of the ridiculousness in people and events" ("How to Love People Who Have No Use," *Life*, 58 April 9, 1965, pp. 6–7).

8. David Goldsmith observes that Eliot's obsessive involvement with volunteer fire departments expresses sublimated guilt over the horrors he has committed as a soldier *(Fantasist of Fire and Ice*, p. 23).

9. *City of Words*, p. 192.

10. *Civilization and Its Discontents*, p. 49.

11. John Tilton says that Vonnegut allows an easy resolution to the tensions between Eliot and his father. To the contrary, Eliot exhibits compassion, but he is no closer to solving his deepest psychic needs. See *Cosmic Satire in the Contemporary Novel*, p. 100.

Chapter 6

1. *Breakfast of Champions*, p. 219.

2. *Wampeters*, p. 235.

3. "Age of Vonnegut," *New Republic*, 12 (June 1971), p. 31. Cited in Hume, "The Heraclitean Cosmos of Kurt Vonnegut," p. 208.

4. "Vonnegut's Self-Projections," p. 178.

5. *Kurt Vonnegut, Jr.*, pp. 172, 173. Tony Tanner comments that through the integration in *Slaughterhouse-Five* of scenes and characters from all previous novels, Billy Pilgrim not only slips backwards and forwards in time, "he is also astray in Vonnegut's own fictions" *(City of Words*, p. 195).

6. John Tilton says that to analyze the narrative mode of *Slaughterhouse-Five* is to analyze its primary subject—its author. But he presents a thoroughgoing argument that despite their similar birthdates and shared ceremonial Luftwaffe saber, Vonnegut and Billy Pilgrim are vastly different people. While Billy fails to bring his nightmare to consciousness, Vonnegut visits his war buddy Bernard V. O'Hare for the express purpose of recalling Dresden. At the same time Billy claims he is kidnapped by a flying saucer and taken to Tralfamadore, Vonnegut actually travels to Dresden as an act of responsibility. *(Cosmic Satire in the Contemporary Novel*, pp. 72, 89, 103). In *Fates Worse Than Death*, while providing extensive details supporting the autobiographical importance of *Slaughterhouse-Five*, Vonnegut explains that it was his fellow ex-Dresden POW Joe Crone who served as the model for Billy Pilgrim (106).

7. "The Swiftian Satire of Kurt Vonnegut, Jr." in *Voices for the Future*, ed. Thomas D. Clareson (Bowling Green, Ohio: Bowling Green University Popular Press, 1976), vol. 1, pp. 238–62, esp. pp. 243–53, 259–62. See also Wymer's extension of this argument in "Machines and the Meaning of Human in the Novels of Kurt Vonnegut, Jr.," in *The Mechanical God: Machines in Science Fiction*, ed. Thomas P. Dunn and Richard D. Erlich (Westport, Conn.: Greenwood Press, 1982), pp. 11–52.

8. *Wampeters*, p. 161. Vonnegut speaks of his youthful optimism before the war and how it changed after the bombings of Dresden and Hiroshima: " 'Hey, Corporal Vonnegut,' I said to myself, 'maybe you were wrong to be an optimist. Maybe pessimism is the thing.' I have been a consistent pessimist ever since, with a few exceptions." Cited in *The Vonnegut Statement*, p. 13. More recently, in *Palm Sunday*, Vonnegut comments that while he had certainly been pessimistic, he was astonished to find "myself an optimist now"—underestimating the intelligence and resourcefulness of his fellow human beings (p. 209).

9. Vonnegut describes the emotional difficulty of dealing with repressed memories of his Dresden experience, for instance, the five thousand pages he has thrown away. For valuable discussion of the way Vonnegut releases these memories gradually over the course of his early novels, see Peter Reed, *Kurt Vonnegut, Jr.*, pp. 177, 178, 186–95; and David Goldsmith, *Fantasist of Fire and Ice (Popular Writers Series*, Pamphlet No. 2, Bowling Green, Ohio: Bowling Green University Popular Press, 1972).

10. "Study Guide for *Slaughterhouse-Five*" (English Department, Miami of Ohio University).

11. This reference appears in an unpublished essay by William H. Pahika, "The Vehicle and the Thing Conveyed: A Commentary on *Slaughterhouse-Five.*"

12. Billy's understated response to horror is not a sign of Vonnegut's stylistic "cuteness," as Sandford Pinsker says, but an expression of schizophrenic withdrawal. Billy attempts to prevent himself from thinking of gory realities in the manner of Hemingway's wounded heroes. In both cases the psychic defense becomes a moral deficiency. See Pinsker, *Between Two Worlds: The American Novel in the 1960s* (New York: The Whitston Publishing Company, 1980), p. 98.

13. Time tripping for Billy is a matter of acute regression. Explanations by J. G. Keogh and Edward Kislaitus about the function of sci-fi conventions in *Slaughterhouse-Five* apply throughout Vonnegut's work. They explain that the novel's many space warps and time jumps create the kind of surrealism one finds in the dream-visions of Graham Greene, and that Vonnegut's sci-fi methodology works like medieval allegory "with the content adjusted to the twentieth century" (*"Slaughterhouse-Five* and the Future of Science Fiction," *Media and Methods*, January, 1971, pp. 38–39, 48). Cited in Reed, "Kurt Vonnegut, Jr.," *Dictionary of Literary Biography, Documentary Series*, pp. 351–52. John Tilton comments that no matter how erratic or eccentric Billy's disordered thoughts appear, nothing is "extraneous, whimsical, or disconnected" in this perfectly crafted novel (*Cosmic Satire in the Contemporary Novel*, p. 88).

14. *Cosmic Satire in the Contemporary Novel*, p. 102. The fictional conflict between Eros and Thanatos has an eerie analogue in Vonnegut's personal experience as a prisoner of war in Dresden. The Dresden factory where he was assigned work—turned into an inferno by allied fire-bombing—made vitamin-enriched malt syrup for pregnant women.

15. Tony Tanner explains that Billy's "serene, conscienceless passivity" contributes as much to such tragedies as Dresden as does the violence of Lazzaro and Roland Weary (*City of Words*, pp. 312, 313). Vonnegut continues in *Slaughterhouse-Five* to explore what Doris Lessing calls "the ambiguities of complicity," which cause the reader to think carefully about degrees of responsibility for violence and injustice ("Vonnegut's Responsibility," *New York Times Book Review*, 4 February, 1973, p. 35). Cited in Reed, "Kurt Vonnegut, Jr.," *Dictionary of Literary Biography Documentary Series*, p. 327."

16. Roland Weary's name, with its allusion to the medieval *Song of Roland*, suggests the haze of romance through which Weary sees his life. His vision of himself as one of the three Musketeers is woefully delusive. Nearly everyone in the novel becomes trapped in romantic conventions of some kind. I take this insight from Pahika's essay, "The Vehicle of the Thing Conveyed. . . . "

17. In chapter 1, Vonnegut associates his condition with Billy's through a reference to Tralfamadorian clocks. As "somebody" plays "with the clocks" against his will, Vonnegut becomes "a non-person," suggesting schizophrenic disembodiment and will-lessness (20).

18. "The Excrement Festival: Vonnegut's *Slaughterhouse-Five,*" *Scholia Satyrica,* 2, no. 3 (1976), p. 5.

19. Ibid.

20. Ibid.

21. *Fantasist of Fire and Ice,* p. 26.

22. Ibid., p. 28.

23. "Easy Writer," *The New York Review* (July 2, 1970), p. 8. Richardson sees Vonnegut as a "too easily understood parabalist," conjuring up "mindless worlds" like Tralfamadore to teach "unenlightened earthlings" a tolerance for pain. Stanley Kauffmann decries Vonnegut's philosophy as "sophomoric" and undemanding, then describes the "wise spacefolk," the Tralfamadorians, who enlighten earthlings. In "Stanley Kauffmann on Films," *New Republic* (May 13, 1972), p. 35. A majority of critics assume that the Tralfamadorians speak for Vonnegut, that the author is as resigned to Tralfamadorian fatalism as Billy Pilgrim. In an article entitled "The American War Novel from World War II to Vietnam," Kalidas Misra sees Vonnegut's vision as so dark, his characters so powerless, that she uses *Slaughterhouse-Five* to describe a shift in the modern war novel from "hope to final despair." "The American War Novel from World War II to Vietnam," *Indian Journal of American Studies,* vol. 14 (2) (1984), p. 76. See the introduction to Robert Merrill's *Critical Essays on Kurt Vonnegut* (Boston, Mass.: G. K. Hall, 1990) for a superb overview of the debate about Vonnegut's alleged espousal of Tralfamadorian fatalism.

24. John Irving provides valuable counterpoint to the argument by Josephine Hendin, Roger Sale, Jack Richardson, John Gardner, et al., that Vonnegut infects his readers with despair and world weariness. Irving agrees that Vonnegut "hurts" us with visions of a ruined planet and evaporated sunny dreams. But Vonnegut's "bleak impoliteness" provokes us to be more thoughtful, creative, and kind. See "Kurt Vonnegut and His Critics," *New Republic* 181 (September 22, 1979): 41–49.

25. *Cosmic Satire in the Contemporary Novel,* pp. 79–101.

26. Ibid., p. 101

27. Through the mindless, erotic satisfactions of Montana Wildhack's hallucinated bosoms (a porno version of Aamons Monzano), Billy achieves the Oedipal fulfillment he has always sought. John Tilton observes that Vonnegut's biographical exposition of Billy's formative years implies that Billy was, at twelve, already on his way to Tralfamadore *(Cosmic Satire in the Contemporary Novel,* p. 76).

28. *Wampeters,* pp. 280, 281.

Chapter 7

1. References to "clocks" appear prominently in *Breakfast of Champions.* The movie version of *Slaughterhouse-Five* follows the spirit of the novel by having a huge clock fall on Billy Pilgrim, suggesting that Billy is psychologically damaged by accepting a Tralfamadorian view of time, that is, time that is inflexible and predetermined. In *Breakfast of Champions,* the author describes human beings who have been turned into emotional and physical grotesques, standing directly beneath a "clock which my father designed" (p. 3). This "father" may be the designer of the universe, the author's architect father, or the father of the country. In any case, the "father" represents a warping influence—one that breeds a fatalistic acceptance of mechanistic systems in which free will has no place.

2. Midland City—Vonnegut's cultureless society—represents *every* city U.S.A. When Francine says to Dwayne Hoover, "We could go to some other city," Dwayne responds, "They're all like here. They're all the same" (167). Patricia Waugh explains that Vonnegut's crude diagrams replace

language in order to express the poverty of Midland City's culture, which is available through representations of "assholes . . . underpants . . . and beefburgers" *(Metafiction,* p. 8).

3. Vonnegut's one play, *Happy Birthday, Wanda June* (1970), contains his clearest statement of belief that humankind can become anything it wants to become (1971; rpt. New York: Dell, Delta [1971]). In contrast to Harold Ryan's assertion that he must act in accordance with a rigidly structured set of values ("That's the way this particular clock is constructed"), the Hemingway look-a-like is turned from a man of violence into a man of peace (p. 116).

4. Leslie Fiedler says that according to the *Book Review Index* from 1952 to 1963, no book of Vonnegut's is recorded as having appeared or been reviewed—hence, Vonnegut's persistent defensiveness underlying his "playful-bitter" references to critical neglect. See "The Divine Stupidity of Kurt Vonnegut," cited in Peter Reed's "Kurt Vonnegut," *Dictionary of Literary Biography Documentary Series,* ed. Mary Bruccoli (Detroit: Gale Research, 1983), p. 339. *Breakfast of Champions* itself has been negatively reviewed. David Ketterer calls it a novel composed apparently of what would not fit into *Slaughterhouse-Five* ("Vonnegut's Spiral Siren Call," p. 297). Robert Merrill faults reviewers for seeing only "textual irrelevances" and "facile fatalism" and for missing the point that *Breakfast of Champions* is about rather than illustrative of fatalism. "Vonnegut's *Breakfast of Champions:* The Conversion of Heliogabalus," *Critique* 18, no. 3 (1977), p. 99.

5. Kathryn Hume explains that Vonnegut uses Trout's fluctuating identity from novel to novel as a means of integrating potentially overwhelming fragments of his own psyche ("Vonnegut's Self-Projections," p. 186).

6. Vonnegut continues to discuss the source of schizophrenia as both biochemical and rooted in life experience. Hoover's craziness is a combination of "bad chemicals" *and* bad ideas, the "Yin and Yang of madness" (14). I think that Trout's mind poisoning of Hoover contradicts the author's comment in *Fates* that he never had an event or another person drive a character crazy (33).

7. Lynn Buck notes that the usual hostility between the protagonist and his father is projected through Dwayne and Bunny Hoover, candidates for a "booby hatch." Bunny is accused of trying to kill his father with hatred and then redirecting his hatred toward his mother (204). Bunny is the first person Dwayne attacks when he goes berserk ("Vonnegut's World of Comic Futility," p. 190).

8. Vonnegut's fears seem based more on his readers' inability to see beyond the dark surfaces of his work than on intrinsic pessimism. Nevertheless, he apparently sees himself as a man who like Howard Campbell has served evil too openly and good too secretly.

9. Vonnegut says in *Palm Sunday,* "As for real death—it has always been a temptation to me, since my mother solved so many problems with it. The child of a suicide naturally thinks of death. . . . Answer: I think I'll blow my brains out" (p. 304). We should keep in mind the obvious fallacy of absolute equations between Vonnegut the author and the Vonnegut persona who lives in his novels. Nevertheless, the reference to "hiding," "void," and "dematerialization" tends to verify the schizophrenic plight of Vonnegut's protagonists as his own.

10. Chaos, the subject of Rabo Karabekian's painting, functions paradoxically as a force of disintegration and a force of renewal. It renders closed systems open and dynamic and thus allows for a creative restructuring of identity. Paradox, contradiction, irony, incongruity are linguistic devices by which Vonnegut achieves the same ends as Rabo's painting.

11. Vonnegut repeats the mirror motif as an expression of reality as flux, and identity and meaning as self-created. He watches the meeting of Kilgore Trout and Dwayne Hoover in the Holiday Inn through sunglasses whose lenses were "mirrors to anyone looking my way" (192). Looking at Vonnegut, Dwayne and Trout will see only themselves, as will the reader. Vonnegut writes, "Anyone wanting to know what my eyes were like was confronted with his or her own twin reflections" (192, 193). As "an equilateral triangle" (236), Dwayne, Trout, and Vonnegut exist both as separate and merging identities—as literary characters as well as psychic projections of Vonnegut. Vonnegut uses this as a structuring principle for the entire novel, the three characters moving in and out of focus.

12. Lynn Buck observes that this defiant gesture against God the Father portrays the Oedipal situation of the author paradoxically becoming the father of his own father. Buck shows that Vonnegut consistently associates God with the protagonists' cold and indifferent, often destructive earthly fathers to show that both are creators of a world of pain and suffering. ("Vonnegut's World of Cosmic Futility," pp. 189, 190, 195). See Freud's *Civilization and Its Discontents* for discussion of the psychological interrelatedness of terrestrial and celestial fathers (pp. 19–21).

13. Phoebe Hurty and Philboyd Studge represent the polarities in Vonnegut's personal psychodrama, the will to love, compassion, humility, conscience versus the will to self-destruction. They equally suggest Vonnegut's ambivalence toward his own parents, who were, he says, good at making jokes and, like Phoebe, contemptuous toward racial prejudice and organized religion, but also the source of "bone-deep sadness." Cited by James Lundquist in *Kurt Vonnegut* (New York: Frederick Ungar Publishing Co., Inc., 1977), p. 6.

Chapter 8

1. *Joyce in Nighttown: A Psychoanalytic Inquiry into Ulysses* (Berkeley: University of California Press, 1974), p. 238.

2. Kurt Vonnegut, personal letter, 30 November 1982.

3. Kathryn Hume sees Eliza as partly Vonnegut's sister and partly himself—a projection of anima, the unconscious creative force which must be raised to consciousness, "Vonnegut's Myths and Symbols," p. 433.

4. Charles Berryman, "After the Fall: Kurt Vonnegut," *Critique* (Winter 1985), p. 98. This essay excels in illuminating psychological tensions interwoven throughout Vonnegut's work. Vonnegut follows Poe, Twain, Hemingway, and Faulkner in the tradition of psychological horror.

5. In his overview of Vonnegut's fiction from *Player Piano* to *Deadeye Dick* Richard Giannone sees Vonnegut's later protagonists as disintegrating rather than reconstructing. The violence of Vonnegut's world, he argues, continues to create only dupes and victims and precludes the possibility of inner wholeness. Vonnegut's protagonists have become "ethnologists, watchers of a disappearing species." "Violence in the Fiction of Kurt Vonnegut," *Thought* (March 1988), pp. 58–76.

6. Vonnegut sees his once close and comfortable family ruined by the loss of their Germanic cultural heritage after World War I, and by the Great Depression, when they lost all their material wealth and accumulation of a lifetime. Marc Leeds reports that further estrangement resulted from the family's inability to support Kurt's artistic endeavors. For example, though *Sirens* was dedicated to Vonnegut's Uncle Alex, he would not read the book, suggesting that beatniks would think it was wonderful. See "What Goes Around, Comes Around: The Naive Schizophrenic-Resurrected Cycle." For comment upon Vonnegut's relatives' response to his books, see *Palm Sunday,* pp. 186–87, 189. In *Bluebeard,* the protagonist refers to his blood relatives as "alienated descendants all" (7).

7. Christopher Lehmann-Haupt's review of *Deadeye Dick* reflects the typically negative response to Vonnegut's work since *Breakfast of Champions,* which he sees as "facile and mannered," with *Deadeye Dick* a slight improvement over *Slapstick* and *Jailbird.* See "Books of the Times," *The New York Times* (November 5, 1982), p. C23. A sampling of reviews suggests no improvement in the understanding of Vonnegut's affirmative vision or the subtlety of his art. Each repeats the charge that Vonnegut's worldview is shallow, nihilistic, undeveloping, and that his artistic method is simplistic or clever at best. See R. Z. Sheppard, "Goodbye Indianapolis." *Time* (Oct. 25, 1976), p. 84; Michael Wood, "Vonnegut's Softer Focus," *The New York Times Book Review* (Sept. 9, 1979), p. 1, 22; Roger Sales, "Kurt Vonnegut: Writing with Interchangeable Parts" *(The New York Times Book Review* (Oct. 3, 1976), p. 3; Andrew Kelly, "Slapstick: Or Lonesome No More!"

America, vol. 135 (December 18, 1976), p. 450; James Wolcott, "Mad Apostle," *New York Review of Books* (November 22, 1979), pp. 11–23; Joseph Browne, "Jailbird," *America* (May 10, 1980), p. 402. In his assessment of Vonnegut criticism from *Player Piano* to *Bluebeard,* Robert Merrill observes that critical response to *Galápagos* and *Bluebeard* has been typically sparse and unappreciative *(Critical Essays on Kurt Vonnegut).*

8. *Metafiction,* p. 9.

9. As Wilbur has his mansion in Vermont converted into a clinic, he acknowledges that his mother is battier than ever, feeble, afraid, and profoundly delusional (143). More and more, the ability of Vonnegut's protagonists to recognize the insanity of people around them, particularly that of destructive parents, throws their own sanity into relief.

10. Vonnegut observes that extended families may become dynamite bouquets when a person stops thinking in order to join a family of like-minded people that happens to be crazy, such as the Ku Klux Klan, Jim Jones' Guyana, the homicidal "family" of Charles Manson, and members of the National Rifle Association.

11. Wilbur comments, "Every so often in my opera . . . the stage would turn mud-colored with uniforms. That would be a war. And then it would clear up again" (17).

Chapter 9

1. Kathryn Hume notes that while Christian ideas form a valid and workable "paradigm for right action" for Walter, Vonnegut defines such action by Christian ethics, not Christian theology ("Vonnegut and the Myths and Symbols," p. 442). Leonard Mustazza similarly notes Vonnegut's more optimistic attitudes after *Breakfast of Champions,* explaining that "Vonnegut's serious interest is to affirm that goodness and justice and altruism and love are rewards in themselves" (155).

2. Charles Berryman discusses Vonnegut's use of "history to support the personal narrative which in turn reinforces the fiction." "After the Fall: Kurt Vonnegut," *Critique* (Winter 1985), p. 98. This essay explains the autobiographical significance of Vonnegut's concern with violence and death.

3. The preface establishes that Walter's battling voices are Vonnegut's own. On the one hand, Vonnegut identifies the loss of that youthful socialist self who believed in employing unions to achieve economic justice. On the other hand, he says that resisting the pull of his defeatist self was necessary to life itself. If he is to go on living, he says, he had better follow the lead of idealistic labor leaders like Powers Hapgood (xiii).

4. During his first meeting with Mary Kathleen, Walter says that "I was as immobilized and eye catching as Saint Joan of Arc at the stake" (139).

5. "Futile defense" suggests not only that the defense failed, but that it failed because passivity or futility is an inadequate response to suffering.

6. Several of Walter's prison mates illustrate the way in which RAMJAC's corporate greed and cruelty corrupt the values of public officials—commenting again upon the interrelationship of public and private crimes. HEW's secretary Virgil Greathouse makes his personal fortune as a RAMJAC associate, pretending to serve the public good. Nixon's most dreaded hatchet man, Evil Larkin, discovers Jesus Christ just as he is about to be prosecuted and makes a deal with Heartland House, a RAMJAC publisher of religious books, to publish his autobiography, *Brother, Won't You Pray with Me* (35).

7. Kathryn Hume points out that Kilgore Trout is not only back in this novel, but, like Walter, a man more sinned against than sinning ("Vonnegut's Self-Projections," p. 185). Changed from his usual despairing, cynical self, he is more innocent, sensitive, and kind, expressive, Hume explains, of Vonnegut's own "inner vicissitudes and developments" (188). Leonard Mustazza alerts us to the fact that Vonnegut's autobiographical projections are always complex and ironically presented.

8. *Jailbird* is Vonnegut's most direct indictment of American capitalism since *God Bless You, Mr. Rosewater*. Its bold portraits of social injustice and personal suffering duplicate the shock of defamiliarization achieved by Vonnegut's drawings in *Breakfast of Champions*. Images of Mary Kathleen O'Looney as one of "tens of thousands of shopping bag ladies in major cities throughout the United States of America" (140), and of the "great engine of the economy . . . spitting out unrepentant murderers ten years old, and dope fiends and child batterers" (140) are as stark and unnerving as Vonnegut's drawing of an electric chair or handgun in *Breakfast of Champions*. All are "tragic by-products of the economy" (140).

9. Walter observes that the tie he puts on upon leaving prison, one he had worn during the Second World War, identifies him also as an officer in the Royal Welsh Fusiliers of World War I. It bears a spirallike design (65). Such intertextual references refute the common view of Vonnegut's world as characterized by random violence rather than by correctable human aggression and greed. See Kathryn Hume's essay, "The Heraclitean Cosmos of Kurt Vonnegut," for the best discussion of Vonnegut's genius for creating seemingly unconnected patterns of events, words, people, and ideas that turn out to be complexly interrelated.

10. "Vonnegut and the Myths and Symbols," p. 442.

11. Descent into the catacombs is yet another example of what Kathryn Hume describes as Vonnegut's frequent symbolic use of the death-rebirth hero monomyth to represent cleansing and renewal. She observes that the toilet stall under the train station is notably Dantesque ("Vonnegut's Self-Projections," p. 188).

12. "Vonnegut and the Myths and Symbols," p. 442.

13. This equation of water with fertility provides at least one exception to Kathryn Hume's view that water in Vonnegut's vocabulary remains "stubbornly nonmystical" ("Vonnegut and the Myths and Symbols," p. 438).

14. "Vonnegut's Self-Projections," p. 184.

Chapter 10

1. Andre Bleikasten's analysis of paternal failure refers to the figure of a ghost replacing the father figure as a major literary convention in the absent father motif. See "Fathers in Faulkner," *The Fictional Father: Lacanian Readings of the Text*, ed. Robert Con Davis (Amherst: University of Massachusetts Press, 1981), p. 122. Significantly, the narrator of Vonnegut's next novel, *Galápagos*, exists entirely as a ghost.

2. *Wampeters, Foma, and Granfalloons*, p. 238.

3. Charles Berryman directs us to a passage in *Palm Sunday* in which Vonnegut himself admits to a version of this nightmare: the "bad dream I have dreamed for as long as I can remember . . . I know that I have murdered an old woman a long time ago" (189). In "After the Fall: Kurt Vonnegut," Berryman calls the repeated fictional recasting of Vonnegut's mother's suicide, associated with her artistic dreams and madness, a "ritualized attempt to exorcise the ghost" (99).

4. "Bathed in ink" compresses drowning and rebirth imagery, signifying the paradox of deep suffering converted to art. The antithetical meanings of bathed—death versus cathartic rebirth—illustrate Saussure's proposition that signs function not through their intrinsic value but through their relative position. Cited in Belsey, *Critical Practice*, p. 40. In *Bluebeard*, such language conventions become like the war medals described as the "junk jewelry of warfare" (235), divorced from the realities they supposedly represent.

5. Robert Con Davis, "The Discourse of the Father," *The Fictional Father*, pp. 4–16. Davis acknowledges a direct debt to the theories of Jacques Lacan for his own views of the absent father motif.

6. Robert Con Davis, "Post-Modern Paternity: Donald Barthelme's *The Dead Father,*" in *The Fictional Father,* p. 169. Davis remarks that *Ulysses, Absalom, Absalom!,* and Barthelme's *The Dead Father* are the most important "father novels" in twentieth-century fiction. *Deadeye Dick* seriously qualifies for this list of rogues gallery father figure texts.

7. See Ernest Hartmann, *Adolescents in a Mental Hospital* (New York: Greene and Stratton, 1968), p. 24. Hartmann shows that withdrawal—becoming uncommunicative or not caring—is the chief symptom of childhood psychological disorder. See also John Weir Perry's description of the schizophrenic individual who has been hurt early in life and left with fragile self-esteem. In *Roots of Renewal in Myth and Madness,* p. 44.

8. The portrait fits Vonnegut's own father, a frail architect and painter, but also, Vonnegut says, "a gun nut, which used to amaze me." *Wampeters,* p. 214. Vonnegut expresses further dismay in *Fates* over his father's gun collection and "the deathly still attic of our house in Indianapolis" (38). Lynn Buck observes that this inner struggle possibly has its origin in Vonnegut's own rebellion in becoming a writer rather than a scientist as his father had hoped. Vonnegut notes that his brother and father both insisted that the arts were silly and impractical and that he should concentrate on chemistry. "Vonnegut's Comic Futility," p. 185.

9. When Rudy's father calls Rudy's teacher an obvious "siren" who lures sailors to shipwrecks, he brings the term into dynamic tension with its usual signification in Vonnegut's work. The siren is associated with volunteer fire departments and therefore wholly good; here, it is both an entrapment and a warning. In repudiation of those who see Vonnegut advocating mental regression in *Galápagos* the author disdains people who "throw away their brains" (*Fates* 200).

10. Delusional syndromes due to amphetamines are in fact often associated with schizophrenia. *DSM-III,* p. 186.

11. Benjamin De Mott, "A Riot of Randomness," *The New York Times Book Review* (October 17, 1982), pp. 32, 34.

12. "Books of the Times," p. C23.

13. "A Riot of Randomness," p. 34.

14. It is paranoia as a creative force that allows Rudy to make such connections. Rudy refers to those "superstitious souls" who were unconvinced that "the beauty" of a neutron bomb explosion was the absence of lingering radiation afterwards (226). About the fact that the city has been closed off by barbed wire and turned into a potential detention center, called by the president "a golden opportunity," Rudy asks, "Do you honestly believe that fence is ever coming down?" (234). As an artist who is aware and accountable for the visions he projects, Rudy completes the hero's existential education in art as a "game" with both destructive and constructive potential.

15. The dysfunction of Eros creates a collective death wish. The mind of one of Midland City's most famous citizens, the Babbitlike Dwayne Hoover, is so eaten away by the termites of materialism and mechanization that he views sex as like having his teeth cleaned—something everybody should do "at least twice a year" (156).

16. "The Discourse of the Father," in *The Fictional Father*, p. 211.

17. *The Works of Jacques Lacan: An Introduction,* p. 153.

Chapter 11

1. *Beyond the Pleasure Principle,* p. 106.

2. Ibid, p. 82.

3. The Captain is a carrier of Huntington's Chorea (85), an inherited, incurable brain disease that produces convulsions and hallucinations.

4. *Civilization and Its Discontents,* p. 91. We are told that Ecuador experiences "a spasm of imperialistic dementia" (18).

5. This is the grotesquely inverted paradise for which Vonnegut's protagonist has always longed—paradoxically a womblike condition where "people—forget who their mothers were" (105).

6. "Maybe Our Brain Is Too Big?" *Pediatric News,* vol. 20, no. 4 (April 1986), pp. 38, 39.

7. Decapitation, in Freudian terms, is an unconscious castration image.

8. Vonnegut comments, "My mother knocked herself off with sleeping pills . . . my father thought she had walked out on him. Father was right" *(Wampeters,* p. 183).

9. Vonnegut identifies the danger of blind adherence to biological drives by associating "dancing" with both the courtship dance and Huntington's Chorea. Vonnegut further disputes mechanical reproduction through Mandarax's poem about human beings who have a child "who will say exactly what the parents did" (108).

10. *Civilization and Its Discontents,* pp. 70–84.

11. Thanks to my colleague, Frank Mason, for this insight.

Chapter 12

1. This term is employed by Ernest Suarez in his book, *James Dickey and the Politics of Canon: Assessing the Savage Ideal* (Columbia: University of Missouri Press, 1993).

2. Rabo, too, is influenced by Hollywood versions of reality. He explains a married life to which he felt unsuited by saying: "That's the way the postwar movie goes" (210).

3. In "The Second Coming."

4. Rabo associates himself primarily with the Abstract Expressionists. The term was used in 1929 by Alfred H. Bar, Jr., founder of the Museum of Modern Art in New York, in reference to the early improvisations of Wassily Kandinsky. The term was popularized in the late forties and fifties. Its chief practitioners, Mark Rothko, Willem de Kooning, Jackson Pollock, were all influenced by ideas on the workings of the unconscious mind based on the theories of Freud and Jung, as well as existentialist philosophy and theories of symbolist poetry and Oriental art and ideas. Characterized by very bold uses of color and mass to convey such basic human emotions as joy and sorrow, it claims as its most significant element the always tentative interrelationship between subject and viewer. Given its intensely psychological nature, its subjective epistemology, and its existential ethic, Abstract Expressionism proves to be a powerfully instructive analogue to Vonnegut's own literary constructions. See Vonnegut's praise for Jackson Pollock and an extensive discussion of Abstract Expressionism in *Fates Worse Than Death.* Vonnegut says that Pollock, like all great Jazz musicians, was a connoisseur of those "appealing accidents" which more formal artists worked to exclude from their performances (42).

5. "Laid" is possibly a pun, indicating an organic as opposed to mechanical relationship between artist and subject.

6. This reaffirms the "Universal Will to Believe" in *Sirens of Titan,* the Lamarckian creative will by which Malachi Constant escapes the spirallike caves of Mercury. This novel provides numerous examples of the UWTB at work—the premise that one attempts, consciously and unconsciously, to make real one's mental images of life.

7. This confirms Bernard Shaw's contention in *Back to Methuselah* that the writer's primary challenge in the twentieth century was to overcome a potentially paralyzing fatalism and to construct a life-affirming iconography to replace that of failed Christianity. This suggests one of many links between the work of Shaw and Vonnegut—art as a constant deconstructive process necessary to the creation of more vital, humanizing systems of belief. See Richard Dietrich's essay, "Deconstruction as Devil's Advocacy," *Modern Drama,* vol. xxix, no. 3 (Sept. 1986).

8. "Deep breathing" ironically adumbrates Rabo's renewal, suggesting one about to give birth.

9. The black woman who discovers Rabo's lost canvas, an art historian, sympathetic and nurturing, is another member of the "rescue squad" (272). Circe Berman appears to be based on Vonnegut's wife Jill, "Xanthippe," described as a "life force woman" without whom, Vonnegut says, "I probably would have died of too much sleep long ago" (*Fates* 188).

10. Lacan and Freud both speak of the castration complex representing itself in the form of a rent, tear, or primal hole, which could only be filled imperfectly by a patch. *An Introduction to the Works of Jacques Lacan,* pp. 152, 153.

11. Rabo is the most human of all Vonnegut's characters, a flesh-and-blood being we can truly care about. Ironically, in this novel about the unreality of reality, there is more gut-level emotion than in any of Vonnegut's other novels.

12. Vonnegut makes numerous references in *Fates* to the autobiographical significance of Rabo's Dresden painting in *Bluebeard.* "We found ourselves in the valley I describe at the end of ... *Bluebeard*" (107), he says. "It wasn't imaginary. It was real. O'Hare and I were there" (171).

13. Illustrating the mechanical cycle of cruelty and violence that links the Holocaust, the Armenian massacre, the death camps, the bombing of Hiroshima, the planting of land mines, the slaying of American Indians, the burning of witches, the feeding of Christians to wild animals (240), Rabo observes, "As for Innocenzo 'the Invisible' de Medici, he was a banker, which I choose to translate as 'loan shark and extortionist' or 'gangster' " (218). While Vonnegut notes that one might go "mad" looking for connections among such horrors, that is precisely what he provokes us to do (216).

14. The phrasing is Patricia Waugh's in *Metafiction: The Theory and Practice of Self-Conscious Fiction,* p. 138. Some theorists maintain that there is no way to distinguish between autobiography and fiction, that the "self" is an ever-changing enterprise constructed and reconstructed in the mind. Paul de Man says that autobiography "demonstrates . . . the impossibility of closure and of totalization of all textual systems made up of topological substitutions." In "Autobiography as De-Facement," *Modern Language Notes* 94 (1979), p. 922. See also Albert Stone, *The American Autobiography* (Englewood Cliffs: Prentice-Hall, 1981), and *The Female Imagination* (New York: Avon, 1976). See Maribeth Mobley, "Fictions of Self in the Language of Lillian Hellman," Dissertation, University of South Florida, 1989.

15. Ibid., p. 133. See also Norman Holland's discussion of "Identity Theory" in *The Dynamics of Literary Response* (New York: W. W. Norton and Co., 1975). Holland argues that the fluid, dynamic, and ambiguous identity of the reader prevents him from getting outside himself to experience others. The reader further constructs meanings to match his own psychological defenses and fantasies, editing what fits and discarding what does not. Yet while the interaction of eye and text changes according to the reader's energy, experience, and capability, Holland believes that a holistic analysis, a central theme, may emerge from the shared symbolic space of reader and text. Holland's observation that the primary identity is capable of infinite variations is central to the identity transformation of Vonnegut's protagonists. See further discussion of identity re-formation in Marshall W. Alcorn, Jr., and Mark Bracher, "Literature, Psychoanalysis, and the Re-Formation of the Self: A New Direction for Reader-Response Theory," *PMLA* 20 (1985), pp. 342–54.

16. Ibid., p. 86.

17. Vonnegut raises the question of problematical artistic evaluation. What Circe applauds, Rabo calls "kitsch" or bad taste. Some works to Rabo's housekeeper have no meaning at all. Yet when Circe asks him how to tell a good picture from a bad one, he answers: "all you have to do . . . is look at a million paintings, and then you can never be mistaken" (156).

18. For a superb discussion of parallels between Cubism and modern literature, see Jo-Anna Isaak's "The Cubist Esthetic," 14 *Mosaic,* vol. 14 (1) (Winter 1981), pp. 61–90. Though the subject is Joyce, Isaak's commentary is specifically relevant to *Bluebeard.*

19. Cited in "The Cubist Esthetic," p. 75. I wish to thank Constance Pedoto for this insight and for others in this chapter as well.

20. Patricia Waugh notes that readers of the French New Novel will recognize this strategy in the novels of Alain Robbe-Grillet. The repetition of incidents within new contexts, slightly shifted, exposes their mutual fictionality. Waugh's observations of Doris Lessing's use of frames in *The Golden Notebook* to express inner division and a desire for wholeness apply directly to *Bluebeard.* See *Metafiction: The Theory and Practice of Self-Conscious Fiction,* pp. 75, 127.

Chapter 13

1. See Lisa Anderson (2H). This reference by Vonnegut highlights the author's frequent use of drowning imagery to represent loss of moral identity. Characters see themselves as "deluged," overwhelmed by "tidal waves," sucked into whirlpools or sewers.

2. Vonnegut reports in *Fates Worse Than Death* that Jane Cox, his first wife, like Mark, was an "hallucinator" and that her mother went periodically insane (155–6).

3. I have adopted Vonnegut's own literary license in the use of the term *schizophrenia.* I show that, as Jerome Klinkowitz has observed, schizophrenia becomes Vonnegut's most graphic and compelling metaphor for the madness devouring Vonnegut's world, but that Vonnegut *also* uses the imagery of schizophrenia to describe the psychic malaise of protagonists who range from the severe depression of Paul Proteus to the dangerously withdrawn state of characters like Eliot Rosewater and Billy Pilgrim. Vonnegut utilizes *both* the figurative and literal possibilities of mental division.

4. "I am reminded," says Vonnegut, "of the late sculptress Louise Nevelson, who told me that she was seventy years old before people 'realized that I really meant it.' 'People won't pay attention,' she said, 'until they realize that you really mean it.' Chris Lehmann-Haupt said to me a couple of years back that he was sorry, but that he could no longer read me. . . . As far as the *Times* is concerned, and the *Washington Post,* too, I have nothing to mean" (personal letter, June 11, 1989). Reviews of *Hocus Pocus* indicate little improvement in an understanding of Vonnegut's affirmative vision or artistic complexity. Vonnegut was particularly dismayed by Salman Rushdie's unflattering review, in which Rushdie complains not only of Vonnegut's "deep pessimism" (360), but that the author appears burned out, facile and repetitious (see *Fates* 131). The fact is that what Peter Reed and Leonard Mustazza have observed about Vonnegut's increased affirmation after *Breakfast of Champions* seems even more true of *Hocus Pocus* and *Fates Worse Than Death:* that Vonnegut appears more confident, more comfortable with the world and himself (Mustazza 132).

5. It is my view that *Hocus Pocus* and *Fates Worse Than Death* are essentially one book, the "big book" both Vonnegut and Eugene Debs Hartke propose will exonerate them from the charge of pessimism. Vonnegut has chosen to take his case directly to his readers, as judge and jury.

6. I have proposed that in *Slapstick, Jailbird, Deadeye Dick,* and *Galápagos,* Vonnegut summons up deeply repressed childhood experiences—a legacy of coldness, morbidity, guilt, and suicide—which needed to be faced as Vonnegut had faced the traumatic experience of war in *Slaughterhouse-Five.* In *Hocus Pocus,* Vonnegut continues to work out tensions between himself and parents who, he says in *Galápagos,* "made psychological cripples of their . . . children" (78), parents described in *Fates* as the sad and broken father, perpetually nine years old, in full retreat from life, and the mother who surrenders to spiritual void (22, 23). The author encourages an autobiographical reading, writing to me that in describing the family tensions in his work, "You have me dead to rights" (February 12, 1990).

7. We learn in *Fates* that Vonnegut's father, the "gutted architect" (23), the defeated "unawakable prince" for whom challenges never came (25), probably serves as the model for Vonnegut's characters for whom artistic failure translates to apathy or aggression. Vonnegut reports that during the war his father stopped being an architect entirely and went to work in inven-

tory control at the Atkins Saw Company, "which was making weapons of some sort, maybe bayonets" (23). The portrait of the father is nevertheless sympathetic.

8. Vonnegut again fuses his message of psychic and social trauma. Eugene's personal suffering reflects the nation's larger decline. As Eugene battles tuberculosis, sees his wife and mother-in-law put into an asylum, and is imprisoned for treason, the country is swept by the plague of AIDS, oil spills, radioactive waste, poisoned acquifiers, looted banks, and liquidated corporations. The warden of Athena prison wonders whether "the whole place was finally going insane" (235). Throughout *Fates,* Vonnegut indicts the blatant hypocrisy and brutality of those he calls the "neo-Cons," a central subject of *Hocus Pocus,* the naked racist and classist upper class white people (e.g., Buckley, Kirkpatrick, Bush) who believe themselves to be the most highly evolved animals on earth and the poor people and the dark people to be "monkeys without tails" (200). Suggestive of the moral schizophrenia of such characters as Lionel Jones and Bernard B. O'Hare in *Mother Night,* Vonnegut portrays the bizarre contradictions in the characters of George Will (the A+ student who criticizes Vonnegut for "trivializing" the Holocaust [99]), Henry Kissinger (winner of the Nobel Peace Prize, who recommends bombing Hanoi at Christmas [103]), and Thomas Jefferson (patriot and slave owner [115]). This is how "Crazy" we *all* are, he concludes (103).

9. Eugene adopts the "false self system" of previous heroes. In this light, a significant moment for Eugene comes when he achieves what Carl Rogers calls "the stripping away of false facades." "It was as though you took off a mask," Muriel Spark tells him, "and you seemed as though you were suddenly all wrung out" (209). Refusing to wear "gloves and a mask" at Athena, Eugene remarks: "who could teach anybody . . . while wearing such a costume?" (117).

10. The perversion of creative or sexual energies by such unfeeling, mechanistic activities as characterize the impersonal world of Tarkington, Athena, Dupont, West Point, and Griot represents the basic psychic disturbance of protagonists from Paul Proteus to Eugene Hartke. Eugene's personal dilemma is symbolized by the "bell clappers" on the library wall of Tarkington identified as "petrified penises" (127).

11. What West Point does to Eugene resembles what Martian brainwashing does to Malachi Constant in *Sirens of Titan,* causing Malachi to murder his best friend in a test of loyalty of his Martian puppetmasters.

12. Vonnegut's most ingenious example of imaginative hocus pocus comes in the form of numerous linguistic tricks that connect these two communities, showing that whereas to the Athenian prisoners Tarkington appears as a "paradise" (83) of harmony and love, its life is only visibly less futile than that of the prison. Each year, thirty inmates die for every student who graduates from Tarkington, the number of sloops (30) the college is given by a parent who had "cleared out the biggest savings and loan bank in California" (264). A major irony is that neither community recognizes its mirror reflection in the other, nor that their tragic alienation is self-induced. When Robert W. Mollenkamp loses his fortune, Eugene notes that he and his wife "were as broke as any convict in Athena" (109). The worlds merge again when a son of one of Tarkington's trustees is sent to Athena for strangling a girlfriend behind the Metropolitan Museum of Art (216). In *Fates,* Vonnegut observes that the neo-Cons, the forces of Beelzebub who were liquidating businesses and natural resources, were putting a greater proportion of its citizens in jail and prison than even the Soviet Union or the Republic of South Africa (192).

13. Eugene's interest in middle-aged women appears at least partly Oedipal in nature, a continuance of what Paul Proteus describes as "the unpleasant business between me and . . . my father" (97), what Eliot Rosewater's psychiatrist calls "crossed wires" (73), "the most massively defended neurosis I've ever attempted to treat" (28), and what Eugene identifies as "the something wrong with me" (149). Jacques Lacan explains that to escape the Oedipal relationship with the mother and constitute his own identity, the subject must accept the name ("the paternal metaphor") of the father. To that end, Vonnegut remarks that his father died eventually, and "in an act of Freudian cannibalism, I dropped the 'Jr.' from my name. Thus in lots of my works do I appear to be both my father and my son" *(Fates* 22).

14. In contrast to those who see "randomness" at the center of Vonnegut's world view, Vonnegut continues in *Hocus Pocus* to explore what Doris Lessing calls "the ambiguities of complicity" (135), which cause the reader to think carefully about degrees of responsibility for violence and injustice. As John Leonard notes, we take leave of *Hocus Pocus* "feeling . . . reflective, as if emerging from the vectors of a haiku" (421). The kind of complacency that prevents readers from establishing causal relationships in Vonnegut's fictional world characterizes as well a society whose self-righteousness blinds it to the criminality of racism, illiteracy, greed, or the suffering of the homeless. Eugene reflects that the American rich "had managed to convert their wealth . . . into a form so liquid and abstract . . . that there were few reminders . . . that they might be responsible for anyone outside their own circle of friends." "Being an American," Paul Slazinger says, "means never having to say you're sorry" (225).

15. See note 1 to Chapter 7. Vonnegut continues in *Hocus Pocus* to use clock imagery to symbolize the timeless and mindless impulse to aggression and the mechanistic structures that promote aggression.

16. The situation was, in actuality, morally compromising. The American lives Eugene saves are at the expense of Vietnamese left behind.

17. "Unhappy strangers" (225). In *Forever Pursuing Genesis,* Leonard Mustazza rightly asserts that the *Sermon on the Mount* becomes the mythic subtext—the heart of Vonnegut's plea for common decency—from *Slapstick* onward. Mustazza indicates a mythic movement toward "judgement" that clearly culminates in *Hocus Pocus.* An actual concept of a judgment day does not appeal to Vonnegut, Mustazza explains, but gentleness, mercy, and justice do (153).

18. In an apparent jibe at the inability of critics to read his works seriously or attentively, Vonnegut has Eugene remark that "the lesson I . . . learned was the uselessness of information to most people, except as entertainment." Suggesting that such a failure of critical perception and sympathy is a major subject of *Hocus Pocus,* Vonnegut interweaves intertextual references to his own stories and novels throughout Eugene's narrative, e.g., "Wanda June" (282), the "Shah of Bratpuhr" (289), "Mark Rothko" (209), "Ed Bergeron" (138), "James Watt" (191), "Midland City" (250), "slapstick comedies" (142), etc. Midland City is Hartke's childhood home. A reference to "the rise of the Vonnegut Memorial Fountain" (137) suggests the identity of Vonnegut's novel as an ironic "memorial" to the career-long obtuseness of critics as "comatose" or just "plain stupid" as the learning-disabled students at Tarkington.

19. Calling these fire fighters "the last shred of faith people have . . . an amazing instance of civic responsibility" (276), Vonnegut repeats his career-long belief that volunteer firemen are humanity's purest expression of disinterested charity, i.e., sanity.

20. Prior to the appearance of Rabo Karabekian, the hero's inability to experience sex as a positive act is a major symptom of his general emotional malaise. This affirmation of Eros—a fusing of flesh and spirit—marks a degree of psychic healing that distinguishes Rabo Karabekian and Eugene Hartke from all of Vonnegut's previous heroes. Vonnegut's declaration, "How feminine I have become" *(Fates* 119), supports Kathryn Hume's observation that Vonnegut came to accept the female principle in himself.

21. This reference calls to mind the "Nation of Two" in *Mother Night,* a form of moral retreatism that reduces life to an endless game of hide and seek.

22. It is Howard Campbell's belief that the ability to imagine the "cruel consequences" (74) of his lies determines that he is sane and hence morally responsible. Eugene's moral accounting corresponds with Campbell's view that in an amoral world, the moral man must create order and meaning and justice where none seems to exist.

23. The novel's most telling example of realities that transform us for better or worse is the grotesquely alienated world of Scipio, a microcosmic representation of American democracy. As imagined by its founding fathers, the utopian community of 1869, with Tarkington its democratic hub, would offer a free education to either sex, of any age, regardless of race or religion, and a modest fee to those farther away (24–25). Even the prison across the lake was intended to improve

the bodies and souls of youthful offenders—a mystic work camp for criminals from big city slums. With the passing of time, materialistic lusts bankrupt the society's spiritual ideals, turning the once sympathetic relationship between Scipio's haves and have-nots to distrust and hatred. Both societies are duped by the promise of paradise at the end of the Capitalistic rainbow, dehumanized by the indifferent machinery of free enterprise and the vicious class system it breeds. Eugene attributes the misery of the "poor and powerless" (67) of Athena directly to the greed of the American rich, no better themselves than "robbers with guns" (264). Vonnegut calls them "unarmed robbers" in *Fates*. For the exploited convicts, Athena becomes the terrible alternative to accepting whatever their "greedy paymasters" gave them in the way of subsistence or working conditions. Many of the prisoners are there, in fact, because of the social irresponsibility of the American business community. When they were little, Eugene says, and had eaten chips or breathed dust from old lead-based paint, the brain damage from lead poisoning had made them capable of the "dumbest crimes imaginable" (201). At the same time, reminiscent of the rebellion of *Player Piano's* "reeks and wrecks" or the futility of Pisquontuit County's disinherited in *God Bless You, Mr. Rosewater,* the desperation of poverty and social inferiority causes Scipio's social rejects to reciprocate in kind—meeting cruelty and insensitivity with the bloodbath of terror and death that follows the Athenian insurrection. Suggesting that, to the last, Athenians and Tarkingtonians are alike victimized by Capitalistic "delusions of grandeur" (96), Alton Darwin inspires the attack on Tarkington with promises of glory and riches, dreaming of using his freedom to restore Scipio's industry. During the siege, the escapees slaughter teachers and trustees but are careful not to damage the physical campus because they believe that its treasures would be theirs for generations to come (28).

24. In reference to several sketches, Eugene's editor informs us that Eugene has made only one such drawing; the others are but "tracings" of the "original" (7–8). Such superimpositions correspond to the multiple layers of reality that constitute the telling of Eugene's story.

25. Eugene's numbering of pages to create the illusions of sequentiality (7) and the self-conscious framing of passages further foreground the text as an artifact, a purely human construction. John Leonard notes that Eugene's scraps of paper remind one of those odds and ends of thoughts that Dr. Reefy in *Winesburg, Ohio* scribbled on bits of paper and then stuffed away in his pockets to become "little hard rubber balls," or self-created truths (421).

26. Eugene sees himself as a "sort of non-combatant wiseman" (91), reflecting Vonnegut's view of himself as a "Shaman," one who provides illumination. But Vonnegut's textual strategies are meant primarily to stimulate thinking, and so he describes his love of building "elaborate theories so closely reasoned as to seem inevitable and then, self-mockingly, to knock them down" (*Fates* 37).

27. According to the testimony of Leon Trout in *Galápagos,* it is fatalism and apathy—the failure "to give a damn" (80)—that steers the characters of *Galápagos* into an apocalyptic nightmare. Vonnegut's survey of recent American history in *Fates* finds several signs of improved mental health—the rights of citizens to worship or not worship however they please, an increasingly educated public that makes for democratic strength, the treatment of censorship as a loathsome disease, and the tendency to consider the discharge of firearms a low form of sport.

Selected Bibliography

Primary Sources

Vonnegut, Kurt. *Player Piano*. New York, New York: Dell Publishing Co., Inc., 1959; rpt. ed. 1971.
_____ . *The Sirens of Titan*. New York, New York: Dell Publishing Co., Inc. 1959; rpt. ed. 1971.
_____ . *Mother Night*. New York, New York: Dell Publishing Co., Inc., 1961; rpt. ed. 1974.
_____ . *Cat's Cradle*. New York, New York: Dell Publishing Co., Inc., 1963; rpt. ed. 1975.
_____ . *God Bless You, Mr. Rosewater*. New York, New York: Dell Publishing Co., Inc., 1965; rpt. ed. 1981.
_____ . *Wampeters Foma & Granfalloons (Opinions)*. New York, New York: Dell Publishing Co., Inc. 1965; rpt. ed. 1975.
_____ . *Slaughterhouse-Five*. New York, New York: Dell Publishing Co., Inc., 1969; rpt. ed. 1972.
_____ . *Happy Birthday, Wanda June*. New York: Seymour Lawrence/Delacorte, 1971; rpt. ed., New York: Dell, 1971.
_____ . *Breakfast of Champions*. New York, New York: Dell Publishing Co., Inc., 1973; rpt. ed. 1975.
_____ . *Slapstick or Lonesome No More*. New York, New York: Dell Publishing Co., Inc., 1976.
_____ . *Jailbird*. New York, New York: Delacorte Press/Seymour Lawrence, 1979.
_____ . *Palm Sunday*. New York, New York: Dell Publishing Co., Inc., 1981.
_____ . *Deadeye Dick*. New York, New York: Delacorte Press/Seymour Lawrence, 1982.
_____ . *Galápagos*. New York, New York: Delacorte Press/Seymour Lawrence, 1985.
_____ . *Bluebeard*. New York, New York: Delacorte Press, 1987.

Secondary Works

Alcorn, Marshall W., Jr., and Mark Bracher, "Literature, Psychoanalysis, and the Re-Formation of the Self: A New Direction for Reader Response Theory." *PMLA* 20 (1985): 342–54.
Aldridge, John W. *After the Lost Generation*. New York: The Noonday Press, 1963.
American Psychiatric Association. *D.S.M. III. Diagnostic and Statistical Manual of Mental Disorders*. 3rd edition. Library of Congress #79–055868, 1980.
Barnard, G. C. *Samuel Beckett: A New Approach*. New York: Dodd, Mead and Company, Inc., 1970.
Barthes, Roland. *Mythologies*. London: Annette Lavers, 1972.
Beckett, Samuel. *Three Novels*. New York: Grove Press, 1965.

Bellow, Saul. *Mr. Sammler's Planet*. Greenwich: A Fawcett Crest Book, 1970.

Belsey, Catherine. *Critical Practice*. New York: Methuen, 1980.

Benvenuto, Bice and Roger Kennedy. *The Works of Jacques Lacan: An Introduction*. New York: St. Martin's Press, 1986.

Berryman, Charles. "After the Fall: Kurt Vonnegut." *Critique* 26 (Winter 1985): 96–102.

Bleikasten, Andre. "Fathers in Faulkner." *The Fictional Father: Lacanian Readings of the Text*. Robert Con Davis, ed. Amherst: University of Massachusetts Press, 1981.

Buck, Lynn. "Vonnegut's World of Comic Futility." *Studies in American Fiction* 3 (Autumn 1975): 182–98.

Browne, Joseph. *"Jailbird." America* (May 10, 1980): 402.

Calvino, Italo. *Mr. Palomar*. Trans. William Weaver. New York: Harcourt Brace Jovanovich, 1985.

Campbell, Robert Jean, M.D. *Psychiatric Dictionary*. 5th edition. New York: Oxford University Press, 1981.

Camus, Albert. *The Myth of Sisyphus*. New York: Vintage Books, 1955.

Carroll, Lewis. *Alice's Adventures in Wonderland and Through the Looking-Glass*. New York: Lancer Books, Inc., 1968.

Crider, Andrew. *Schizophrenia: A Biopsychological Perspective*. Hillsdale: Lawrence Erlbaum Associates, Publishers, 1979.

Davis, Robert Con. "The Discourse of the Father." *The Fictional Father: Lacanian Readings of the Text*. Amherst: University of Massachusetts Press, 1981.

———. "Post Modern Paternity: Donald Barthelme's *The Dead Father*." *The Fictional Father: Lacanian Readings of the Text*. Amherst: University of Massachusetts Press, 1981.

De Man, Paul. "Autobiography as De-Facement." *Modern Language Notes* 94 (1979): 922.

De Mott, Benjamin. "A Riot of Randomness." *The New York Times Book Review* (17 October 1982): 34.

———. "Vonnegut's Otherworldly Laughter." *Saturday Review* 54 (May 1, 1971): 29–32, 38.

Del Vecchio, John M. *The 13th Valley*. New York: Bantam Books, 1982.

Derrida, Jacques. *Of Grammatology*. Trans. Gazatri Chakravorty Spivak. Baltimore: Johns Hopkins, 1974.

Dietrich, Richard Farr. "Deconstruction as Devil's Advocacy: A Shavian Alternative." *Modern Drama* 19, no. 3 (Sept. 1986): 431–51.

Donleavy, J. P. *The Ginger Man*. New York: Berkley Medallion Books, 1968.

Eagleton, Terry. *Literary Theory: An Introduction*. Minneapolis: University of Minnesota Press, 1983.

Erlich, Richard. "Unpublished Teaching Notes to *Slaughterhouse-Five*." Department of English, Miami of Ohio University.

Fiedler, Leslie A. "The Divine Stupidity of Kurt Vonnegut." *Esquire* 74 (September, 1970): 195–97, 199–200, 202–4.

Fish, Frank. *Schizophrenia*. 2nd ed. Bristol: John Wright and Sons, 1976.

Freud, Sigmund. *Civilization and Its Discontents*. Trans. James Strachey. New York: W. W. Norton and Company, Inc., 1961.

———. *Beyond the Pleasure Principle*. Trans. James Strachey. New York: Bantam Books, 1967.

———. *The Interpretation of Dreams*. Trans. James Strachey. New York: Avon, 1965.

Giannone, Richard. *Vonnegut: A Preface to His Novels*. Port Washington: Kennikat Press, 1977.

———. "Violence in the Fiction of Kurt Vonnegut." *Thought* (March 1981): 64.

Goldenson, Robert M., *Encyclopedia of Human Behavior*. Garden City: Doubleday & Co., 1970.

Goldsmith, David. *Fantasist of Fire and Ice*. Bowling Green, Ohio: Bowling Green University Popular Press, 1972.

Goldstein, Michael, Bruce Baker and Kay Jamison, eds. *Abnormal Psychology: Experiences, Origins, and Interventions*. Boston: Little Brown, 1980.

Gould, Roger. *Transformations: Growth and Change in Adult Life*. New York: Simon and Shuster, 1978.

Harmon, Gary. "The Scene with Kurt Vonnegut, Jr.: A Conversation." Stephans College, ed. Jack Lazebrick.

Hartmann, Ernest. *Adolescents in a Mental Hospital*. New York: Grune and Stratton, 1968.

Hassan, Ihab. "The Character of Post-War Fiction in America." *On Contemporary Literature*, Richard Kostelanetz, ed. New York: Avon Books, 1964.

Heller, Joseph. *Catch-22*. New York: Dell, 1969.

Hendin, Josephine. *Vulnerable People: A View of American Fiction since 1945*. New York: Oxford University Press, 1978.

_____ . *The Harvard Guide to Contemporary American Writing*. Daniel Holfman, ed. Cambridge: Belknap Press, 1979.

Hemingway, Ernest. *Across the River and into the Trees*. New York: Charles Scribner's Sons, 1950.

Hoffman, Thomas. "The Theme of Mechanization in Player Piano." *Clockwork Worlds: Mechanized Environments in Science Fiction*, Richard D. Erlich and Thomas P. Dunn, eds. Westport: Greenwood Press, 1983.

Holland, Norman. *The Dynamics of Literary Response*. New York: W. W. Norton and Co., 1975.

Hume, Kathryn. "Vonnegut's Self-Projections: Symbolic Characters and Symbolic Fiction." *The Journal of Narrative Technique* 12 (Fall 1982): 177–90.

_____ . "Kurt Vonnegut and the Myths and Symbols of Meaning." *Texas Studies in Literature and Language* 24, no. 4 (Winter 1982): 429–46.

_____ . "The Heraclitean Cosmos of Kurt Vonnegut." *Papers on Language and Literature* 18 (1982): 208–24.

Hutcheon, Linda. *A Theory of Parody: The Teachings of Twentieth-Century Art Forms*. New York: Methuen, Inc., 1985.

Irving, John. "Kurt Vonnegut and His Critics." *New Republic* 181 (September 22, 1979): 41–49.

Isaak, Jo-Anna. "The Cubist Esthetic." 14 *Mosaic* 14 (1) (Winter 1981): 61–90.

Kauffmann, Stanley. "Stanley Kauffmann on Films." *New Republic* (May 13, 1972): 22, 35.

Kazin, Alfred. "The Alone Generation." *The American Novel since World War II*. Marcus Klein, ed. Greenwich: A Fawcett Premier Book, 1969.

Kelly, Andrew J. "Slapstick: Or Lonesome No More!" *America* 135 (December 18, 1976): 450.

Keogh, J. G. and Edmund Kislaitis. *"Slaughterhouse-Five* and the Future of Science Fiction." *Media and Methods*. (January 1971): 38, 39, 40.

Kesey, Ken. *One Flew over the Cuckoo's Nest*. New York: New American Libarary, 1975.

Ketterer, David. *New Worlds for Old: The Apocalyptic Imagination, Science Fiction, and American Literature*. Garden City: Anchor Books, 1974.

Klinkowitz, Jerome and John Somers. *The Vonnegut Statement*. New York: Delacorte/Seymour Lawrence, 1973.

Klinkowitz, Jerome and Donald L. Lawler, eds. *Vonnegut in America: An Introduction to the Life and Work of Kurt Vonnegut*. New York, New York: Delacorte Press/Seymour Lawrence, 1977..

_____ . "Kurt Vonnegut, Jr. and the Crime of his Times." *Critique* 12, no. 3 (1971): 38–53.

Knickerbocker, Conrad. "How to Love People Who Have No Use." *Life* 58 (April 9, 1965):6–7.

Krutch, Joseph Wood. *The Modern Temper*. New York: Harcourt, Brace, and Co., 1956.

Lacan, Jacques. *Ecrits: A Selection*. Trans. Alan Sheridan. New York: W. W. Norton, 1977.

Laing, R. D. *The Divided Self*. New York: Random House, Pantehon Books, 1969.

Langer, Lawrence L. *The Holocaust and the Literary Imagination*. New Haven: Yale University Press, 1975.

Leeds, Marc. *What Goes Around, Comes Around: The Naive Schizophrenic-Resurrected Cycle in the Novels of Kurt Vonnegut*. Dissertation, University of New York at Buffalo, 1987.

Lehmann-Haupt, Christopher. "Books of the Times." *The New York Times* (November 5, 1982):C23.

Lessing, Doris. "Vonnegut's Responsibility." *The New York Times Book Review,* 4 (February 1973):35.

Lidz, Theodore, M.D. *The Origin and Treatment of Schizophrenic Disorders.* New York: Basic Books, Inc., Publishers, 1973.

Lorenz, Konrad. *Evolution and Modification of Behavior.* Chicago: University of Chicago Press, 1965.

Lundquist, James. *Kurt Vonnegut.* New York: Frederick Unger Publishing Co., 1977.

Mailer, Norman. "The White Negro." *Advertisements for Myself.* NewYork: G. P. Putnam's Sons, 1959.

―――― . *An American Dream.* New York: H. Holt and Company, 1987.

Mathews, Richard. "Vonnegut Explores Terrain beyond Guilt and Shame." *Tampa Tribune* (October 11, 1987):5C.

Merrill, Robert. "Vonnegut's *Breakfast of Champions:* The Conversion of Heliogabalus." *Critique* 18, no. 3, (1977):99–108.

―――― . "Vonnegut's *Slaughterhouse-Five:* The Requirements of Chaos." *Studies in American Fiction* 6 (Spring 1978):65–76.

Misra, Kalidas. "The American War Novel from World War II to Vietnam." *Indian Journal of American Studies* 14(2) (1984):73–80.

Mobley, Maribeth. "Fictions of Self in the Language of Lillian Hellman." Dissertation. University of South Florida, 1989.

Nicholi, Armand. *The Harvard Guide to Modern Psychology.* Cambridge: Belknap Press of Harvard University Press, 1978.

Olderman, Raymond. *Beyond the Waste Land: A Study of the American Novel in the Nineteen Sixties.* New Haven: Yale University Press, 1972.

Pahika, William H. "The Vehicle and the Thing Conveyed: A Commentary on *Slaughterhouse-Five.*" Unpublished essay.

Perry, John Weir. *Roots of Renewal in Myth and Madness.* San Francisco: Jossey-Bass Publishers, 1976.

Pieratt, Asa B., Julie Huffman-Klinkowitz and Jerome Klinkowitz. *Kurt Vonnegut: A Comprehensive Bibliography.* Hamden, Conn.: Anchor Books, 1987.

Pinsker, Sandford. *Between Two Worlds: The American Novel in the 1960s.* New York: The Whitston Publishing Company, 1980.

Pynchon, Thomas. *Gravity's Rainbow.* New York: The Viking Press, 1973.

Ralph, Clyde, M.D. "Maybe Our Brain Is Too Big?" *Pediatric News* 20, no. 4 (April 1986):38, 39.

Reed, Peter J. *Writers for the 70s: Kurt Vonnegut, Jr.* New York: Warner Paperback Library, 1974.

―――― . *Dictionary of Literary Biography, Documentary Series* 3, Mary Bruccoli, ed. Detroit: Gale Research, 1983.

Reich, Wilhelm. *The Function of the Orgasm.* Trans. Vincent R. Carfago. New York: Pocket Books, 1978.

Richardson, Jack. "Easy Writer." *The New York Review* (July 2, 1970):7–8.

Rogers, Carl. *On Becoming a Person.* Boston: Houghton Mifflin, 1961.

Rosen, Ephraim, and Ian Gregory. *Abnormal Psychology.* Philadelphia: W.B. Saunders Co., 1965.

Sachs, Hanns. *The Creative Unconscious.* Cambridge, Mass: Sci-Art Publishers, 1951.

Samuels, Charles Thomas. "Age of Vonnegut." *New Republic* (June 12, 1971):30–32.

Sales, Roger. "Kurt Vonnegut: Writing with Interchangeable Parts." *The New York Times Book Review.* (October 3, 1976):3.

Saussure, Ferdinand de. *Course in General Linguistics.* Trans. Wade Baskin. New York: Philosophical Library, 1959.

Schatt, Stanley. *Kurt Vonnegut, Jr.* Boston, Massachusetts: Twayne Publishers, 1976.

Scholes, Robert. *Fabulation and Metafiction*. Urbana: University of Illinois Press, 1979.

Selinger, Bernard. *Le Guin and Identity in Contemproary Fiction*. Ann Arbor: UMI Research Press, 1988.

Shaw, Bernard. *Back to Methuselah*. Baltimore: Penguin Books, 1961.

Shaw, Patrick. "The Excremental Festival: Vonnegut's *Slaughterhouse-Five*." *Scholia Satyrica* 2, no. 3 (Autumn 1976):3–11.

Shapiro, Sue A. *Contemporary Theories of Schizophrenia*. New York: McGraw-Hill, 1981.

Shechner, Mark. *Joyce in Nighttown: A Psychoanalytic Inquiry into Ulysses*. Berkeley: University of California Press, 1974.

Sheppard, R. Z. "Goodbye Indianapolis." *Time* (Oct. 25, 1976):84.

Shields, James, and Eliot Slater. "Heredity and Psychological Abnormality." *Handbook of Abnormal Psychology: An Experimental Approach*. H. J. Ezsenck, ed. New York: Basic Books, 1961.

Spacks, Patricia Meyer. *The Female Imagination*. New York: Avon, 1976.

Spenser, Sharon. *Space, Time, and Structure in the Modern Novel*. New York: New York University Press, 1983.

Stone, Albert. *The American Autobiography*. Englewood Cliffs: Prentice Hall, 1981.

Suarez, Ernest. *Politics, Culture, and the South in Literature*. Dissertation, University of Wisconsin, 1988.

Tanner, Tony. *City of Words*. London: Jonathan Cape Ltd., 1971.

Tilton, John. *Cosmic Satire in the Contemporary Novel*. Lewisburg: Bucknell University Press, 1977.

Updike, John. "All's Well in Skyscraper National Park." *New Yorker Magazine* (October 1976).

Van den Berg, J. H. *The Phenomenological Approach to Psychiatry*. London: Routledge and Kegan Paul, 1955.

Vonnegut, Kurt. Personal letter. November 30, 1982.

———. "The Art of Fiction LSIV: Kurt Vonnegut." *Paris Review*, No. 69 (Spring):56–103.

Vonnegut, Mark. *The Eden Express*. New York: Praeger Publishers, Inc., 1975.

Waugh, Patricia. *Metafiction: The Theory and Practice of Self-Conscious Fiction*. New York: Methuen, Inc., 1984.

Wolcott, James. "Mod Apostle." *New York Review of Books* (Nov. 22, 1979):11–12.

Wood, Michael. "Vonnegut's Softer Focus." *The New York Times Book Review* (September 9, 1979):1, 22.

Wymer, Thomas. "The Swiftian Satire of Kurt Vonnegut, Jr." *Voices for the Future*. Thomas D. Clareson, ed. Bowling Green, Ohio: Bowling Green University Popular Press, 1976.

Young, Philip. *Ernest Hemingway: A Reconsideration*. University Park: The Pennsylvania State University Press, 1966.

Index

About the Author

Lawrence R. Broer is Professor of English, University of South Florida. He received his bachelor's and master's degrees from Florida State University and his doctorate from Bowling Green State University. He is author of *Counter Currents: An Introduction to Current Fiction* (1973) and *Hemingway's Spanish Tragedy* (1973), editor of *The First Time: Initial Sexual Experiences in Fiction,* and coauthor (with Jack Walthar) of *Dancing Fools and Weary Blues: The Great Escape of the Twenties* (1990). He served as a Fulbright lecturer at the University of Paris in 1981 and 1984, and he received the Faculty Award for Excellence in Teaching at the University of South Florida in 1986 and 1992 and the Theodore and Venette Askounes-Ashford Distinguished Scholar Award for 1989.